A BATTLEFIELD ATLAS

OF THE CIVIL WAR

By Craig L. Symonds

A BATTLEFIELD ATLAS

OF THE CIVIL WAR

By Craig L. Symonds

Cartography by William J. Clipson

THE NAUTICAL AND AVIATION PUBLISHING COMPANY OF AMERICA

Baltimore, Maryland

Published in the United States by the Nautical & Aviation Publishing Company
of America, Inc., 8 W. Madison Street, Baltimore, MD 21201.

Library of Congress Catalog Card Number: 93-086931

ISBN: 1-877853-25-9

Printed in the United States of America

Third Edition, First Printing, 1994
Second Printing, August 1995

Symonds, Craig L.
  A battlefield atlas of the Civil War.

  Bibliography: p.
  1. United States—History—Civil War, 1861-1865—
Campaigns. 2. United States—History—Civil War,
1861-1865—Battle-fields—Maps. 3. United States—
History—Civil War, 1861-1865—Battle-fields—
Guide-books. I. Clipson, William. II. Title.
EA70.S975   1983   973.7   93-086931
ISBN 1-877853-25-9

FOR JEFF

Contents

Key to Map Symbols

▬	Infantry units
▨	Former position of infantry units
⚑	Cavalry units
▲	Infantry attacking
• • • • •	Skirmish line
■ ■ ■ ■ ■	Dispersed infantry units
⚑ ⚑	Army headquarters
≣	Artillery (depicts location, not precise number of guns)
⛵	Sea-going warships
⛴	River gunboats
■ ☐	Forts
wwwww	Field Fortifications
•••••➤ ⇨	Intended line of advance
⇢	Actual line of advance
✝	Church
—○—	Lighthouse
✡	Site of skirmish or battle

Introduction

The idea for this volume originated with my students. Frustrated in their efforts to follow my chalkboard maneuvers in the classroom, they asked if I could pass out sketches of the principal campaigns. This volume is the result. Throughout its preparation it has been a particular pleasure to work with Bill Clipson, a skilled perfectionist whose renderings faithfully portray the movements we wanted to highlight. Rather than produce maps that could be deciphered only with a magnifying glass, we have tried to keep the execution simple, so that the critical tactical movements could be perceived at a glance. All maps have a north-south axis but are drawn to different scales. For this reason, a bar scale is included on each.

It is important to be aware that the boxes used to indicate the infantry and cavalry units (shown at left) are *not* intended to show the precise number of brigades or divisions involved. Rather, they illustrate the *proportional* strength on each side. Because the strength of units varied so greatly, not only between the armies but also within each army, any attempt to portray the location of every unit would lead to the same kind of crowding and confusion that frustrated my efforts at the chalkboard. In the Civil War, unit size and designation varied considerably. At the beginning of the war, neither side had any unit larger than a brigade. Only gradually did the table of organization indicated below emerge. Even then, the strength of any of these units varied widely. Divisions, for example, could be as small as 2,000 or as large as 7,000.

The following terms are used throughout the text to refer to the units of both sides.

ARMY—A term applied to any force operating independently in a theater. The main armies, Lee's Army of Northern Virginia or the Army of the Potomac, for example, were generally commanded by a major general (two stars) in the Union Army, and a full general (four stars) in the Confederate Army. The strength of any army could vary from 10,000 or less in a secondary theater to in excess of 100,000.

CORPS—Commanded by a major general in the Union Army and by a lieutenant general (three stars) in the Confederate Army. Usually composed of two or three divisions and totalling between 15,000 and 20,000 men.

DIVISION—Commanded by major generals in both armies. Usually composed of two or three brigades and totalling around 5,000 men.

BRIGADE—Commanded by a brigadier general (one star) in both armies. Composed of two or more regiments and totalling between 1,200 and 3,000 men.

REGIMENT—Commanded by a colonel. Usually composed of ten companies of fifty to a hundred men each. Depending on how long they had been in the field, regiments varied from 200 to 800, with some veteran regiments as low as 50.

The text accompanying each map is necessarily brief, but I have made an effort to go beyond the mere description of troop movements. In most cases the text is written from the perspective of the attacking army, and whenever relevant, the personalities of the commanders on the opposing sides are explored. In every case the interpretations offered are my own.

Of course not every battle of the war is included. The selection represented here was my own and I apologize in advance to those students of the war who note the absence of their "favorite" battle. Several battles were known by different names North and South; while the North tended to name battles after a nearby geographical landmark, especially rivers, the South named battles after the closest community. In such cases, I have listed the battle as it was known in the North with the Southern name in parentheses afterward: i.e., Bull Run (Manassas).

The casualty figures cited for each battle are rounded off from the best estimates of the leading authorities. In the last two years of the war it became very difficult to account for Confederate wounded and missing. Lightly wounded soldiers—those who could still march and fight—were generally not included in lists of wounded submitted by unit commanders. Thus Confederate losses were almost always more severe than the precise numbers reported. On the other hand, many southern soldiers listed as missing after important battles were men who more than likely would return to the ranks after a visit home or a brief unauthorized liberty. By 1864 the armies of the Confederacy had simply stopped keeping precise records of battle losses. Estimates, therefore, vary greatly.

As noted above, I am especially grateful to Bill Clipson for his fine work on the maps. Errors on any map are my responsibility alone, for his careful rendering was done to my specifications. I would also like to thank my colleagues in the History Department of the U.S. Naval Academy, including Professor Bill Darden, Dr. Roger Zeimet, and especially Captain Don Alexander, a scholar and professional soldier who contributed several ideas to the book and provided an interested and tolerant ear when necessary. The project was encouraged to completion by Jan Snouck-Hurgronje of The Nautical & Aviation Publishing Company, who remained faithful to the original proposal to produce a clear, simple, and inexpensive battlefield atlas.

Craig L. Symonds
May 20, 1983

Introduction to the Third Edition

Ten years ago, when this slim volume first appeared, I had envisioned that it would be used primarily—perhaps exclusively—by those students who took my course on the Civil War at the U.S. Naval Academy. Because of that, my goal was to ensure that the book was 1) clear, and 2) cheap. Inflation has ensured that it is no longer "cheap" (although it is still less expensive than its competitors), but I hope that it continues to be clear. Indeed, uncluttered clarity and simplicity is both its principal characteristic and its greatest strength as a teaching tool. I was astonished when, soon after publication, the book provoked strong interest in a much wider audience. I have encountered literally hundreds of individuals who have told me that they have found the book useful while exploring battlefields, as a handy reference when perusing other histories, or even as a general (if admittedly brief) history of the war. It is very gratifying that now, a decade later, it is going into a Third Edition.

This Third edition contains six new maps (#40–45), all dealing with the war in the western theatre, and an updated suggested reading list. Like earlier editions, this book grinds no interpretive ax, except to note those areas where scholars of the war disagree. In the decade since it first appeared, scores of Civil War scholars have uncovered new material and cast new interpretive light on many aspects of the war. But except to correct the occasional fact when the evidence warranted, I have not changed the interpretive thrust of what I wrote in 1983. There is certainly enough human drama in the events themselves, and the personalities who played the principal roles, to allow the chronology to stand on its own. I hope, then, that readers will continue to rely on this book as a reference, as a battlefield guide, or—as was originally intended—as a teaching tool.

Craig L. Symonds
Annapolis, 1993

Prologue: Fort Sumter

As Charlestonians like to explain to outsiders, Charleston Harbor is where the Ashley and Cooper Rivers flow together to form the Atlantic Ocean. In the spring of 1861, the attention of most of the nation was focused on Charleston Harbor and in particular on the three Federal forts guarding it: the Revolutionary War-vintage Fort Moultrie on Sullivan's Island, the equally ancient Castle Pinckney near the mouth of the Cooper River, and the still-unfinished Fort Sumter on a man-made island near the entrance to the harbor (*see* Map 1). For although South Carolina now insisted that it was no longer part of the United States, the government in Washington maintained titular control over these three pieces of Federal property.

Governor Francis W. Pickens, who considered himself a head of state after secession, sent envoys to Washington to negotiate the transfer of the forts to South Carolina. Lame-duck President James Buchanan refused to meet with them officially, though unofficially he let it be known that he would avoid any action that would precipitate a crisis. Buchanan's principal goal in 1861 was to pass on his office to Lincoln without bringing on a war. After all, he reasoned to himself, it was Lincoln's election that had brought on the crisis; it was only fitting that Lincoln deal with it.

The man on the spot in this situation was Major Robert Anderson, who commanded the tiny Federal garrison at Fort Moultrie. He had been hand-picked by Buchanan's Virginia-born Secretary of War John B. Floyd, partly because Anderson's father had successfully defended Moultrie against a British invasion during the American Revolution, and partly because Anderson was himself Southern-born and a former slaveholder. Floyd's subsequent actions suggest that he hoped Anderson would be cooperative with his Charleston hosts and gracefully surrender the forts when the time came. Anderson, however, was a serious and determined professional who regarded his assignment as a special trust.

Concluding that Moultrie was indefensible, on December 26, 1860, Anderson transferred his garrison to the incomplete but nearly impregnable Fort Sumter. South Carolinians were furious. Recalling Buchanan's "pledge" to maintain the status quo, they charged that the Federal government had gone back on its word. Secretary Floyd was nearly as outraged and wanted to order Anderson to return to Moultrie. But after wavering for a week, Buchanan finally concluded that Anderson had acted in accordance with his discretionary instructions, and refused to order his recall. Meanwhile, South Carolina troops occupied both Moultrie and Castle Pinckney and began to erect a ring of batteries around Sumter. Principal works were built at old Fort Johnson and on Cumming's Point, where the Charlestonians erected a battery protected by an iron shield; both sides called it the Iron Battery. In addition, shells could reach Sumter from Fort Moultrie and from a floating battery moored off the tip of Sullivan's Island.

In January the Buchanan administration sent the merchant steamer *Star of the West* to Charleston with reinforcements and supplies for Anderson's beleaguered garrison. Forewarned by southern sympathizers in Buchanan's cabinet, South Carolina artillerists were ready and waiting and opened fire on the unarmed vessel—the first shot being fired by a young Citadel cadet. Torn by doubts about his duty in this situation, Anderson hesitated to return fire, and the *Star of the West* reversed course and headed back out to sea.

The Stars and Bars of the Confederacy fly over Fort Sumter on April 14, 1861. (NA)

Confederate President Jefferson Davis assumed responsibility for the situation in Charleston Harbor in February. His order to Beauregard to demand the surrender of Fort Sumter and if refused to reduce the fort precipitated the final crisis. (NA)

From January until Lincoln's inauguration in March, both sides maintained an uneasy truce in the harbor. Charlestonians worked hard to improve their fortifications ringing the fort, and Anderson's men worked to complete Sumter's works and mount several more pieces of artillery.

On February 18, 1861, in Montgomery, Alabama, Jefferson Davis was sworn in as the first and, as it would turn out, the only president of the Confederacy. The burden of determining Sumter's fate thus passed from Pickens to Davis. The new president sent envoys to Washington to negotiate, but he also sent Brigadier General P. G. T. Beauregard to Charleston to take over command of the Southern forces there. Two weeks later in Washington, Abraham Lincoln was sworn in as the sixteenth president of the United States and vowed in his inaugural address to "hold, occupy, and possess" Federal property in the South. The lines were clearly drawn.

Acting on information that Anderson's supplies were low, Lincoln in early April ordered the preparation of a relief expedition to Sumter. Despite the obstructionism of Secretary of State William Seward, who had promised the Confederate envoys that the administration would evacuate the fort, the expedition got underway on April 6. Moreover, Lincoln notified Governor Pickens of the expedition, thus deftly tossing the ball into the South's court. Pickens forwarded the information to Davis who on April 10, after discussing the issue with his cabinet, sent Beauregard a telegram ordering him to demand Sumter's surrender, and if he were refused, "to reduce the fort."

The next day Beauregard dutifully made his demand. Anderson refused to surrender, but in an effort to prevent bloodshed he informed Beauregard's envoys that his provisions were so low that starvation would necessitate his surrender in a few days in any case. Here was a possible solution. After several hours' delay while Beauregard checked with Davis, the envoys returned to Sumter after midnight (now April 12) to ask Anderson precisely *when* the fort would be surrendered. By noon on April 15, Anderson replied, if the fort was not resupplied in the meantime. Alas, Beauregard's envoys considered this reply unsatisfactory and at 3:30 A.M. they informed Anderson that they would open fire in an hour. At 4:30 a single gun from Fort Johnson sent a shell arching toward Fort Sumter to burst a hundred feet above the ramparts.

The bombardment lasted all day and into the night. The Federals did not return fire until 7:00

Major Robert Anderson, the commander of the beleaguered Federal garrison in Fort Sumter, felt duty and honor tugging him in two directions. As a southerner he believed that slavery was no sin and that secession was a constitutional right. As a professional officer in the U.S. Army, he was determined to do his duty. (NA)

A.M., when Abner Doubleday, Anderson's second-in-command and the reputed inventor of baseball, sighted a 32-pounder at the Iron Battery and gave the order to fire. But Federal fire was ineffective because Anderson refused to use his heavy-caliber guns on the exposed parapet and because he had no fuses for the exploding shells of his smaller guns. He therefore had to rely on round shot, which proved utterly useless against the rebel batteries.

In the early afternoon of the second day (April 13) a rebel shot struck Sumter's flagpole and brought down the colors. Though they were soon rehoisted, Colonel Louis T. Wigfall (lately Senator Wigfall of Texas) rowed out to Sumter to ask once again if Anderson would surrender. With fires burning out of control inside the fort, and with no prospect of aid from the Federal relief squadron, Anderson agreed.

On April 14 the Federal garrison marched out of the fort to Confederate boats, which transferred the men to the Union squadron offshore. Incredibly, the only casualties on either side resulted from the explosion of a Federal gun during the salute to the flag after the surrender.

PART ONE

The Amateur Armies

The news from Charleston prompted President Lincoln to issue a call to the individual states for 75,000 volunteers who would serve for a period of three months, in order to suppress "combinations too powerful to be suppressed by the ordinary course of judicial proceedings." Lincoln's proclamation was considered a declaration of war by the Southern States, and led to the secession of Virginia, North Carolina, Tennessee, and Arkansas, thus bringing the total number of seceded states to eleven. (The Confederate flag, however, bore thirteen stars: one each for Kentucky and Missouri, which did not secede formally but which provided large numbers of troops to the South as well as to the North.)

The next three months were taken up by the efforts of both sides to put armies in the field. In this effort, though there was no shortage of enthusiasm, it soon became clear that both sides lacked the organizational and logistical machinery to support the mass armies that flocked to the colors. Jefferson Davis would later be criticized for turning away over 200,000 Confederate volunteers that first year because the government could not clothe, arm, or even feed them. Likewise, Lincoln's disorganized and unimaginative Secretary of War, Simon Cameron, discovered that his staff of two clerks was wholly inadequate to meet the administrative demands of fielding an army of 75,000.

A sense of urgency was added to Cameron's efforts by the geographical location of the Federal capital. From the windows of the White House Lincoln could see Confederate battle flags across the Potomac on Arlington Heights, where Beauregard, fresh from his triumph over Fort Sumter, had encamped his army. Moreover, unrest in Baltimore (Maryland being a slave state) threatened to cut off Washington from the North.

The arrival of the first few regiments from Northern States eased fears that the rebels would seize the capital, but it created a whole new set of problems. Troops arrived faster than the government could provide them with camp sites, rations, supplies, and arms. Moreover, regiments came attired in uniforms of their own design: some in gaudy silken Zouave uniforms, some in blue wool, some in outfits of no recognizable uniformity at all. At least one regiment—the Eighth New York—arrived in civilian clothes. The Union "army" was more nearly an armed mob than a disciplined military force.

Over half a million men enlisted in the armies of one side or the other at the outset of the American Civil War, and only a handful—fewer than 16,000—were regular soldiers. Many of the volunteers had never before borne arms. There were farmers, mechanics, and tradesmen, and a smattering of professional men. Nearly all were brazen amateurs at the art of war—enthusiastic and naïve. Their officers, who were generally elected from the ranks, were also amateurs. Even those few with professional training—West Point graduates—had never commanded anything larger than a regiment in battle. It was a classic example of the blind leading the blind.

In a possibly apocryphal story, the great Prussian chief of staff, Helmut von Moltke, commented that it would be useless to send Prussian officers as observers to the American Civil War. What could they possibly learn from watching armed mobs of civilians pursue each other through the wilder-

Charging Federal Troops at Bull Run drive the Confederates off Matthew's Hill in this artist's conception from *Harper's Weekly*. Unlike later battles, Bull Run was a stand up fight reminiscent of eighteenth century warfare. (LC)

] 1 [

can military prowess. The military was an honorable profession for the sons of the South, but ironically it was their sense of honor that helped ensure that the first year of the war would be marked by unprofessional leadership. The Southern understanding of honor led Confederate commanders to eschew staff work and rely instead on setting examples of personal bravery. At First Bull Run the Confederate commander issued orders so confusing they were barely comprehensible, and then responded to the crisis by riding toward the sound of the guns, and urging his men to greater acts of courage. It is no coincidence that both Albert Sidney Johnston, the Confederate commander in the West, and Joseph E. Johnston, his Eastern counterpart, were wounded in early battles, the former mortally. They had been leading regimental-sized charges at the fighting front—where no army commander had any business being.

The Federal high command, if somewhat less reckless, was no more acute. The Union failure at Bull Run resulted, at least in part, from the inability of the Federal commander to recognize the limiting influence on his paper-perfect plan of what Clausewitz called "friction." And in the West,

Brevet Lieutenant General Winfield Scott was a 6′5″ 350 pound septugenarian who was plagued so badly by gout that he often had difficulty walking, and he was completely incapable of mounting a horse—even if one could be found that was sturdy enough to carry him. But he was the senior military officer in the country and he was the principal architect of the so-called Anaconda Plan (see Map 2). (NA)

ness? The comment is generally cited to illustrate Moltke's cultural prejudice, but there is more than a grain of truth in it. The early Civil War battles at Bull Run (Manassas) in the East and Shiloh in the West were gigantic open-field clashes between armies of spirited amateurs.

On the Union side, the small professional army might have been broken up to provide a cadre of veterans for the new units, but Brevet Lieutenant General Winfield Scott argued that it was essential to keep these veteran units intact, thus assuring the presence of at least a few reliable regiments on the battlefield. Nearly all students of the war agree now that this was a grave error, and assured a longer incubation period for the Grand Army of the Republic. Of course, there were no veteran units to be preserved on the Confederate side, which was perhaps an advantage, in the early years, but the rebels also suffered from a lack of clear organization and experienced leadership in handling large numbers of troops. Moreover, though the South might claim a greater percentage of volunteers who could ride a horse and shoot a gun, nearly all of its recruits were equally inexperienced in the practice of organized warfare.

The South considered itself the cradle of Ameri-

Brigadier General Pierre Gustave Toutant Beauregard was an energetic and flamboyant southern commander who enjoyed his reputation as the conqueror of Fort Sumter. At Bull Run (Manassas) he did not so much direct the battle as react to it. His staff work was poor and, like many southern officers in early battles, he believed leadership was best demonstrated by riding to the sound of the guns and displaying courage under fire. (NA)

Flag Officer Samuel F. DuPont commanded the Union fleet that successfully captured Port Royal in November 1861. Five months later he attempted to employ similar tactics at Charleston and found those defenses much tougher. As a result his ascendency was halted and his star eclipsed by that of David Glasgow Farragut (*see* Maps 1, 6, and 9). (USNA Museum)

none other than Ulysses S. Grant was caught absolutely flat-footed at Shiloh, where he managed to avoid disaster by the narrowest of margins. Only on the water did the Federals achieve anything worthy of a good cheer. At Port Royal and New Orleans important victories were won with virtually no loss by a Federal Navy that possessed unchallenged command of the sea. (The CSS *Virginia* would not sortie until the spring of 1862.)

The lessons of these early battles were that the war would be neither short nor bloodless, and that the scale of the conflict would surpass anything anticipated by the leaders on either side; before the war was over nearly four million men would serve in the Union and Confederate armies. A third lesson—that the advent of the minie ball and rifled musket had made frontal assaults against prepared lines virtually suicidal—took the generals on both sides a little longer to learn. The failure by commanders on both sides to appreciate this lesson helps account for the staggering death toll of the American Civil War. Two recent scholars have argued that the irrational predilection of Confederate generals for the attack accounts in large measure for the South's defeat.

By the end of the first year of war, the green recruits of 1861 had become hardened veterans, full of scorn for the draftees brought to their armies by the conscription acts which both sides required to fill their ranks. But in that first year, the early volunteers had to depend more on luck and pluck than on either the skill of their leaders or the support of their governments.

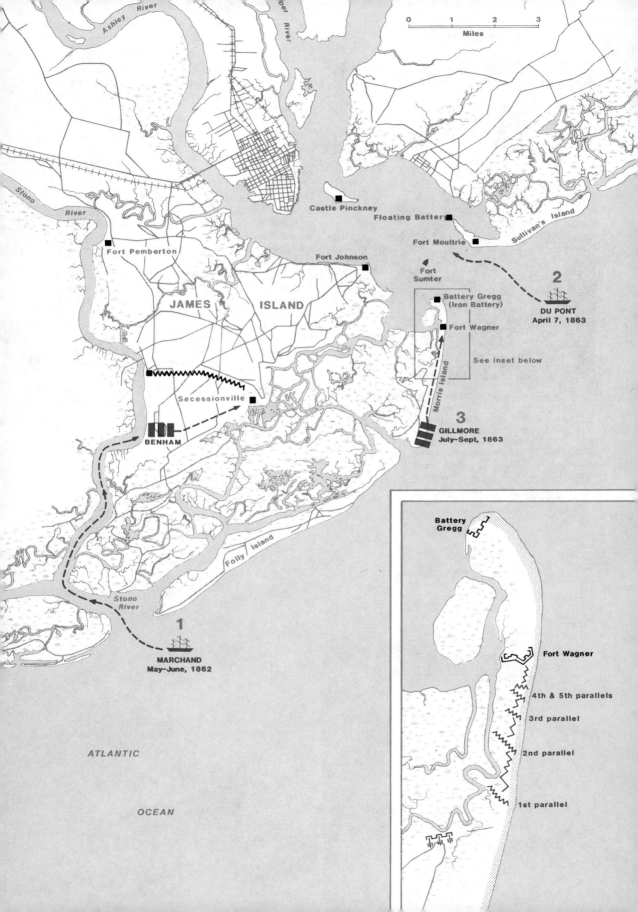

Ashley River

Chapel River

0 1 2 3
Miles

Stono River

Castle Pinckney

Floating Battery

Fort Moultrie

Sullivan's Island

Fort Pemberton

Fort Johnson

Fort Sumter

JAMES ISLAND

Battery Gregg (Iron Battery)

Fort Wagner

2
DU PONT
April 7, 1863

See inset below

Secessionville

BENHAM

Morris Island

3
GILLMORE
July–Sept, 1863

Stono River

Folly Island

1
MARCHAND
May–June, 1862

ATLANTIC

OCEAN

Battery Gregg

Fort Wagner

4th & 5th parallels

3rd parallel

2nd parallel

1st parallel

MAP 1

Charleston Harbor

Because South Carolina was the first state to secede, and because the first shots of the war were fired in its harbor, Charleston held a special significance for both sides. During the war, Union forces mounted three large-scale efforts to capture Charleston, all of them unsuccessful.

1. Secessionville, June 16, 1862

In May 1862 the commander of the Union blockading squadron off Charleston, Captain John B. Marchand, took some of his lighter-draft vessels over the bar at the entrance to the Stono River. After a brief survey, he dispatched a report to his superiors asserting that Union troops landed on the banks of that river could march across James Island and take Fort Johnson from the rear. Possession of that fort, Marchand argued, would make Sumter untenable and lead to the capture of Charleston itself.

Troops for just such an operation were quickly gathered, but their advance was blocked by a line of hastily erected Confederate entrenchments across the island, anchored by a fort at the small community of Secessionville. Not only did the fort at Secessionville command the road to Fort Johnson, but from that position, the rebels maintained a harassing fire on the Federal encampments along the banks of the Stono River. The commander of the growing Federal army, Brigadier General Henry W. Benham, therefore determined that the fort, called Battery Lamar by the Confederates, would have to be seized. Benham's plan was not strongly supported by his subordinates, especially Brigadier General Horatio Wright, who argued in a staff meeting that volunteer troops were incapable of storming prepared works like those at Secessionville. Benham nevertheless ordered the advance, which took place in the early-morning hours of June 16.

It was a fiasco. Only two Federal regiments succeeded in reaching the enemy positions at all and,

unsupported as they were, they were soon driven out. There was a great deal of recrimination afterward, and Benham was even arrested for ordering the advance without specific approval from the theater commander, Major General David Hunter. The mismanaged battle at Secessionville ended the Federal threat to Charleston from the south.

2. The Naval Battle, April 7, 1863

The Navy had its turn next. In April 1863 a fleet of ironclads and wooden steamers under the command of Rear Admiral Samuel F. Du Pont conqueror of Port Royal (see Map 6), tried to force the entrance to the harbor. But the Confederates had spent almost two full years sighting their guns on the ship channels, and easily turned back the Union armada while receiving very little punishment in return. After a lengthy one-sided cannonade, this attack was also abandoned. Even the presumed "unsinkable" monitors proved vulnerable, as the twin-turreted Keokuk, struck by over one hundred shots, rolled over and sank. Du Pont was made the scapegoat for the failure and replaced by John A. Dahlgren, inventor of the Dahlgren gun. But Dahlgren had no better luck and though he continued to tighten the blockade around Charleston, he could not battle his way into the harbor.

3. Fort Wagner, July-September, 1863

The third Union effort was the most serious. A Federal army under the command of Major General Quincy Adams Gillmore attacked across Lighthouse Inlet from Folly Island to Morris Island in July 1863. Supported by naval gunfire, the Union army advanced to the outer defenses of Fort Wagner, but an attempt to storm this position on July 18 failed. For over a month Gillmore advanced regular siege lines against Wagner and, aided by the Union blockading fleet, bombarded it regularly. The sappers were subjected not only to artillery fire from Wagner, but also to plunging fire from the heavy guns at Fort Sumter. To silence those guns, Gillmore aimed his own batteries toward Sumter and in a period of fifteen days virtually knocked it to pieces.

By early September, Gillmore was ready to launch a final assault on Wagner, but on September 7 he discovered that the Confederates had abandoned both Wagner and Battery Gregg on Cumming's Point. The next night Gillmore tried to take Sumter itself in a surprise night attack, but the attempt failed. Charleston held out for another full year, falling only when Sherman cut its rail lines to the interior during his march through South Carolina in 1864 (see Map 41).

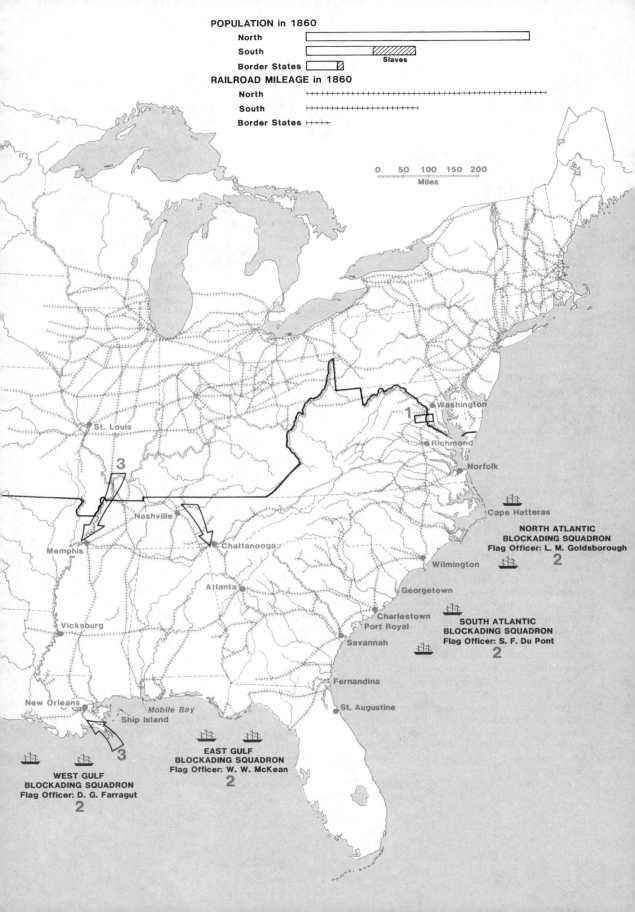

POPULATION in 1860

North

South

Slaves

Border States

RAILROAD MILEAGE in 1860

North

South

Border States

0 50 100 150 200
Miles

Washington

Richmond

Norfolk

1

3

St. Louis

Nashville

Chattanooga

Memphis

Atlanta

Vicksburg

Cape Hatteras

NORTH ATLANTIC
BLOCKADING SQUADRON
Flag Officer: L. M. Goldsborough
2

Wilmington

Georgetown

Charlestown
Port Royal

SOUTH ATLANTIC
BLOCKADING SQUADRON
Flag Officer: S. F. Du Pont
2

Savannah

Fernandina

St. Augustine

New Orleans

Mobile Bay
Ship Island

3

EAST GULF
BLOCKADING SQUADRON
Flag Officer: W. W. McKean
2

WEST GULF
BLOCKADING SQUADRON
Flag Officer: D. G. Farragut
2

MAP 2

The Anaconda Plan

Spring, 1861

The onset of armed conflict made Lincoln a war president. He was a man with no first-hand military experience, except for a brief tour as a volunteer during the Black Hawk War in 1832 when, by his own admission, the only enemies he had seen were mosquitos. The man to whom he turned for military advice in the spring of 1861 was the aging veteran of both the Mexican War and the War of 1812, Major General Winfield Scott.

Initially, Scott proposed that the Southern states should be allowed to go in peace, even suggesting the possibility that the country be fragmented into four or five discrete nations. But recognizing that this was thoroughly unacceptable to Lincoln, Scott confined himself to specifically military advice. The plan he offered to the President consisted of three elements, all designed to achieve not so much a military victory as a reconciliation:

(1) A major army should be created to operate in northern Virginia, both to protect the Federal capital and to tie down the principal rebel army. Scott did not advocate an early offensive, however, largely because he knew that the spilling of blood was the surest guarantee of rendering a reconciliation impossible.

(2) A naval blockade should be established to cut the Confederacy off from European military aid and diplomatic support. The subsequent isolation would demonstrate to the rebels their dependence on the Northern states and perhaps force them to reconsider their rashness.

(3) A combined Army–Navy operation to control the Mississippi River should be mounted to split the Confederacy in half both physically and economically.

Scott's recommendations were based on his belief that once the North demonstrated the futility of rebellion, the Southern states might voluntarily re-enter the Union. Though his assessment proved inaccurate, his specific recommendations were accepted and formed the basis of Federal strategy throughout the war. The only major modification resulted from Lincoln's insistence that military pressure be applied in East Tennessee as well. Lincoln's motive was political—Eastern Tennessee being heavily Republican and Unionist in sentiment—but his modification served an important military function as well, since it prevented the Confederates from concentrating their numerically inferior armies.

Amateur strategists, newspaper editorialists in particular, judged Scott's plan too passive. They called it the Anaconda Plan, likening it to the South American reptile that strangled its prey with slowly constricting coils. Far better, they argued, to assert national authority immediately by a rapid descent on Richmond.

The greatest difficulty, of course, was the raising of armies and the expansion of the the Navy. The problem of naval expansion included the purely physical one of somehow acquiring a sufficient number of vessels. A Federal Strategy Board headed by Flag Officer Samuel F. DuPont established four blockading zones (*see* map at left), but since the Union navy then comprised only a handful of ships, a successful blockade of the 3,500-mile Confederate coastline would first require a monumental construction program. In addition, the government purchased dozens of merchant vessels, private yachts, and even ferry boats, and converted them all to warships. The result was a rapid growth in the size of the U.S. Navy and in the effectiveness of the naval blockade. Whereas there were only eighty-two U.S. Navy ships in commission in July 1861, by December there were 264, and a year later the Navy could boast of 427. By 1864, with a U.S. Navy of over 600 ships, only a few Confederate ports remained open to blockade-runners.

In addition to their reliance on an expanded Navy, both Lincoln and Scott recognized the strategically significant role railroads would play in the conflict. In this, as in so many other quantifiable categories, the Union held a huge advantage. There were over 20,000 miles of track in the Northern States at the outset of the war, nearly all of it of a uniform gauge. By contrast, the South had only 9,283 miles—less than half that of the North—much of it non-standard gauge. During the war both sides added to their rail networks, but considering the North's overwhelming advantage in industrial capacity, the building of new roads (and the repair of old ones) was much easier for the North. The map at left shows the railroads existing in 1864 at the height of the war. Despite the South's inferiority in this category, its ability to use interior lines of communication made its railroads important targets of early Union offensives.

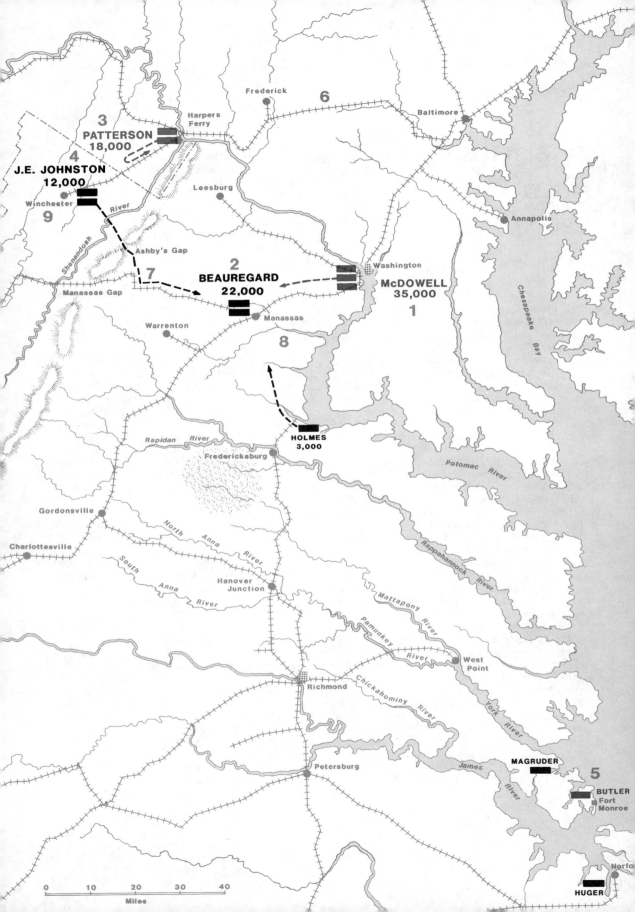

MAP 3

The Strategic Situation in the East

June, 1861

Despite the essential cogency of Scott's military advice, Lincoln knew that the seventy-five-year-old warrior was not the man to command Union armies in the field. Even Scott recognized his own limitations in this regard; he would remain in Washington to coordinate the armies. For the principal field commmand, Scott urged the appointment of Major Irvin McDowell. To be sure, McDowell had never commanded anything larger than a regiment, but few Americans had. Breveted to Major General, McDowell was tasked with the job of turning into an army the motley assemblage of militia regiments flooding into Washington. Moreover, he came under a great deal of popular and political pressure to mount an immediate offensive to crush the rebellion. Horace Greeley's New York *Tribune* urged daily that the army march "Forward to Richmond." McDowell protested to Lincoln that his troops were too green to undertake an offensive, but the President responded by saying: "You are green, it is true, but they are green also; you are all green alike." Thus prodded, McDowell examined the possibilities inherent in the strategic situation in the summer of 1861.

There were four armies in the field: (1) McDowell's own force at Arlington, numbering about 30,000 at the beginning of June, but growing to 37,000 by mid-month; (2) the somewhat smaller Confederate army of Major General P.G.T. Beauregard at Manassas Junction; (3) a second Union army under Major General Robert Patterson near Harpers Ferry; and (4) a Confederate army in the Shenandoah Valley under the command of General Joseph E. Johnston. A third Union force (5) under Major General Benjamin Butler was at Fort Monroe across the James River from Norfolk, too far away to affect the strategic situation in northern Virginia.

Each Federal army outnumbered its Confederate foe, though imperfect intelligence hid this fact from the commanders. But the key to success for either side would be its ability to exploit the available railroad network. McDowell's force was linked to Patterson's via the Baltimore and Ohio Railroad (6) while Johnston and Beauregard could reinforce one another via the Manassas Gap Railroad (7). If one side could concentrate its two armies against one of the other's, it could produce the superiority needed for victory.

McDowell's initial plan was to maneuver Beauregard away from Manassas Junction by moving around his right and placing himself between Manassas and Richmond (8). Forced to defend either Richmond or Manassas, Beauregard would presumably choose the former and thereby cut himself off from the rail link to Johnston's army, allowing McDowell to attack him in the open field with superior numbers. But the public mood would not wait for such a detailed plan to develop. Instead, McDowell was urged by Scott to advance directly against Beauregard at Manassas. Patterson would be tasked with the responsibility of pinning down Johnston's army in the Shenandoah Valley. At a cabinet meeting where the plan was discussed, Scott was reassuring: "I assume the responsibility for having Johnston kept off of McDowell's flank," he announced.

McDowell's force set out from Fairfax on Tuesday morning, July 16. On the same day, Patterson advanced cautiously southward toward Winchester (9). But, convinced that Johnston's forces outnumbered his own by a ratio of two to one, Patterson soon retraced his steps back to Harpers Ferry, where he called for reinforcements. Thus, while McDowell advanced slowly toward his showdown with Beauregard, Patterson had wholly failed to carry out his responsibility for holding Johnston in the Valley.

Major General Irvin McDowell was a former classmate of Beauregard's at West Point. He was known in the regular army for three attributes: a wide knowledge of military theory, a mastery of staff work, and an enormous appetite at the dinner table. (NA)

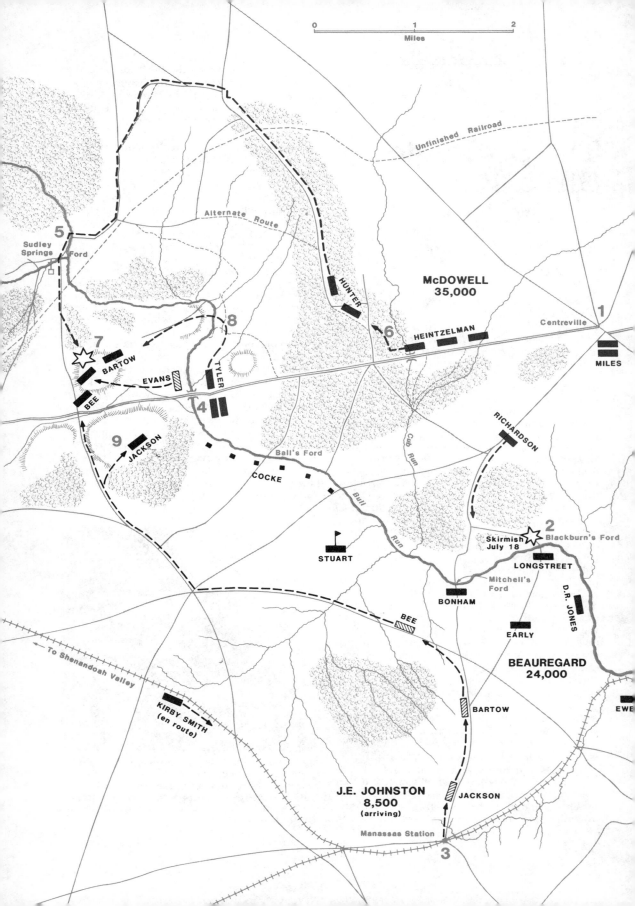

MAP 4

The First Battle of Bull Run (Manassas)

July 21, 1861

McDowell's army, some 35,000 strong, reached the vicinity of Centreville, Virginia (1) on July 18, 1861. Initial contact with Beauregard's Confederate army came that day along the banks of Bull Run Creek near Blackburn's Ford (2). A probing Federal column was thrown back with losses and the two armies faced each other across the winding shallow creek. Both McDowell and Beauregard now made plans for an offensive. McDowell sent out scouts to find a way to outflank the Confederate position, and Beauregard telegraphed General Joseph E. Johnston to come with reinforcements. The first elements of Johnston's army arrived at Manassas Junction (3) by rail on the afternoon of the 19th and Johnston himself arrived the next day. Though Johnston was senior, he allowed Beauregard to maintain command of the battlefield and to continue his plans for an offensive.

That night (July 20) McDowell invited his brigade and division commanders to his tent to discuss his plans for battle the next day. Many of his officers argued that a confrontation should be postponed or cancelled because all day long they had heard the sounds of trains arriving and departing Manassas Junction, a few miles to the south. Surely the Confederates were bringing elements of Johnston's army from the Valley! But McDowell was determined. He knew that if he did not attack now, the expiring enlistments of a large number of his troops would make another advance impossible for at least six months. McDowell spread a large map on the dirt floor of his tent to point out the particular assignments of each unit. Three brigades under Brigadier General Daniel Tyler were to mount an assault on the stone bridge across Bull Run Creek (4) while a brigade under Colonel Israel B. Richardson made a demonstration south toward the Confederates defending Blackburn's and Mitchell's Fords. Both of these movements, however, were intended to draw Confederate attention away from the main effort, which was a giant flanking movement across Sudley Springs Ford several miles to the north (5).

The Federal movement began shortly after 2:00 A.M. but not until 6:30 were Tyler's brigades in position near the stone bridge. Firing three cannon shots, they announced the beginning of the battle. Meanwhile the flanking column of two full divisions (those of Brigadier Generals David Hunter and Samuel Heintzelman), some 13,000 men, set off on the daring and dramatic maneuver around the Confederate left flank (6). The road was narrow and blocked by felled trees. Moreover, the Federal guide directed the column to the longer of two possible routes, believing that the shorter road would expose the movement to the enemy. Not until 9:30 did the lead brigade reach the ford at Sudley Springs. The men had been marching for seven hours and still had more than a mile to go before they reached the enemy flank.

While the two Union divisions were on the march, Beauregard continued to plan an offensive of his own: an attack against the Federal left from Blackburn's Ford. But his orders were vague and confusing, and his staff disorganized. By mid-morning he had decided, reluctantly, to call it off. Meanwhile Confederate Brigadier General Nathan G. "Shanks" Evans, charged with the defense of the stone bridge, was warned by a semaphore flag signal that his flank was about to be turned by the Federal column probing southward from Sudley Springs. Evans reoriented his front ninety degrees to face northward, and at a little after 10:00 when the Federals emerged from thick woods into the open, they were hit by heavy fire from Evans' men on the high ground known as Matthew's Hill (7). The brigades of Barnard Bee and Francis S. Bartow came to Evans' support and the Confederates established a stable line across the crest of Matthew's Hill. Both Hunter and Colonel Henry W. Slocum fell wounded. The flanking movement stalled.

The situation was saved by Tyler's decision to send two brigades across Bull Run Creek via an unmarked ford near the stone bridge (8). The arrival of these two brigades (one of which was commanded by William Tecumseh Sherman) and the almost simultaneous arrival of the rest of the Federal flanking column under Heintzelman gave the Union attack the impetus it needed to drive the Confederates off Matthew's Hill, across the Warrenton Pike, and onto Henry House Hill (9).

At a quarter past eleven, Johnston became convinced by the sound of increasing fire to the north that the real battle was being fought there, and he and Beauregard quitted Blackburn's Ford and rode northward. The two generals arrived in time to help place the retreating Confederate units into a line across the top of Henry House Hill, the dominant geographical feature on the battlefield. But the situation was nothing less than desperate, for if the Confederates were driven from this rise, there was no good ground behind them to make another stand. Moreover, the Federals appeared to have gained the momentum they needed to sweep up and over the thin Confederate line. The climax of the battle, then, took place atop this hill.

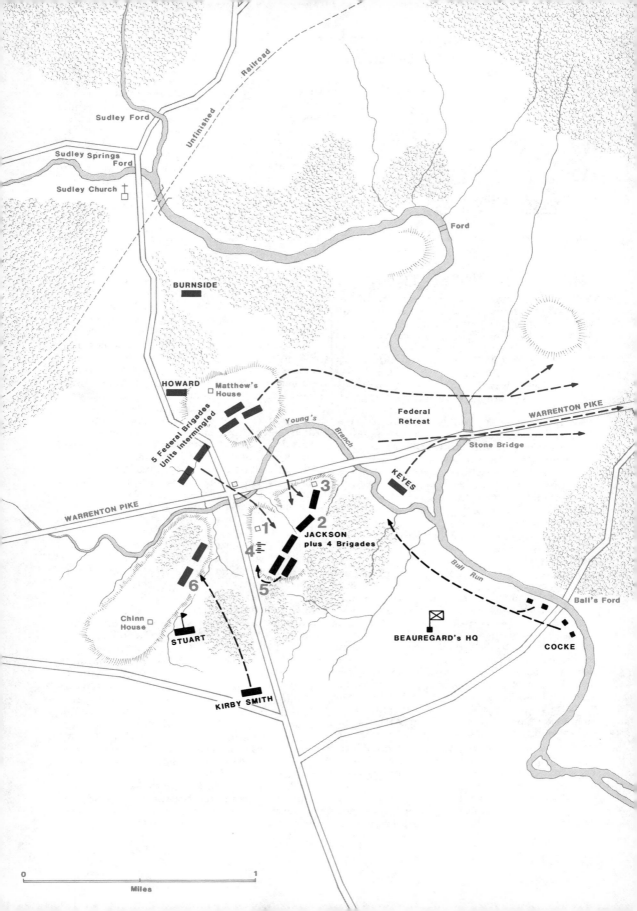

Sudley Ford

Sudley Springs Ford

Sudley Church

Unfinished Railroad

BURNSIDE

Ford

HOWARD   Matthew's House

5 Federal Brigades Units Intermingled

Young's Branch

Federal Retreat

WARRENTON PIKE

Stone Bridge

WARRENTON PIKE

KEYES

3

1

2

JACKSON plus 4 Brigades

4

5

6

Chinn House

STUART

Bull Run

Ball's Ford

BEAUREGARD's HQ

COCKE

KIRBY SMITH

0   1

Miles

MAP 5

Bull Run Continued: The Battle for Henry House Hill

July 21, 1861 (noon to 4 P.M.)

Henry House Hill is an undulating piece of open high ground overlooking the Warrenton Turnpike where it intersects the Manassas–Sudley Road. It received its name from the home of Mrs. Judith Henry (1), an aged widow who lived in a white frame house near the crest of the hill and who was destined to become the first civilian casualty of the Civil War.

While Union troops were breaking through the Confederate line on Matthew's Hill, Confederate Brigadier General Thomas J. Jackson was placing his brigade atop Henry House Hill with great care. He deployed his men in a shallow depression on the reverse slope where they would be protected against Union artillery, but where they could still sweep the crest of the ridge in front of them (2). When the disorganized remnants of the Confederate forces from Matthew's Hill straggled back to Henry House Hill, Jackson's brigade was nearly the only Southern unit to maintain cohesiveness. Brigadier General Barnard Bee rode up to Jackson and pointed out the obvious: Confederate units were falling back, unable to contain the Federal advance. Exuding calm amidst the turmoil, Jackson suggested that Bee rally the men around his own brigade. Bee rode into the mass of retreating Confederates and urged them to rally behind the Virginians. "There stands Jackson like a stone wall!" he cried, pointing to the stolid former V.M.I. mathematics professor. The appeal worked and the Confederates managed to assemble a more or less continuous line across the crest of Henry House Hill from the Manassas Road to the Robinson House (3). There the Confederates awaited the Federal attack.

They did not have long to wait. A little after noon, five Union brigades—nearly ten thousand men—stormed up the hill. Bee was killed in the first rush but by this time both Beauregard and Johnston had arrived from Blackburn's Ford and, under the eye of their generals, the Confederates stood their ground. After a short pause, the Union soldiers

regrouped and came on again in furious but unco-ordinated attacks. For over an hour the crest of the hill blazed with musketry and the acrid smoke of the muzzle loaders drifted about in clouds as Union and Confederate soldiers battled at close range.

Sensing victory, McDowell at about 2:00 P.M. ordered two artillery batteries (those of Griffin and Ricketts) up onto Henry House Hill to enfilade the Confederate left (4). Their position was dangerously exposed and, as it turned out, their fire had little effect on the rebel line because of the uneven ground. Moreover, the gunners themselves were subject to a flank attack from the woods along the Manassas Road (5). At the height of the battle, a blue-clad regiment marched out of those woods to a point only 50 or so yards from the Federal guns. Believing these troops to be their own infantry support, the gunners continued to concentrate on the center of the Confederate line to their front. But the regiment was the 33rd Virginia, under the command of Colonel Charles Cummings, who had his men dress ranks before ordering a volley and a bayonet charge. The Confederates seized the guns and turned them on their former owners. The Federals counterattacked and re-captured the guns. Hand-to-hand fighting around the guns brought the two sides face-to-face and the battery changed hands no less than three times. The outcome of the battle hovered in the balance.

By 4:00 P.M., however, Federal soldiers had been up and on the march or in battle for 14 consecutive hours. Many had dropped out of the battle from sheer exhaustion and by late afternoon there was very little fight left in any of them. Though McDowell still believed that victory was in his grasp, Union troops began falling back down the slope of Henry House Hill and across Young's Branch toward the stone bridge. A Confederate attack by fresh rein-forcements on the Union left near the Chinn House (6) hurried them along.

The Union soldiers were no longer moving in cohesive units now, but as an undirected river of men streaming across the bridge and even swim-ming the river itself. A Confederate battery ad-vanced to the stone bridge and lobbed several shells after the retreating enemy. One lucky shot landed square on the bridge over Cub Run, two miles to the east, overturning a wagon and clogging the Warrenton Pike. At this point, the withdrawal became a rout. Soldiers abandoned the road to seek safety by fleeing through the countryside in the general direction of Washington.

There was no Confederate pursuit, for the battle had disorganized the victors almost as much as it had the vanquished. Only Jackson, now wearing his new nickname, seriously suggested a pursuit. But Beauregard and Johnston overruled him, and a jubilant but exhausted Confederate army settled down to bask in the afterglow of a hard-won victory.

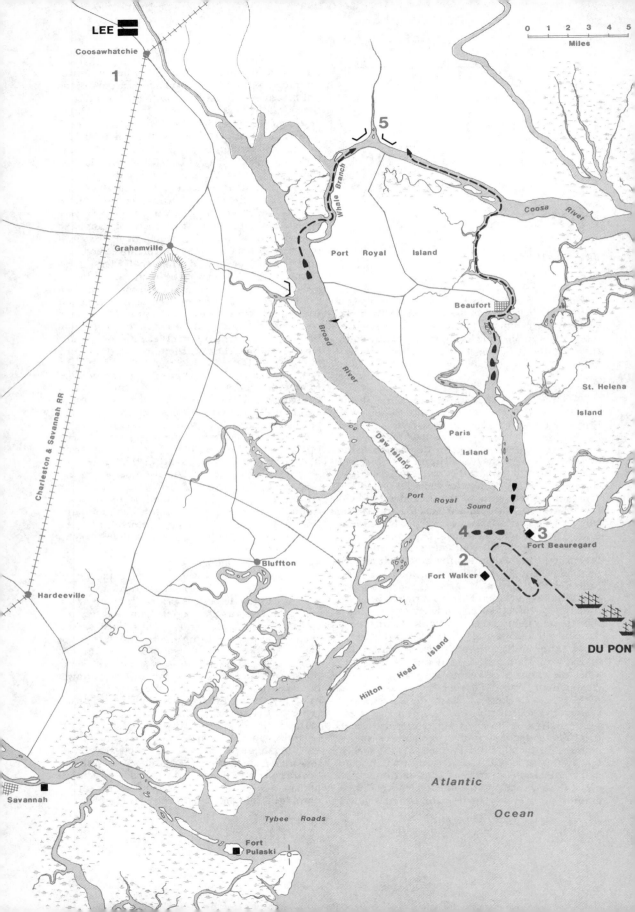

LEE

Coosawhatchie

1

Grahamville

Charleston & Savannah RR

Hardeeville

Bluffton

Savannah

Fort
Pulaski

Tybee Roads

Whale Branch

Broad

River

Daw Island

Port Royal

Sound

Hilton

Head

Island

Port Royal Island

Beaufort

Coosa River

Paris

Island

St. Helena

Island

5

4

2
Fort Walker

3
Fort Beauregard

DU PON

Atlantic

Ocean

0 1 2 3 4 5
Miles

MAP 6

Port Royal

November 7, 1861

Practically the first strategic decision made by the Lincoln administration upon the outbreak of war was that the Southern coastline should be declared to be in a state of blockade. Some members of the government worried that the use of the term "blockade" might imply recognition of the Confederacy. Navy Secretary Gideon Welles suggested that closing the southern ports might be construed as a domestic municipal duty made necessary by the fact that import duties could not be collected at those ports. But this legal nicety was soon discarded and the government had to accept the name as well as the fact of the blockade. The four blockading zones established by the Strategy Board at this time (*see* Map 2) were maintained throughout the war. But in addition, the Board recommended that at least one major harbor in each zone be seized by Union forces for use as a base. The first such base to be seized was at Port Royal, South Carolina, midway between Savannah and Charleston, and the attack was led by DuPont himself.

Port Royal was chosen as a target for three reasons. First, its location between Savannah and Charleston made it a convenient base for Union vessels blockading those cities. Second, Port Royal Sound was an enormous roadstead, large enough to accommodate the entire Union Navy. Third, Port Royal was a watery wedge to the interior that offered a possible means of breaking the Charleston and Savannah Railroad at Coosawhatchie (1).

In October 1861 DuPont assembled a mixed fleet of eleven regular warships, a few converted merchantmen, and a large number of Army transport vessels carrying the 12,000-man occupation force of Brigadier General Thomas W. Sherman (no relation to the more famous William Tecumseh Sherman). The original plan was to conduct a joint Army–Navy attack with DuPont's warships providing covering fire for Sherman's troops. But a storm encountered off the Carolina coast on November 1 drove ashore the ships carrying the landing craft. DuPont determined that a naval attack would have to be attempted without the army.

The entrance to the Sound was guarded by two earthen forts hastily thrown up by the Confederate defenders. Fort Walker (2) on the southern headland was the stronger of the two and DuPont believed (correctly, as it would prove) that if Walker fell, Fort Beauregard on the northern headland (3) would have to be abandoned. Leaving the transports at anchor offshore, the Commodore's flagship, the *Wabash*, led the Union warships in single file into the Sound on November 7.

The Union squadron steamed up the center of the channel in line-ahead formation beyond the range of all but a few of the Confederate guns. Then DuPont led the squadron in a broad turn to the left, passing Fort Walker at a range of 800 yards. DuPont possessed several advantages in this contest. The Union warships carried 123 guns whereas the fort mounted only nineteen. Moreover, DuPont's ships were a moving target for the inexperienced Confederate gunners. Finally, the smaller Union gunboats were able to enfilade the defenders from the north (4). On only the third pass, the Confederates hoisted a white flag. With Fort Walker's surrender, the garrison of Fort Beauregard withdrew to Port Royal Island.

Eventually Union naval forces followed up this victory and seized the city of Beaufort and all of Port Royal Island. But, except for a well-executed amphibious assault on Confederate batteries at Port Royal Ferry (5), they did not succeed in using their foothold at Port Royal to advance into the interior. The commander of the Confederate forces, none other than Robert E. Lee, concluded from the Port Royal operation that it was futile to attempt to defend the Confederacy at the water's edge, and adopted instead a flexible defensive system anchored by a mobile force at Coosawhatchie and at Pocataligo, just to the north. He gave up the navigable inlets to the Union gunboats. But whenever Union soldiers attempted to push inland, the mobile force was rushed to the danger spot to drive them back. The result was that the Union Navy used Port Royal Sound as a major base for four years, but did not succeed in seizing the railroad between Charleston and Savannah until after Sherman's army occupied Savannah in December, 1864 (*see* Map 41).

Nevertheless, the Union naval victory at Port Royal was significant, for in addition to providing an important base for the South Atlantic Blockading Squadron, it demonstrated that steam-powered warships firing explosive shells were more than a match for hastily erected fortifications along the coast. Port Royal was to be merely the first of a long series of Union victories along the South Atlantic coast and in the Gulf of Mexico, which would enhance the blockade and effectively seal off the Confederacy from the outside world. By 1864 only Charleston and Wilmington, North Carolina, on the Atlantic seaboard, remained open to Confederate blockade-runners.

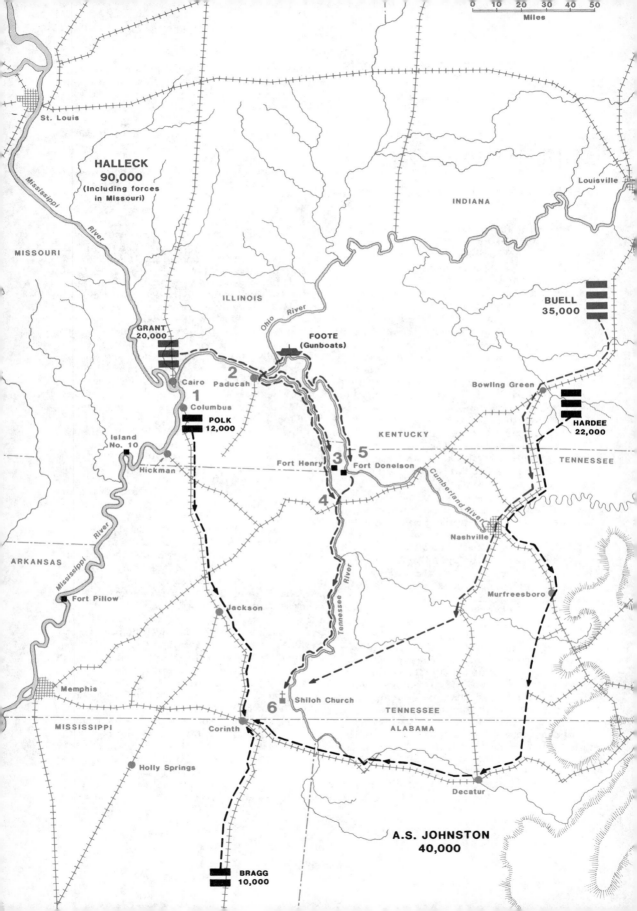

MAP 7

The Strategic Situation in the West

February-March, 1862

In the West the strategy of both sides was influenced by the ambiguous status of Kentucky. As the native state of both Lincoln and Davis, Kentucky epitomized the dilemma of the border states. The unhappy situation of the Crittenden family illustrated this dilemma. Senator John J. Crittenden, who had led the unsuccessful last minute compromise attempts in Congress, had two sons: One became a Major General in the Confederate Army, the other held the same rank in the Union Army. Following Fort Sumter, Kentucky declared itself neutral, though both sides recruited troops within its borders. After several months of an uneasy truce, the Confederates made the first overt military move when rebel forces seized the town of Columbus on the Mississippi River (1) in September 1861. Soon afterward, Union forces under Brigadier General Ulysses S. Grant occupied Paducah (2).

Both sides now moved large forces into the state. The Confederate commander, General Albert Sidney Johnston, established a defensive barrier which came to be known as "the long Kentucky line" running from Columbus through Forts Henry and Donelson to Bowling Green and east to the Cumberland Gap. Johnston's unfortunate decision to adopt a passive defense and to disperse his numerically inferior forces exposed him to piecemeal defeat at the hands of the two Union armies in the field.

Union concentration was also made difficult by a command situation that divided authority between Major General Henry W. Halleck, who commanded the Department of the Missouri headquartered in St. Louis, and Brigadier General Don Carlos Buell, who commanded the Department of the Ohio from Louisville. Operating independently, each commander embarked on a campaign of his own: Buell edged cautiously south toward Bowling Green while Halleck dispatched Grant against Forts Henry and Donelson.

Grant was the most aggressive of the Union commanders in the West and was destined to make his name in this campaign. In conjunction with gunboats under Flag Officer Andrew H. Foote, Grant compelled a quick Confederate evacuation of Fort Henry on the Tennessee River (3). Then, while Foote steamed upriver to destroy the Memphis and Ohio Railroad bridge (4), Grant crossed overland to lay siege to powerful Fort Donelson on the Cumberland River (5).

At this point, Johnston was still in a position to concentrate his centrally located forces against either Grant or Buell with a fair hope of success. Instead he made the worst possible decision: he detached 12,000 men from his main army at Bowling Green and sent them to Brigadier General John B. Floyd at Fort Donelson. It was too small a reinforcement to assure Floyd of success against Grant, and the detachment lengthened Johnston's own already-long odds against Buell. Even with these reinforcements, Floyd's position at Fort Donelson was hopeless. Floyd hesitated past the point when he might have escaped with his entire garrison, then fled upriver with only a handful, leaving to Brigadier General Simon Bolivar Buckner the dubious honor of surrendering. Grant's terms to Buckner—"unconditional and immediate surrender"—made great play in the Northern press and turned Grant into a war hero.

The loss of Fort Donelson smashed Johnston's "long Kentucky line" and forced both Polk and Johnston himself (with Hardee's Corps) to withdraw southward. Indeed, with the destruction of the Memphis and Ohio Railroad bridge across the Tennessee River, the Confederacy now lacked any east–west rail communications in Tennessee, forcing the rebels to fall back all the way to Corinth, Mississippi. As Johnston retreated, Buell followed slowly, accepting the surrender of Nashville in late February.

In March Halleck reacted to rumors that Grant had a drinking problem by replacing his most successful commander with Brigadier General C. F. Smith. Soon convinced that the rumors were exaggerated, however, Halleck reinstated Grant. In the meantime William T. Sherman, the senior division commander, had led the army's advance southward up the Tennessee River to Pittsburg Landing, which became the site of a major Union encampment dubbed Camp Shiloh after a nearby church (6).

On March 11, Lincoln elevated Halleck to the command of all Union troops in the theater, including Buell's. Almost immediately, Halleck ordered Buell's forces to march overland and join Grant's army at Pittsburg Landing. Halleck let it be known that once the two armies were united, he would take command personally and lead an offensive to smash the rebels at Corinth. Buell obediently began his move on March 16, unaware that Albert Sidney Johnston was planning an offensive of his own against Grant's exposed camp at Shiloh.

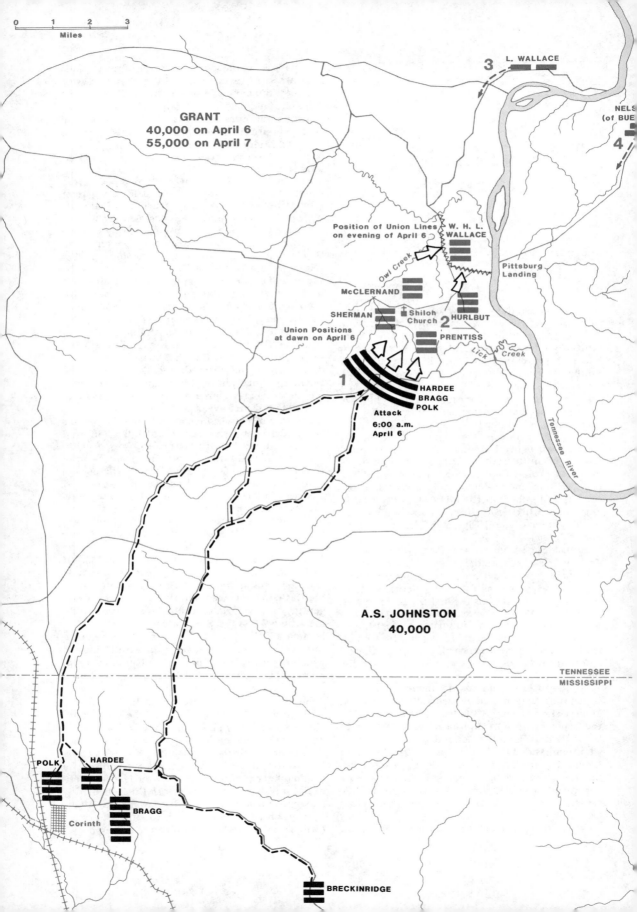

0 1 2 3
Miles

3 L. WALLACE

GRANT
40,000 on April 6
55,000 on April 7

NELS
(of BUE

4

Position of Union Lines
on evening of April 6

W. H. L.
WALLACE

Pittsburg
Landing

Owl Creek

McCLERNAND

SHERMAN

■ Shiloh
Church

2 HURLBUT

Union Positions
at dawn on April 6

PRENTISS

Lick   Creek

1

HARDEE
BRAGG
POLK

Attack
6:00 a.m.
April 6

Tennessee River

A.S. JOHNSTON
40,000

TENNESSEE
MISSISSIPPI

POLK   HARDEE

Corinth   BRAGG

BRECKINRIDGE

MAP 8

Shiloh

April 6-7, 1862

The Confederate "Army of the Mississippi," which concentrated around the vital railroad junction at Corinth in March, was divided into three groups: four brigades under Major General Leonidas Polk (an Episcopalian Bishop), six under Major General Braxton Bragg, and three under Major General William J. Hardee. Three additional brigades under former Vice President (and 1860 Presidential candidate) John C. Breckinridge were moving up from the south, and a handful of troops arrived from Jackson, Tennessee, with Lieutenant General P. G. T. Beauregard, who had been dispatched to the western theater from Virginia to serve as Johnston's second-in-command. All together, Confederate forces numbered just over 40,000. Johnston and Beauregard were aware that Grant's forces at Camp Shiloh were at least as strong as their own. But they also knew that with Buell moving west to link up with Grant, they had to strike now while the odds were relatively even. To delay would almost surely mean that they would be overwhelmed by the superior numbers of the combined Union armies.

The rebel army got underway on April 3, advancing on roughly parallel roads to avoid congestion, but the troops made little progress the first day and Beauregard, who had drawn up plans for a Confederate attack on the 4th, despaired of meeting his timetable. In fact, it was the afternoon of April 5 before the Confederates were in position to launch their attack. By that time, Beauregard felt sure that the Yankees must have discovered the Confederate movement and were dug in, ready and waiting. He expressed this fear to Johnston and suggested that the operation be cancelled. But Johnston was eager for a fight and set the attack for dawn the next day: April 6.

In fact, Grant had no idea that the rebels were so close. He was not even present in the camp the night Beauregard and Johnston had their discussion, but was down river off Savannah, Tennessee, on a Union gunboat. Sherman was the senior division commander, but he was sure the rebels had had the fight taken out of them at Fort Donelson. He had not required his men to prepare fortifications, and had thrown out only a few pickets. Grant himself later admitted in his *Memoirs* that he had "scarcely the faintest idea of an attack."

At about 6:00 A.M. on April 6 the Confederate line surged forward, crashing out of the trees to surprise most of the Union soldiers at breakfast (1). Johnston had arrayed his host in three ranks—one Corps behind the other in a front nearly three miles wide. The result of this curious formation was a loss of effective command and control over the widely dispersed Confederate units, and the conflict soon dissolved into a confused melee, making it impossible for Johnston to determine where reinforcements were needed. Nevertheless, for several hours the rebels drove the even more disorganized Union troops back toward the Tennessee River. The small creeks that Sherman had believed would guard his flanks now served to hem in the retreating Union soldiers who were threatened with possible annihilation.

At about 9:30 the rebel advance stalled near a grove of trees that both sides would come to call "the hornet's nest" (2). There, elements of Prentiss's and W.H.L. Wallace's divisions fought off a dozen Confederate assaults, inflicting heavy casualties (including a mortal wound to Johnston himself), and winning several valuable hours for the hard-pressed Union army. Though finally outflanked and overwhelmed, the Union soldiers at the hornet's nest probably saved the day for the rest of Grant's army.

Grant was on the field by mid-day, having hurried south at the first sound of the guns. His arrival, plus reinforcements from Lew Wallace's division (3), stiffened Union resistance. By nightfall the Yankees had been pushed back to the river's edge, but they held on grimly. Moreover, with reinforcements that arrived during the night from the advanced elements of Buell's army (4), Grant was able to launch a counter-attack the next day and win back virtually all the ground given up on the 6th.

Badly outnumbered now, disorganized, and having lost the element of surprise as well as the services of General Johnston, Beauregard ordered a Confederate retreat to Corinth. The battle had claimed 13,000 Federal and 10,700 Confederate casualties, a total of nearly 24,000 men—five times the losses at Bull Run. Because the Union army held the field, and because the Confederates had failed in their effort to annihilate Grant's army, the North could and did claim victory. Moreover, the loss of Johnston and the lesson Grant and Sherman learned about the risks of underestimating the enemy, would affect the operations of both sides for the rest of the war. Finally, Buell's arrival completed the concentration of Federal armies in the West and forced the Confederacy to withdraw into its field fortifications around Corinth, leaving the initiative to Buell and Grant.

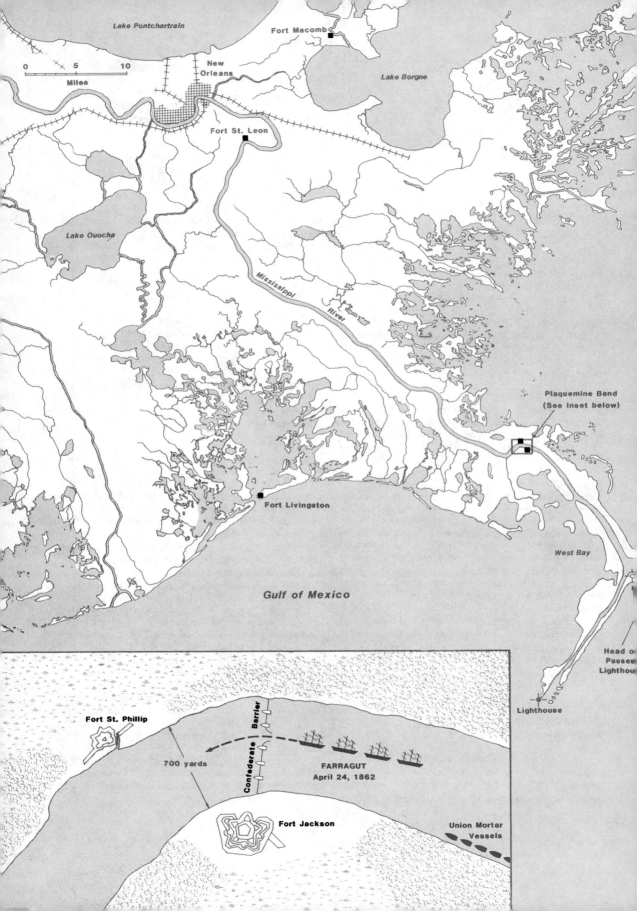

Lake Pontchartrain

Fort Macomb

New Orleans

Lake Borgne

0   5   10
Miles

Fort St. Leon

Lake Ouocha

Mississippi River

Plaquemine Bend
(See inset below)

Fort Livingston

West Bay

Gulf of Mexico

Head o
Passes
Lighthou

Lighthouse

Fort St. Phillip

Barrier

700 yards

Confederate

FARRAGUT
April 24, 1862

Fort Jackson

Union Mortar
Vessels

MAP 9

New Orleans

April, 1862

While Union and Confederate troops battled to a bloody draw at Shiloh, U.S. Navy Flag Officer David Glasgow Farragut, commander of the West Gulf Blockading Squadron, contemplated an assault on the Confederate forts guarding the Mississippi River below New Orleans. Despite the confidence engendered by DuPont's success against Confederate fortifications at Port Royal, the situation on the lower Mississippi seemed to favor the defenders. The key Confederate defenses were at Plaquemine Bend, about ninety miles (as the river winds) south of New Orleans. There the rebels occupied two strong masonry forts (not earthen forts, as at Port Royal) armed with a total of 142 guns. In addition, a boom of logs linked by heavy chains barred the river. Farragut's deep-draft warships would have to steam upriver against a four-knot current and overcome the log boom while sustaining heavy fire. On the other hand, if the Union warships did succeed in getting past the forts, the rebels would be cut off from retreat or supply because the forts were surrounded by swamps and forest and dependent on the river for communications with New Orleans.

Initially, Union planners envisioned a joint Army-Navy operation, but Assistant Secretary of the Navy Gustavus Vasa Fox was eager to enhance the prestige of the Navy by winning a solo victory. His plan was for a fleet of mortar boats under the command of Captain David Dixon Porter to pound the Confederate forts into rubble, after which Farragut's oceangoing steam sloops would run by the forts. The timing of the operation was upset by the month's delay required to nurse Farragut's vessels over the shallow bar at the entrance to the river, but by mid-April the Union armada was finally in position for the assault.

Porter's mortar boats began their bombardment on April 17, and lobbed shells into both forts almost continuously for a week. The exploding shells destroyed most of the flammable wooden structures inside the forts, but did not significantly reduce the forts' firepower. For their part, Confederate gunners damaged several Union gunboats and sank one.

Nevertheless, in the pre-dawn darkness of April 24, Farragut's steam sloops got underway and headed for a break in the log boom made by two of the Union gunboats. The Confederates opened fire and Farragut's warships responded. Gun flashes from both sides lit up the night. It took only about an hour for ten of the Union warships to run the gauntlet; three others, damaged by gunfire, turned back. Two Confederate ironclads which had been rushed to completion entered the battle, but proved too clumsy to have much effect.

Once Farragut had passed the forts, the defenders were trapped. The big Union warships chased the smaller Confederate gunboats upriver or forced them to run themselves ashore. With the river cleared, Farrragut landed the advance elements of Brigadier General Benjamin F. Butler's army above Fort St. Philip. Though the Confederates held out for another week, their capitulation was only a matter of time. Meanwhile, Farragut, unwilling to wait for the army, steamed upriver to New Orleans. With the Mississippi at spring flood, his guns commanded the streets of the city. Even though Butler's soldiers were still ninety miles downriver, New Orleans capitulated on April 25. Butler's army arrived in the city on May 1 to begin a very unpopular military occupation.

The strategic significance of the fall of New Orleans was enormous. Not only did it deprive the Confederacy of a major city and a principal seaport, but combined with Union successes on the upper Mississippi, it brought significantly closer the sundering of the Confederacy along the axis of the Mississippi River.

Flag Officer David Glasgow Farragut commanded the West Gulf Blockading Squadron. His success in capturing New Orleans helped win him a promotion to Rear Admiral, the first in U.S. Naval history. (NA)

PART TWO

The Organized War

By the spring of 1862, civilian and military leaders on both sides had accepted the fact that the war was going to be longer and bloodier than anyone had anticipated. After the Union disaster at Bull Run, President Lincoln issued a call for no less than 400,000 volunteers to serve for a period of three years—a far cry from the three-month enlistments asked of the original 75,000 volunteers. For its part, the Confederacy had required a one-year enlistment from its initial recruits, and in the spring of 1862 that year was coming to an end. With the blush off the rose, recruits were harder to find, and on April 16 the Confederate Congress passed a conscription act that obligated all white males aged 18 to 45 to military service. For a society founded upon the principles of individualism and limited government, the passage of this act was a major concession.

Southerners generally, and Jefferson Davis in particular, discovered that it was extremely difficult to conduct a total war with a limited government. Some members of the administration refused to accept that their system did not function efficiently, and placed the blame for failures on Davis. Governor Joseph E. Brown of Georgia took the government to court to contest the legality of conscription, and even Davis' Vice President, Alexander Stephens, became a vocal critic of the administration.

The Union government also had to adjust during the crisis. Lincoln had declared martial law in Maryland early in the war, and in succeeding months he extended it throughout the border states. Critics of the Lincoln administration wondered aloud about the value of preserving a Union

Federal supply centers like this one at Yorktown testified to the growing domination of logistics and materiel over the conduct of war. (LC)

that did not respect civil liberties. Throughout the war Lincoln had to walk a political tightrope between the "Copperheads," who wanted to let the South go in peace, and the "Radicals," who wanted to use the war to achieve major social changes in the South and in particular to abolish slavery.

The events of the first year of the war led both sides to make important changes in top military command positions. In the North, Scott stayed on temporarily as the titular head of the Army, but for

Major General Henry Wager Halleck, called "Old Brains" for his wide knowledge of military theory, was brought to Washington in 1862 to serve as General in Chief of the Union armies. Lincoln hoped that he would coordinate Union strategy on a national level. Halleck soon discovered, however, that his powers were limited by political pressure and sensitive personalities and he became little more than a military advisor to the President. (LC)

Major General George Brinton McClellan was "the problem child of the Civil War" according to historian T. Harry Williams. Brilliant and flamboyant, he was a superb organizer and skilled at winning the hearts of his men who cheered him spontaneously and called him "Little Mac." He was, however, reluctant to commit his army to battle, and bristled when asked to explain or defend his military decisions. (NA)

General Robert E. Lee succeeded to command of the Army of Northern Virginia when Joseph E. Johnston was wounded at Fair Oaks. Almost immediately he began an offensive known subsequently as The Seven Days that drove McClellan from the gates of Richmond. Lee's political tact and strategic audacity made him invaluable to the Confederacy. (LC)

the field command, McDowell was eased aside to make way for a new man: thirty-six-year-old Major General George Brinton McClellan. McClellan was in many ways an ideal selection. He possessed the organizational and managerial skills needed in a conflict fought by mass armies and requiring the mobilization of national resources. McClellan's talents in training, drill, and logistics would result in the creation of a powerful Union army. Unfortunately for his historical reputation, he was less skilled in wielding that army in battle. One noted scholar has called McClellan "the problem child of the Civil War" and McClellan has almost as many critics as champions. But all agree that his organizational skills helped build the national army that would, in other hands, bring victory.

One of McClellan's principal contributions was the creation of a military staff. Whereas Scott had believed that a staff of two was more than sufficient, McClellan put together a staff of sixty-five with his own father-in-law, Colonel Randolph B. Marcy, as chief of staff. Similar growth was mirrored in the government as a whole. The number of civilian employees of the Federal government multiplied fourfold between 1861 and 1865. Headed by Montgomery Meigs, the Quartermaster General's office alone employed over 7,000 clerks and became a logistical machine that kept McClellan's army clothed, fed, and supplied with ammunition.

In the South, the change in command leadership was partly the result of the fortunes of war. Joseph E. Johnston, who commanded the Confederate armies in northern Virginia, was wounded at the Battle of Fair Oaks (Seven Pines) and Davis turned to Robert E. Lee to replace him. Lee's assumption of command was even more important to the South than McClellan's organizational innovations to the North. In part, this was due to Lee's own organizational skill: he divided his army into two corps (headed by Lieutenant Generals Longstreet and Jackson) and in other ways vastly improved the Confederacy's military command structure. But Lee's greatest contribution was his own personality. Whereas both Beauregard and Johnston had quarreled with Davis—and with each other—often over frivolous matters, Lee's great tact and gentle manner smoothed the machinery of government and reduced the inherent civil-military tensions bound to exist in a society where the head of state considered himself a military expert.

McClellan and Lee handled responsibilities far greater than McDowell, Beauregard, or Johnston. Whereas the generals of 1861 had commanded armies of between twenty-five and thirty-five thousand, McClellan and Lee would command armies of between eighty and one hundred fifty thousand. McClellan is often criticized by historians and military analysts for the failure of his Peninsular

Campaign, and rightly so. But the very act of transporting an army of 120-150,000 men to the peninsula (experts vary on the exact numbers), and maintaining it in the field, was a formidable accomplishment. Likewise Lee's skillful maneuvering of his army required a level of staff work beyond the capability of any organization that had existed in 1861.

Two other characteristics of these rival commanders require comment. The first is McClellan's curious conviction that his enemy's forces nearly always seriously outnumbered his own. McClellan relied heavily on the military intelligence gathered by the famous detective Allan Pinkerton, whose operatives counted campfires and interviewed rebel deserters. Whether he deliberately hedged on the side of caution or was simply confused, Pinkerton consistently exaggerated Confederate strength by as much as 100 percent. Given McClellan's natural sense of caution, this kind of false intelligence made him hesitant, even timid, at critical moments. In February 1862 Lincoln had to issue General War Order No. 1 directing a Union advance on or before Washington's birthday. Such an order only confirmed McClellan's opinion of Lincoln as strategically naive, but the President felt he had to prod his general into action.

The second characteristic that affected the outcome of battles in 1862 was Lee's willingness to take chances: to divide his already numerically inferior army in the face of an enemy, and to launch attacks against strong positions in the belief that superior morale would compensate for inferior numbers. Often he was right. But it must be noted that McClellan's conservative tactics preserved manpower while Lee's expended it, and in the years ahead those expended lives would be missed.

The twelve months after April 1862, then, saw the emergence of "the organized war," which was marked by the ascendancy of Lee's reputation as a military tactician *nonpareil*. The moral value of Lee's presence on the battlefield came to be worth several divisions. In the same period McClellan's reputation declined and near the end of the second campaign season of the war, Lincoln sacked him, explaining that McClellan had "the slows." Any comparison of the two men usually results in an unflattering portrait of McClellan: he was timid, sluggish, perhaps even cowardly. But Lee's own opinion of him was somewhat different. When asked after the war to identify the best Union general he had faced, he did not hesitate: "McClellan," he said, "by all odds."

Major General John Pope briefly commanded the Federal "Army of Virginia" in 1862. He created resentment in his new command almost immediately by issuing an irritating general order that belittled the accomplishments of the eastern troops as compared to their western colleagues. He met with failure at the Second Battle of Bull Run and never again held important command in the army. (NA)

Major General James Ewell Brown ("Jeb") Stuart commanded Lee's cavalry division throughout the campaigns of 1862-63. Only 29 when this photograph was taken in 1862, he grew his luxuriant beard to conceal his youth. Stuart first gained fame by riding completely around McClellan's army during the Peninsular campaign (*see* Map 14). (NA)

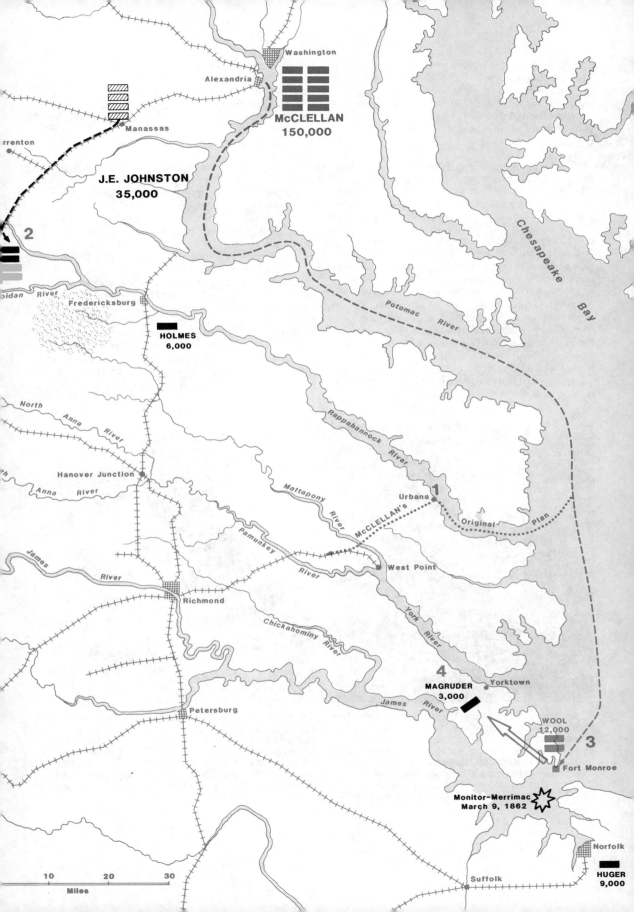

Washington

Alexandria

McCLELLAN
150,000

Manassas

rrenton

J.E. JOHNSTON
35,000

2

oidan   River

Fredericksburg

HOLMES
6,000

North

Anna   River

Hanover Junction

Anna   River

Potomac   River

Rappahannock   River

Mattapony   River

Pamunkey   River

Urbana

McCLELLAN's

1

Original   Plan

West Point

Chesapeake
Bay

James

River

Richmond

Chickahominy   River

Petersburg

York   River

4

MAGRUDER
3,000

Yorktown

James   River

WOOL
12,000

3

Fort Monroe

Monitor-Merrimac
March 9, 1862

Norfolk

Suffolk

HUGER
9,000

10   20   30

Miles

MAP 10

The Peninsular Campaign

March-April, 1862

Prodded by the President's War Order No. 1, McClellan finally divulged a plan of operations to Lincoln in February, 1862. The new Union commander sought to avoid a direct assault on Joseph Johnston's army entrenched at Manassas by using Union naval superiority to outflank the Confederates. He proposed to transport the bulk of the Union army by sea to the small port city of Urbana on the Rappahannock River (1). There he would be between Richmond and Johnston's army and in a position either to make a rapid descent on the Confederate capital or to fight the rebel army on grounds of his own choosing.

Lincoln was pleased that McClellan finally had revealed the existence of a plan, but he was dubious about the wisdom of the plan itself. He wondered aloud what would prevent the rebels from occupying Washington while McClellan was disembarking at Urbana. To McClellan it seemed obvious that Johnston would be compelled to fall back in defense of his own capital, but Lincoln viewed the situation politically and knew that no success by McClellan in the field, even the capture of Richmond, could compensate for the loss of Washington. He therefore insisted that before he could approve McClellan's plan, the general would have to provide assurances that sufficient Federal troops would be left behind to defend the nation's capital. McClellan believed that such a request only betrayed Lincoln's naivete in military matters, but nonetheless made the requested pledges.

Alas for McClellan's careful planning, Joe Johnston did not wait patiently at Manassas for the Federals to take the initiative. Uneasy about the proximity of the huge Federal army at Arlington, he had for some time considered withdrawing to the more easily defended line of the Rappahannock River (2). He undertook the move on March 9, earning much criticism from the patriotic press in Richmond, which pointed out that he had voluntarily surrendered what Southern soldiers had died defending only eight months earlier.

In the wake of Johnston's evacuation, McClellan cautiously advanced toward Manassas and occupied the abandoned Confederate camp. A cursory exploration of the camp, however, revealed that it could not possibly have housed as many enemy soldiers as McClellan had claimed, and that several of the large guns frowning from the earthworks were, in fact, "Quaker guns"—logs painted black. In addition to bearing the embarrassment of these discoveries, McClellan now had to scrap his Urbana scheme. Johnston's selection of the Rappahannock as a defense line made Urbana less desirable as a debarkation site. Unwilling to surrender the idea of an amphibious movement, McClellan selected as his new landing site Federally-occupied Fort Monroe at the tip of the peninsula formed by the York and James Rivers where they flowed into the Chesapeake Bay (3). For a while it appeared that McClellan's amphibious movement to Fort Monroe would have to be postponed or cancelled because of the dramatic success of the Confederate ironclad CSS *Virginia* in Hampton Roads. In their hurry to evacuate Norfolk after the secession of Virginia, the Federals had failed to destroy completely the new U.S. steam frigate U.S.S. *Merrimac.* The Confederates raised it, repaired it, armor plated it, and re-christened it the *Virginia.* On March 8 it steamed out of Norfolk Harbor and attacked the Federal squadron in Hampton Roads. It sunk one Union vessel and severely damaged another. The rest of the Federal squadron withdrew to the safety of deep water where the *Virginia* could not follow, surrendering the control of Hampton Roads to the Confederates. The *Virginia* sortied again on March 9 (the same day Johnston withdrew from Manassas) but this time it was met by a Union ironclad—the oddly shaped *Monitor* which had arrived overnight. Their duel lasted several hours and ended in a tactical draw, but the *Monitor's* ability to stand up to the *Virginia* saved McClellan's seaborne movement.

Lincoln exacted the same pledges from McClellan about his new scheme as he had for the Urbana plan, asking him to provide the Secretary of War with a list of the units that would be left behind to defend Washington after McClellan had departed for the peninsula. McClellan did so, but he exaggerated the numbers, counting some units twice and including other units too far away to be of any real effect in a defense of the capital. Once Lincoln and Stanton discovered this, they made one of the more controversial decisions of the war: they ordered McDowell's corps, earmarked for McClellan's amphibious movement, to remain behind.

Because McClellan himself had already embarked for Fort Monroe, he did not learn of this reduction in his forces until he was already in the field. He was outraged. Unreasoning panic by the government, he believed, had rendered his position precarious. Though the only enemy force in his path when his army arrived in early April was an undersized "army" commanded by Major General "Prince John" Magruder (4), McClellan hesitated to advance and he complained in official and private letters that the government had sabotaged all his plans. His disappointment and sense of betrayal would affect his actions during the ensuing campaign.

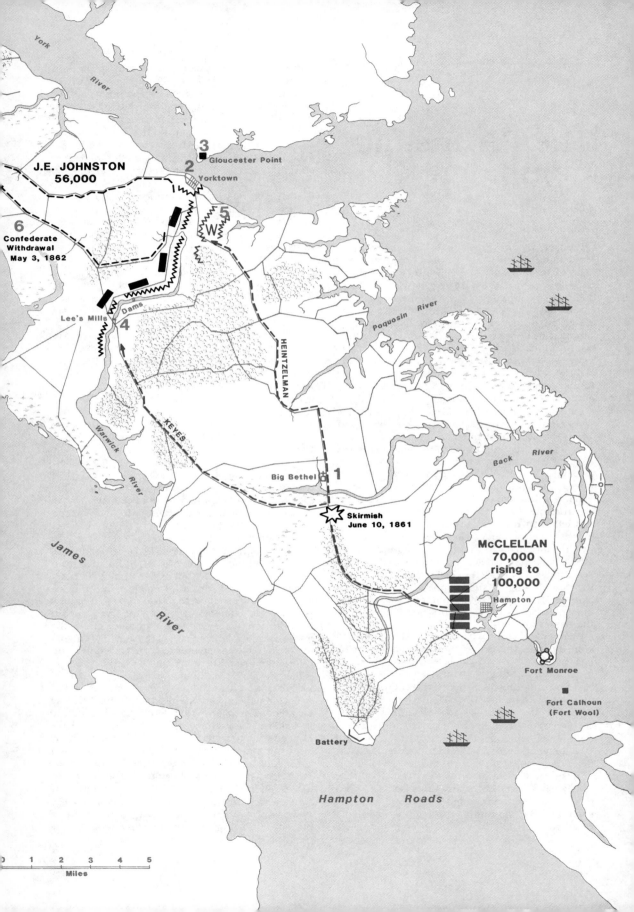

York River

J.E. JOHNSTON
56,000

3 ■ Gloucester Point

2 ▨ Yorktown

5

W

6
Confederate
Withdrawal
May 3, 1862

Lee's Mills   Dams

4

Warwick

River

HEINTZELMAN

KEYES

Poquosin River

Big Bethel ⌂ 1

Skirmish
June 10, 1861

Back   River

McCLELLAN
70,000
rising to
100,000

Hampton

James

River

Fort Monroe

Fort Calhoun
(Fort Wool)

Battery

Hampton   Roads

0   1   2   3   4   5
Miles

MAP 11

The Siege of Yorktown

April-May, 1862

Union soldiers had garrisoned old Fort Monroe on the tip of the Yorktown peninsula since the beginning of hostilities, but up to now Magruder had kept them well bottled up. In June 1861 Union Major General Benjamin Butler had attempted a sortie toward Big Bethel (1), but was driven back in a battle that, though much celebrated at the time, would rank as little more than a skirmish in the long history of the war. The arrival of the first elements of McClellan's army in April 1862, however, put an entirely new complexion on the situation and led Jefferson Davis to call an emergency strategy conference to consider an appropriate response to this threat.

Davis met with his highest-ranking generals in Richmond on April 14. At that conference Johnston reported that Magruder's lines could not possibly withstand a concerted Federal effort, and urged that Confederate forces be withdrawn from the peninsula and concentrated near Richmond. Opposition to Johnston's suggestion came from Davis' military advisor, General Robert E. Lee, who thought the peninsula a fine place to offer battle, and James Longstreet, who urged a Confederate offensive toward Washington. The fact that an offensive was considered at all at this meeting suggests that Lincoln's concern for the safety of Washington was not as foolish or naive as McClellan believed. But in the end Davis sided with Lee and ordered Johnston to join Magruder's forces on the Yorktown line and to hold there as long as possible.

Johnston accepted the assignment with no real enthusiasm or expectation of success. Even counting Magruder's forces already in place on the peninsula, he could field only about 56,000 men against a Federal army that he believed to number over 100,000. Under ordinary circumstances the strength of his defensive position might have made up for his inferiority in numbers, but McClellan's over-whelming superiority in the artillery arm rendered the Confederate situation tenuous. The Union artillery outranged the older smoothbore cannons of the Confederates, a fact that would make it possible for the Federals to batter Confederate defenses at Yorktown (2) and Gloucester Point (3) to pieces, after which McClellan could use his army transport vessels to move up the York River and land in the Confederate rear.

In fact, this was precisely what McClellan had in mind. But in attempting to execute this plan, Little Mac was to be disappointed on two counts. First, the Navy announced that it could not assure him of adequate gunfire support on the York River because the rebel batteries were too strong and because the *Virginia* still posed a threat from Norfolk. Second, the corps which McClellan had planned to use on this amphibious end run was McDowell's. He had even arranged for McDowell's men to be specially trained and equipped for such an operation. But those men had been withheld from McClellan by Lincoln's order and were now utterly beyond his reach.

As a result of these disappointments, McClellan felt he had no choice but to conduct a regular siege. He advanced toward Johnston's lines, attempted a few half-hearted probes at Lee's Mills (4) and at Yorktown, and then settled in for a protracted siege, digging parallels and sapping forward in accordance with the time-honored practices of siege warfare (5).

Johnston continued to advise Davis and Lee in Richmond that his position was untenable. "The result is certain," he wrote, "the time only [is] doubtful." In fact, Johnston had no intention of allowing McClellan the leisure to complete his spade work and open up with his big siege guns. By the end of April he was preparing to evacuate his position and fall back on Richmond, as he had originally suggested.

On the night of May 3, 1862, the Confederate army pulled out of its lines and filed back in good order toward Williamsburg (6). When Federal pickets reported the next day that the quarry had flown, McClellan was jubilant. He ordered a pursuit and reported to Washington that he had won a great victory. He had captured a very strong field position and fifty-six enemy guns without the help of the Navy, without McDowell's Corps, and without losing a single man. What more could the government expect?

In retrospect, however, most historians have viewed the siege of Yorktown as a Federal defeat. Despite overwhelming force, the Union army was held up for nearly a month, gaining for the Confederacy some of the time it would need to raise the manpower necessary to confront the Federal juggernaut head-on near Richmond.

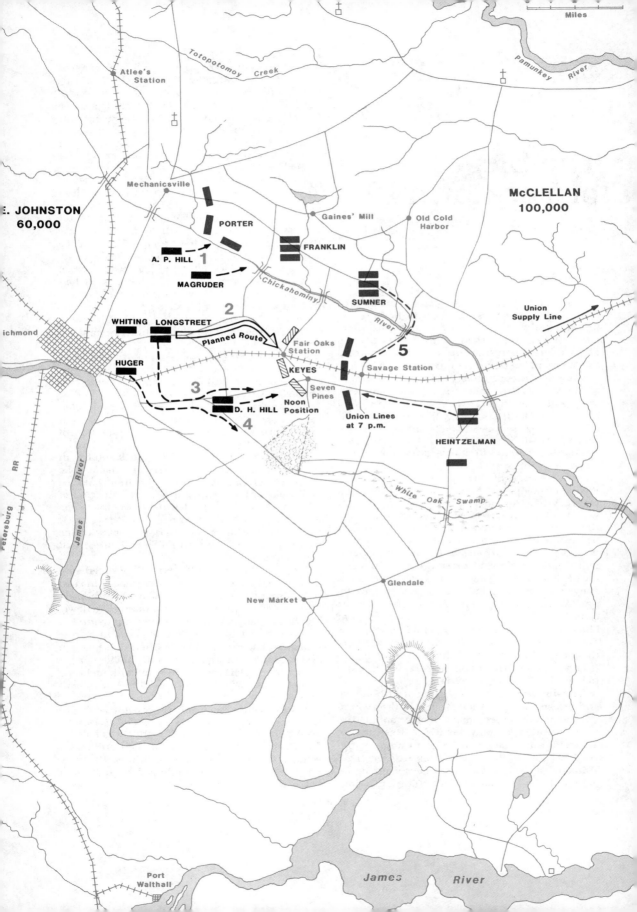

Miles

E. JOHNSTON
60,000

McCLELLAN
100,000

Totopotomoy Creek

Pamunkey River

Atlee's Station

Mechanicsville

PORTER

Gaines' Mill

Old Cold Harbor

A. P. HILL **1**

FRANKLIN

MAGRUDER

Chickahominy

SUMNER

Union Supply Line

River

WHITING LONGSTREET **2**

Planned Route

Fair Oaks Station

ichmond

KEYES

Savage Station

HUGER

Seven Pines

5

3

Noon Position

D. H. HILL

Union Lines at 7 p.m.

4

HEINTZELMAN

Petersburg

James River

RR

White Oak Swamp

Glendale

New Market

Port Walthall

James River

MAP 12

Fair Oaks (Seven Pines)

May 31, 1862

Following its withdrawal from Yorktown, Johnston's army made a brief stand at Williamsburg before retreating all the way back to the outskirts of Richmond. There, beyond the range of Union naval gunfire, Johnston hoped to find an opportunity to attack a portion of the Union army and inflict a defeat decisive enough to convince McClellan to call off his offensive. Certainly the geography of the peninsula aided him in this ambition, for the peninsula was bisected by the Chickahominy River which forced McClellan to split his advancing forces into two unequal groups. He kept the largest portion of the army north of the stream in order to maintain communications with his supply base at White House Landing on the York River. But two full corps, those of Major Generals Samuel P. Heinzelman and Erasmus Keyes, were south of the river. Moreover, though the Chickahominy was spanned by a half-dozen bridges, the spring rains had rendered several of them impassable, effectively isolating Keyes' corps near the railroad junction of Fair Oaks Station and the nearby community of Seven Pines.

Johnston's plan of attack was to use the divisions of Magruder and Ambrose Powell (A.P.) Hill to hold the bulk of the Union army in place north of the Chickahominy (1), and to concentrate the rest of his forces for an attack on Keyes. He planned to hit Keyes with three divisions simultaneously by advancing on three nearly parallel roads: the Nine Mile Road to Fair Oaks (2); the Williamsburg Road to Seven Pines (3); and the Charles City Road (4), which led away from the battlefield, but possession of which was necessary to protect the Confederate right flank. The main assault was to be entrusted to Longstreet. Reinforced by several brigades from Major General W.H.C. Whiting's division, Longstreet was to march via the Nine Mile Road to smash into the Federal right wing at Fair Oaks Station. D.H. Hill's division would advance directly against Seven Pines, and Benjamin Huger's division would occupy the Charles City Road.

Johnston's conduct of the battle brought him little credit. He did not divulge its details to Davis or to Lee and almost petulantly declined to explain his intentions. His orders to his subordinates were confusing and during the battle itself he appeared to be uncertain of the exact dispositions of the units—the enemy's and his own. His plans went awry almost from the outset. Poor staff work explained some of the confusion and misunderstanding, but besides Johnston's errors of omission, the biggest mistake was Longstreet's. Instead of heading east, he turned his brigades south, crossing in front of Whiting's men, cutting Huger off from his assigned road, and finally debouching onto the Williamsburg Road eight hours behind schedule. A.P. Hill and Magruder did their job holding Porter and Franklin north of the Chickahominy, but the planned triple punch against Keyes sputtered into an unsupported attack by D.H. Hill's division.

After waiting several hours, and despairing of Longstreet's arrival, Hill finally sent his men in alone at 1:00 P.M. Hill's men fought aggressively and drove the Federals back a mile or two, but could not inflict the kind of defeat that would require McClellan to suspend his offensive. As Federal reinforcements arrived from Sumner's corps (5), the Confederate attack stalled, and after nightfall the rebels withdrew toward Richmond, having wasted an excellent opportunity to win at least a limited victory. To add to Confederate disappointments, General Johnston was seriously wounded in the battle. Though Johnston would recover, his wound rendered him temporarily incapable of continued command in the field.

Though apparently indecisive, the Battle of Fair Oaks (or Seven Pines) nevertheless had two important consequences quite apart from the battlefield results: First, Johnston's wound removed him from command and led Jefferson Davis to offer the field command to the man who would hold it for the rest of the war and compile an almost mystical reputation as a battlefield commander and tactician—Robert E. Lee. Second, the furiousness of the Confederate assault reinforced McClellan in his belief that the rebels significantly outnumbered his own troops. He did not believe that a responsible commander would attack without clear numerical superiority. The losses were not extravagant compared to the bloodbath at Shiloh: the Federals suffered just over 5,000 casualties in all categories (killed, wounded, and missing), and the attacking Confederates just over 6,000. But this was the first battle which McClellan had conducted where his forces had suffered any serious losses at all. The experience unnerved him and in the coming weeks would make him even more cautious than usual.

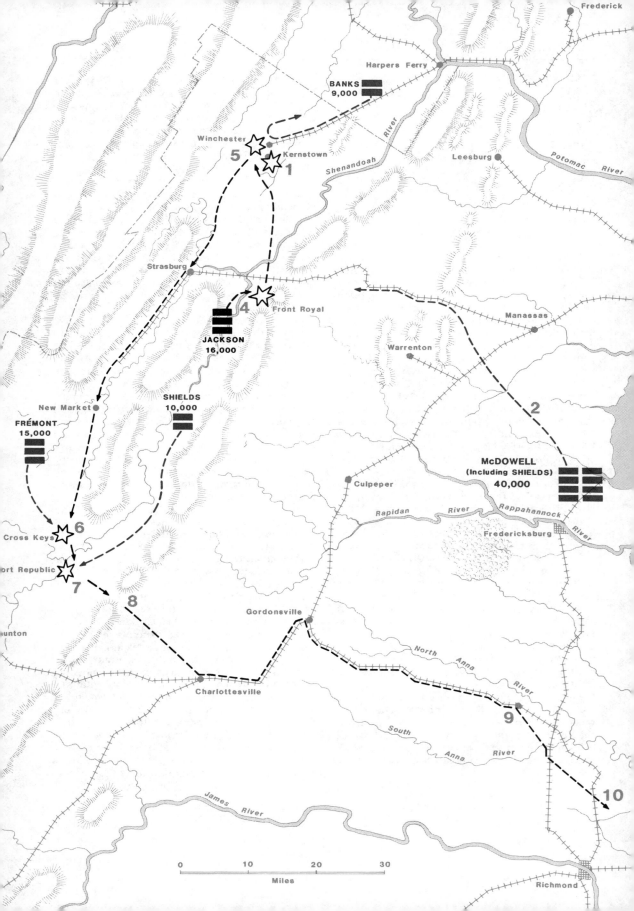

Frederick

Harpers Ferry

BANKS
9,000

Winchester

Leesburg

Potomac River

Kernstown

Shenandoah River

5

1

Strasburg

Front Royal

4

Manassas

JACKSON
16,000

Warrenton

New Market

SHIELDS
10,000

FRÉMONT
15,000

Culpeper

2

Rapidan River

Rappahannock River

McDOWELL
(Including SHIELDS)
40,000

Cross Keys

6

Fredericksburg

Fort Republic

7

8

Gordonsville

9

Staunton

Charlottesville

North Anna River

South Anna River

10

James River

0   10   20   30

Miles

Richmond

MAP 13

Jackson's Valley Campaign

March-June, 1862

When Lee took command of the Confederate Army before Richmond, his principal problem was manpower. The Confederates had lost 10 percent of their strength at Fair Oaks (as compared to 5 percent Federal casualties) and were running out of both space and time. To even the odds Lee looked toward the Shenandoah Valley, where "Stonewall" Jackson commanded a 16,000-man army. Jackson was already fully engaged in the Valley, dealing with no less than three Federal armies whose combined strength was nearly triple his own. Confederate hopes therefore rested on Jackson's ability to keep those Federal armies fully occupied, and then to disengage successfully and transfer his army to Richmond in time for a strike against McClellan.

Jackson had already been performing feats that were little short of miraculous. In late March he had attacked the Federal Army of Major General Nathaniel Banks at Kernstown (1) to prevent Banks from sending reinforcements to McClellan. It was a bold, almost foolhardy, move, for Jackson hurled about 3,000 men against a Federal division of 9,000. Jackson's men were driven off with relative ease, but the battle caused Banks to postpone his move to Washington, thus "freezing" a large body of Union troops in the northern end of the Valley. Moreover, Banks' victory helped convince President Lincoln that Jackson's army could be cut off and destroyed. He therefore ordered McDowell's corps at Fredericksburg to move west to head off Jackson's retreat (2), thereby trapping "Stonewall" in the long narrrow Valley with superior armies above and below him. The decision to dispatch McDowell on this chase was unwise on two counts: First because to catch Jackson, McDowell's men would have to march a longer distance over poorer roads than the force they were attempting to trap; and second because it prevented McDowell's junction with McClellan and denied the latter 40,000 reinforcements.

Easily escaping this gambit, Jackson sped south to deal with a smaller Union force under John C. Fremont, whose army was moving toward the Valley from West Virginia. Frémont's target was Staunton on the Virginia Central Railroad (3). Jackson marched his men southward, used the railroad to transport his men to Staunton, and then marched west to defeat Frémont's detachment on May 8 at the Battle of McDowell (off the map to the west of Staunton).

Jackson's maneuvers now became positively mystifying to the Federals. Marching with the speed that earned his troops the nickname of "foot cavalry," he attacked and defeated a small Union garrison at Front Royal (4) on May 23, and then fell upon Banks' main army at Winchester (5) on May 25. Banks fled northward all the way to the Potomac, with Jackson on his heels most of the way. Breaking off his pursuit of Banks, Jackson headed next for the southern end of the Valley where Federal forces were marching to cut him off; Frémont was approaching again from the west, and a division of McDowell's corps under Brigadier General James Shields from the east. Jackson hit Frémont first at the Battle of Cross Keys (6) on June 8, and then turned on Shields at Port Republic (7) on June 9. In less than three months Jackson had fought six battles and won five of them. But more importantly he had occupied nearly 60,000 Federal soldiers in a fruitless effort to bring him to bay. Now his mission was to break contact, extricate himself from the Valley, and bring reinforcements to Lee.

On June 23, Jackson made a secret visit to Richmond where he sat down with the new commander for the first time. Lee asked him how soon his men could be in position for an attack on McClellan. Somewhat unrealistically, Jackson announced that his men could get to their assigned positions north of Richmond by the next day, June 24. Lee therefore set his plans in motion for a general attack the day after that—the beginning of the Seven Days battles that would decide the fate of Richmond.

Jackson's confidence derived in part from the fact that he already had his men on the move. He had started them out from Brown's Gap (8) toward the Virginia Central Railroad at Charlottesville before leaving for his meeting with Lee. But Jackson had fewer than 200 freight cars at his disposal to move an entire army along the single line of track from Charlottesville to the South Anna River crossing where Federal cavalry had burned the bridge. As a result, most of the army had to march parallel to the railroad as far as the junction at Beaver Dam (9), then across country to Ashland, and finally on to the attack positions near Mechanicsville (10). In making his pledge to Lee, Jackson failed to appreciate the differences between the hard, dry Valley roads and the marshy terrain and narrow roads of the peninsula. For once in his military career, Jackson would be late.

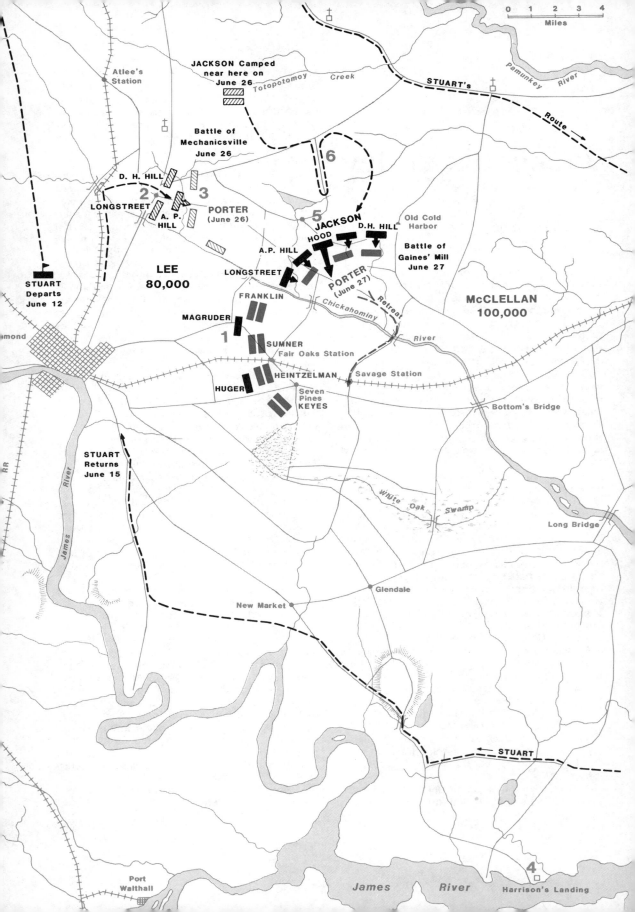

0 1 2 3 4
Miles

JACKSON Camped
near here on
June 26
Totopotomoy Creek

STUART's

Pamunkey River

Atlee's
Station

Route

Battle of
Mechanicsville
June 26

6

D. H. HILL

2

3

LONGSTREET

A. P.
HILL

PORTER
(June 26)

5 JACKSON

Old Cold
Harbor

HOOD

D.H. HILL

LEE
80,000

A.P. HILL

Battle of
Gaines' Mill
June 27

STUART
Departs
June 12

LONGSTREET

PORTER
(June 27)

Retreat

McCLELLAN
100,000

FRANKLIN

Chickahominy

MAGRUDER

1

River

SUMNER

Fair Oaks Station

Savage Station

Bottom's Bridge

STUART
Returns
June 15

HEINTZELMAN

HUGER

Seven
Pines
KEYES

RR

James River

White Oak Swamp

Long Bridge

Glendale

New Market

mond

Port
Walthall

STUART

James River

Harrison's Landing

4

MAP 14

The Seven Days, I

Even before sending for Jackson, Lee's first response when he took command in June was to dig in. He put his men to work building field works—an occupation unappreciated not only by the men in the ranks but by many officers who considered such activity wasteful and vaguely dishonorable. Indeed, many of them chidingly referred to their new commander as the "King of Spades." They seriously mistook their man. In fact, Lee was already planning an offensive. Before he began, however, he needed three things: a secure base, greater manpower, and accurate information of the enemy dispositions. His field works would provide the secure base, Jackson's brilliant maneuvers in the Valley would bring him the manpower, and Lee's young and flamboyant cavalry commander, Brigadier General James E. Brown ("Jeb") Stuart, would bring him the information.

1. J.E.B. Stuart's Raid, June 12-15, 1862

On June 10 Lee summoned Stuart to explain that he was planning an attack against the Union forces north of the Chickahominy and needed to know where the Federal right wing rested. Delighted at the opportunity to lead a scouting raid, Stuart departed on June 12, heading almost due north with 1,200 troopers. Twenty miles north of Richmond his column turned east. Skirmishing with Federal patrols, the rebel cavalry then headed southeast across Totopotomoy Creek. Now behind the Union lines, Stuart resolved to carry out a project that had tempted him from the start: to ride completely around the Union army. For 48 hours the grey-clad troopers rode south, then west along the north bank of the James, finally returning to Richmond exhausted but jubilant on June 15.

The newspapers in Richmond made much of the exploit, but the real value of the raid was the news Stuart brought to Lee: the Federal right wing was "in the air," unsecured by any natural or manmade barrier. If a substantial body of Confederate troops could get around that flank, McClellan's forces could be surprised and routed.

2. The Battle of Mechanicsville, June 26, 1862

Like Johnston at Fair Oaks, Lee hoped to concentrate his army for a decisive blow against an isolated Union Corps—this time Major General Fitz-John Porter's Fifth Corps north of the Chickahominy. Huger and Magruder, with 25,000 men between them, would attempt to immobilize four full Union Corps (some sixty to eighty thousand men) south of the river (1), while Longstreet and the two Hills (A.P. and D.H.) concentrated for an attack on Porter (2). Lee's real ace-in-the-hole, however, was Jackson's 18,000-man Valley army which was to fall upon Porter's exposed right flank.

Confederate success depended on two things: a convincing performance by Magruder in front of the bulk of McClellan's army, and coordination between the two men principally responsible for the attack on Porter—A.P. Hill and Jackson. Magruder did his job splendidly, convincing McClellan to call off a planned attack of his own. But, unfortunately for Confederate hopes, coordination between A.P. Hill and Jackson was nonexistent. The result was that A.P. Hill led an unsupported attack against extremely strong Federal positions along Beaver Dam Creek (3) while Jackson went into bivouac only a few miles away—each unaware of the presence or situation of the other.

Lee was disappointed that his attack had misfired but he was determined to renew his efforts the next day. Surprisingly, it was McClellan—whose men had gotten much the best of it along Beaver Dam Creek—who was worried. Still convinced that his own forces were outnumbered, he resolved to withdraw Porter from his exposed position and at the same time to transfer his own base to Harrison's Landing on the James River (4).

3. The Battle of Gaines's Mill, June 27, 1862

Confederate forces spent most of the day on June 27 getting into position to strike Porter's new defense line along Boatswain's Swamp near Gaines's Mill (5). Once again Jackson was a major disappointment, arriving over two hours late to the battle, partly because of a wrong turn that required him to backtrack for several miles (6). When Jackson finally did join the battle at about 4:30 P.M., Porter's line collapsed under the impetuous assault of Hood's Texas Brigade. For once, Lee had overwhelming numerical superiority; nearly 50,000 Confederates assaulted Porter's 35,000-man corps. Lee's attacking infantrymen suffered heavily, especially from Union artillery, but they drove Porter out of his defensive positions and south across the Chickahominy.

This, Lee's first victory, was won at a terrible cost; some 8,000 Confederates fell in the attack (as against 4,000 Union casualties). The South could not afford many more such "victories." But the significance of Mechanicsville and Gaines's Mill was that they convinced McClellan to abandon his advance on Richmond and seek a secure base on the James. The erstwhile "King of Spades" was determined that McClellan should never get there.

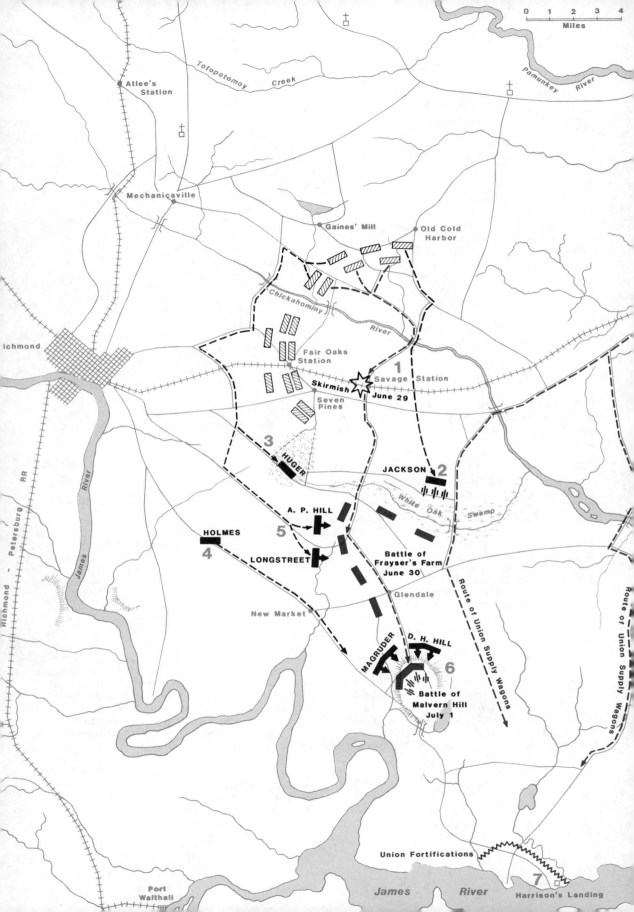

Scale: 0 1 2 3 4 Miles

Totopotomoy Creek

Pamunkey River

Atlee's Station

Mechanicsville

Gaines' Mill

Old Cold Harbor

Chickahominy River

Richmond

Fair Oaks Station

1
Savage Station

Skirmish June 29

Seven Pines

3

HUGER

JACKSON **2**

White Oak Swamp

A. P. HILL

HOLMES

5

LONGSTREET

4

Battle of Frayser's Farm June 30

Glendale

New Market

Route of Union Supply Wagons

Route of Union Supply Wagons

MAGRUDER

D. H. HILL

6

Battle of Malvern Hill July 1

Richmond — Petersburg RR

James River

Port Walthall

Union Fortifications

7

James River

Harrison's Landing

MAP 15

The Seven Days, II

Gaines's Mill might have been a disaster for McClellan's army had he not previously decided to transfer his base from the York River to the James. Indeed, Federal supply wagons were already on the move during the battle. But McClellan's problems were not over. He had to conduct a fighting retreat across the peninsula, fend off Lee's continued attacks, and shield his supply trains. For his part, Lee's objective was to force a decisive battle before McClellan reached the relative security of the James, where U.S. Navy gunboats could guard his flanks and rear.

The clash at Savage Station (1) on June 29 was essentially a rear-guard action in which Confederate forces under Magruder attacked from Seven Pines along the Williamsburg Road and were repulsed rather easily. While this action was underway, Lee was using the road network outside Richmond to direct four converging columns toward McClellan's presumed line of march.

1. The Battle of Frayser's Farm, June 30, 1862

Lee entrusted the direct pursuit to Jackson and ordered three other columns to converge on the Union flank. Jackson was delayed in crossing the Chickahominy by the necessity to rebuild a bridge destroyed by Porter in his retreat. Then, to add to the mystery of Jackson's disappointing performance in this campaign, he allowed himself to be thwarted by Federal defenses behind the bridge across White Oak Swamp (2). Aside from unlimbering his artillery to exchange shots with Federal gunners, Jackson spent the rest of the afternoon of June 30 doing absolutely nothing.

A second Confederate column under Huger was ordered by Lee to advance along the Charles City Road (3). But Huger found his way blocked by thick woods, and rather than send his infantry ahead unsupported, he stopped to cut a road through the woods for his artillery. Like Jackson, he played no part in the day's battle.

The weakest of the Confederate columns was a small division under Holmes moving toward Malvern Hill from New Market (4), but Holmes's force was too small to send in alone. The main effort, therefore, would depend on the combined forces of A.P. Hill and Longstreet (5) which fell upon the Federal flank near Glendale in what became known as the Battle of Frayser's Farm. The two Confederate divisions attacked McClellan's lines and took heavy losses, but aside from capturing some woods, achieved nothing of importance. That night the Federals withdrew to take up new positions atop Malvern Hill (6).

2. The Battle for Malvern Hill, July 1, 1862

The night after the clash at Frayser's Farm, the Confederate army concentrated around the abandoned Federal camp at Glendale. There, Lee pondered his next move—he was beginning to fear that McClellan might make good his "escape." The new Federal position was a strong one, but Lee saw no real option other than to keep up the pressure on his retreating foe, so he planned to renew the pursuit the next day.

The Confederate army came up to Malvern Hill around noon on July 1. The Federal position appeared to be unassailable and Lee sought locations from which Confederate artillery could bombard the heights. Only when (and if) the artillery broke the Union lines would Confederate infantry assault the hill. The artillery duel began at 1 P.M. and lasted for several hours, with the Federals having much the better of it. But owing to a confusion in orders, the infantry divisions of Magruder and D.H. Hill attacked the hill anyway at about 6 P.M. It was a massacre. Southern bravery availed nothing against the well-placed Union guns. That night McClellan's men retreated to an entrenched position at Harrison's Landing. The Seven Days were over.

Lee was deeply discouraged that McClellan had made good his crab-like movement to the James, and McClellan himself considered his maneuver to have been a model of logistical and tactical skill. But in fact the strategic situation had been almost exactly reversed. Though the cost had been heavy (nearly 20,000 Confederate casualties—a fourth of Lee's army), Lee had broken McClellan's spirit and convinced him that he could not take Richmond without massive reinforcements.

Moreover, not only had McClellan lost confidence in himself, but Lincoln was losing confidence in him too. Lincoln's doubts were fueled by a curious letter sent to him by McClellan from Harrison's Landing, charging the President with sabotaging his campaign. Lincoln offered to send McClellan an additional 50,000 reinforcements, but when Little Mac responded that this would not be enough, Lincoln ordered the army recalled. Richmond had been saved.

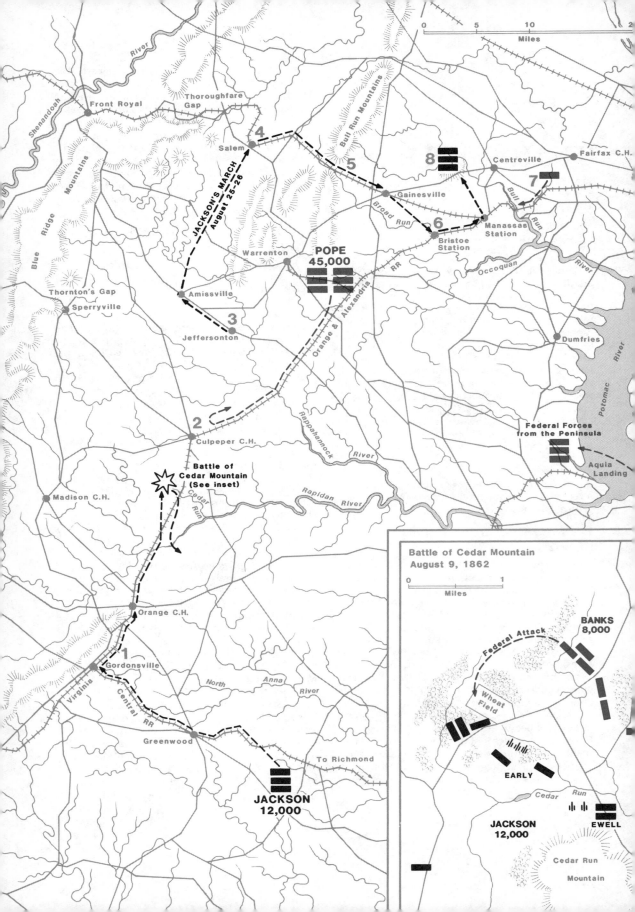

Miles

0   5   10

Front Royal

Thoroughfare
Gap

Bull Run Mountains

Fairfax C.H.

Salem

4

5

8

Centreville

7

Shenandoah

Gainesville

Broad
Run

Blue

Ridge

Mountains

Warrenton

POPE
45,000

6

Bristoe
Station

Manassas
Station

Bull
Run

Occoquan

River

Amissville

Thornton's Gap

Sperryville

3

Jeffersonton

Orange & Alexandria

RR

Rappahannock

River

Dumfries

Potomac

River

2

Culpeper C.H.

Federal Forces
from the Peninsula

Rapidan   River

Aquia
Landing

Battle of
Cedar Mountain
(See inset)

Madison C.H.

Cedar

Run

Orange C.H.

JACKSON'S MARCH
August 25-26

1

Gordonsville

North

Anna

River

Virginia

Central

RR

Greenwood

To Richmond

JACKSON
12,000

Battle of Cedar Mountain
August 9, 1862

Miles

0   1

BANKS
8,000

Federal Attack

Wheat
Field

EARLY

Cedar   Run

JACKSON
12,000

EWELL

Cedar Run

Mountain

MAP 16

Second Bull Run (Manassas): Jackson's March

(July-August 1862)

While McClellan was fending off Lee's furious attacks on the peninsula, Lincoln moved to consolidate the various Union forces elsewhere in Virginia into a new field army. The President looked to the West for a commander for this new army and chose Major General John Pope, conqueror of Island Number 10 on the Mississippi above Memphis. Pope was feted in Washington, where he particularly impressed Secretary of War Stanton with his confident manner and aggressive declarations. He was designated commander of the Army of Virginia on June 26 (the day of the Battle of Mechanicsville), and entrusted with a force of some 45,000 men.

In July, after the Seven Days, Pope pushed his new army southward across the Rappahannock toward Gordonsville (1). Here the Virginia Central Railroad looped northward and possession of that vital rail line would cut the Confederate capital off from the Valley. Because McClellan was quiescent inside his lines at Harrison's Landing, Lee sent Jackson with 12,000 men (later reinforced to 24,000) to counter this new threat. Jackson arrived at Gordonville on July 19, but he was not satisfied to remain on the defensive. Learning that Pope had pushed his advance guard as far as Culpeper (2), he moved his northward to Orange Court House and then to Culpeper.

On August 9 Jackson crossed the Rapidan River and ran into Nathaniel Banks's Federal Corps of about 8,000 men. The result was the Battle of Cedar Mountain (see inset). With the rare luxury of superior numbers, Jackson had a prime opportunity to maul Banks's force. Instead Jackson badly mishandled the affair. Allowing Banks to assume the offensive. The Federals attacked through a wheatfield, turning the rebel left, and were beaten back only by the arrival of Confederate reinforcements. The Confederates managed to rally and drive the Federals from the field (Federal losses were 2,381, the Confederates' 1,276), but the Confederate victory at Cedar Mountain was an empty one. The rebels held the field and drove off the impudent Yankees, but Banks was not routed and Pope had been warned that a substantial enemy force was in his front. Thus warned, Pope withdrew his army north of the Rappahannock, and Jackson also withdrew southward back across the Rapidan.

Four days later on August 13, ten brigades commanded by Longstreet joined Jackson's force. Each man would now command a Wing of the reorganized Army of Northern Virginia. With McClellan clearly engaged in withdrawing from the Peninsula, Lee's goal was to inflict a decisive defeat on Pope before the Federal armies could combine. In this he was aided by McClellan whose ponderous movements were never so slow as on this occasion. McClellan was simply in no hurry to join forces with Pope, a man for whom he felt only disdain.

The combined Confederate army pushed northward and recrossed the Rapidan on August 20. On August 24 Lee visited Jackson in his camp at Jeffersonton (3) and suggested that Jackson take his entire Corps on a flank march around Pope's army. Jackson was immediately enthusiastic. With three divisions he set out on the morning of August 25. The long gray line of men snaked westward and northward to Salem (4) on the 25th. Before dawn the next morning they were off again marching along the tracks of the Manassas Gap Railroad through the gap (5) to Gainesville where they brushed aside the only Federal troops they encountered. Late in the afternoon the lead elements arrived at Bristoe Station (6) on Pope's supply line. They had covered 54 miles in two days. A holiday mood prevailed as the rebels derailed one Federal train and watched a second crash into the wreckage. Pope was thus informed in a particularly spectacular way of the presence of enemy forces on his supply line. Immediately he started northward to drive them off.

Meanwhile Jackson's men learned of the presence of a huge Federal supply depot at Manassas Station three miles northward. Leaving Ewell to hold off Pope at the bridge over Broad Run, Jackson took his other two divisions north to Manassas. There under the indulgent eyes of their officers, the tired and hungry soldiers gathered up all they could carry. The ragged southern soldiers had never seen such bounty. One recorded almost reverently that he "got a toothbrush, a box of candles, a quantity of lobster salad, a barrel of coffee, and other things which I forget."

Despite this good fortune, Jackson was in a precarious spot. Pope with superior numbers was advancing on him from the south while another smaller Federal force probed from the north (7). With the railroad bridges at Bull Run and the Broad River both in ashes, now was the time to withdraw westward and join up with Longstreet who was approaching along the same route Jackson had used. But Jackson chose instead to occupy a gentle hill a mile to the west (8) and implicitly challenge Pope to attack him. In that, Pope would not disappoint him.

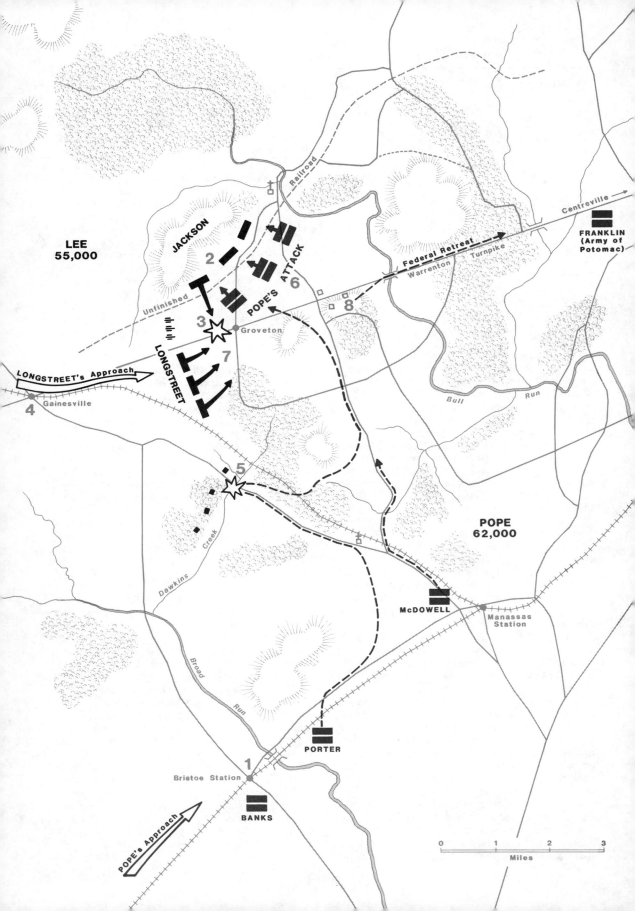

LEE
55,000

JACKSON

2

POPE'S ATTACK

6

3

Groveton

Unfinished

LONGSTREET's Approach

LONGSTREET

7

4
Gainesville

Railroad

Federal Retreat

Warrenton Turnpike

FRANKLIN
(Army of
Potomac)

Centreville

8

Bull Run

5

Creek

Dawkins

POPE
62,000

McDOWELL

Manassas
Station

Broad Run

PORTER

1
Bristoe Station

BANKS

POPE's Approach

0   1   2   3
Miles

MAP 17

Second Bull Run (Manassas)

August 29-30, 1862

When news reached Pope that rebel raiders were across his supply line at Bristoe Station, he set his own troops in motion northward to confront them. No doubt he was concerned about his communications, but he was also anxious to catch the rebels and destroy them. He drove Ewell's division back onto Bristoe Station (1) on the afternoon of August 27, where he learned for the first time that the rebel raiders were nothing less than Jackson's entire corps. Far from being intimidated by this information, Pope believed he saw a chance to inflict a decisive defeat on the brash Jackson if only he could catch him.

Pope did not know that instead of trying to escape westward, Jackson had in fact occupied the forward slope of Sudley Mountain on a line running from Sudley Church to just north of the crossroads community of Groveton. Jackson's position (2) was not especially strong though he was protected by the cut of an unfinished railroad that ran across his front. His greatest strength was that Pope did not know where he was.

Pope meanwhile issued orders to all his far flung divisions to concentrate on Manassas. One of those divisions, King's division of McDowell's corps, marched across Jackson's front on the Warrenton Turnpike on August 28. Jackson watched the blue column passing by and could not resist the opportunity to strike it. He ordered his soldiers forward out of the treeline and the two forces clashed in a hard fought stand up fight known as the Battle of Groveton (3). The Federal force retreated from the field, but Jackson had gained little and more importantly he had exposed his position.

Pope was convinced that King's column had run into Jackson while the latter was in full retreat. Eager to prevent his escape, he issued orders to his corps commanders that were designed to bring about a classic double envelopement: Jackson would be crushed between two federal forces: McDowell's and Porter's Corps, which Pope ordered to occupy Gainesville (4), and the rest of the Army of Virginia at Manassas. But Pope had a faulty understanding of Jackson's intentions, of the disposition of his own troops, and perhaps of the reliability of some of the Federal units recently returned from the peninsula whose loyalty was to McClellan and not to Pope.

Pope issued a joint order to both McDowell and Porter to move from Bristoe Station to Gainesville along the route of the Manassas Gap Railroad. At Gainesville Porter's Corps would block Jackson's escape route along the Manassas Gap Railroad, prevent him from getting any reinforcements along that same route, and Porter's Corps would also serve as the anvil on which Pope's hammer blow would fall.

Porter, however, never got to Gainesville. As he was approaching Dawkin's Creek (5) he was held up by rebel skirmishers. Pope later blamed his subsequent defeat on Porter's failure to push ahead, and Porter would be found guilty by a court-martial for this failure. But even had he been more aggressive at Dawkin's Creek, Porter would have been too late, for Longstreet's divisions were already marching through the streets of Gainesville on their way to the battlefield. The truth of the matter was that Pope had simply lost the tactical picture.

Believing that he was about to issue the coup de grace, Pope launched his assault on Jackson's line at about 1:00 P.M. (6) Pope's attacks were delivered frontally and were not coordinated in such a way as to take advantage of his numerical superiority, and not until late in the day did Pope issue orders designed to turn Jackson's flank. By that time it was too late. Longstreet's Corps—some 30,000 men—was closing in on the battlefield. Characteristically, Longstreet took the time to align his brigades and issue careful orders that would ensure a strong continuous front. His delayed worked to the Confederates' advantage for only when Pope, oblivious to the threat to his flank, had his forces fully engaged, did Longstreet launch his own attack (7). When it came it was irresistible and drove the Federals back on to Henry House Hill (8) where they regrouped and made a stand that finally succeeded in halting the rebel onslaught. That night and the next day, the Federals conducted a well-ordered fighting retreat across Bull Run Creek.

The Second Battle of Bull Run was no Union rout. But it was nevertheless a clear defeat. The Federal Army of Virginia suffered nearly double the casualties of its opponent: 16,000 Federals and 9,000 Confederates. Pope retreated to Washington and soon afterward was relieved of his command. He was never again trusted with another. For his part McClellan was not-so-secretly pleased by Pope's failure. But despite that, little Mac was restored to the command of the reunited armies because Lincoln believed, correctly that McClellan was the one man able to rebuild the shattered Union army.

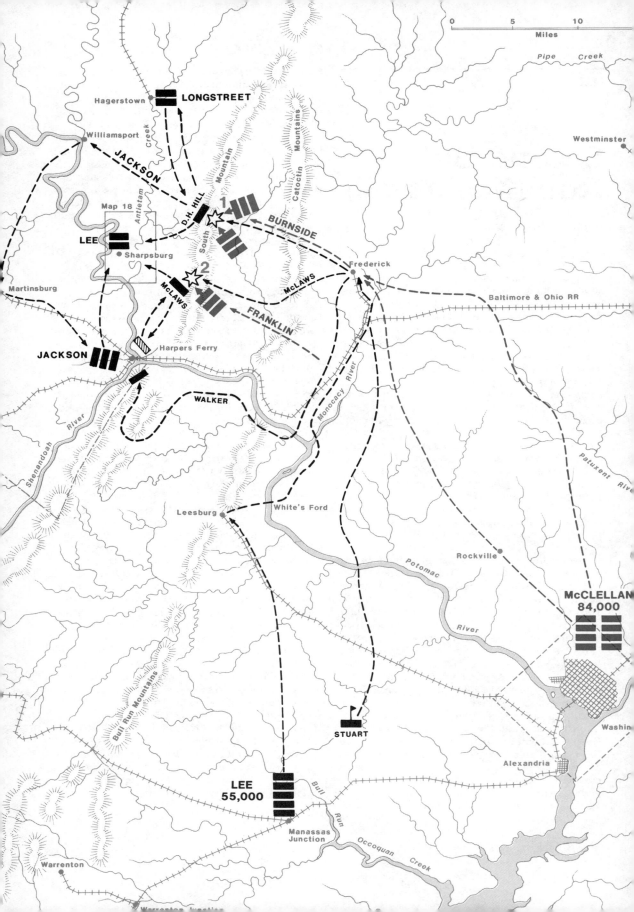

0   5   10

Miles

Pipe   *Creek*

LONGSTREET

Hagerstown

Westminster

Williamsport

JACKSON

Map 18

LEE

D.H. HILL

1

BURNSIDE

Frederick

Sharpsburg

2

McLAWS

Martinsburg

McLAWS

Baltimore & Ohio RR

FRANKLIN

JACKSON

Harpers Ferry

WALKER

Leesburg

White's Ford

Rockville

McCLELLAN
84,000

Potomac

River

Washin

STUART

Alexandria

LEE
55,000

Manassas
Junction

Bull

Run

Occoquan

Creek

Warrenton

Warrenton Junction

MAP 18

Lee's First Invasion

September, 1862

With McClellan's withdrawal from the peninsula and the Confederate victory at Second Bull Run (Manassas), initiative in the East passed to the Confederacy and specifically to Robert E. Lee. Lee could have chosen simply to await the next Federal offensive; after all, the South needed only to avoid being conquered to win the war. But Lee determined instead to retain the initiative and carry the war across the Potomac into Maryland and Pennsylvania.

Screened by Stuart's cavalry, Lee's army moved north from the vicinity of Manassas and began crossing the Potomac on September 4 at White's Ford north of Leesburg, the men singing "Maryland, My Maryland" as they splashed across. Three days later the bulk of the army was concentrated around Frederick. It was in Frederick that the incident involving Barbara Frietchie's impassioned defense of the national ensign is alleged to have taken place.

At Frederick, Lee divided his forces in order to bring about the encirclement of the 12,000-man Federal garrison at Harpers Ferry. He sent one division under Brigadier General John C. Walker to occupy Loudon Heights, east of the city, and two divisions under Major General Lafayette McLaws through the passes in South Mountain to seize Maryland Heights, north of it. The three divisions entrusted to Jackson had the longest march: a roundabout hike through Williamsport and Martinsburg to approach Harpers Ferry from the northwest. Longstreet, with two divisions, would remain in the vicinity of South Mountain. All these orders were written out in Special Order No. 191 and distributed to the various commanders. A few days later, however, Lee learned that a small Federal force was near Hagerstown and he took Longstreet's force off to investigate. By thus dividing his army into four small corps (five, counting Stuart's cavalry), Lee was taking a calculated risk: he was betting that his troops could win limited victories and reunite before the cautious McClellan caught up with him.

For six days his gamble seemed safe. McClellan moved north from Washington with his usual timidity, reaching Frederick on September 13. But at Frederick, McClellan was handed a copy of Confederate Special Order No. 191. A Union soldier had found the order lying on the ground wrapped around three cigars and had passed it up the chain of command. McClellan was elated at his stroke of luck. "Here is a paper with which if I cannot whip Bobbie Lee, I will be willing to go home," he told one witness. He sent couriers flying in all directions to get his huge army on the move.

Warned by a Southern sympathizer that McClellan had obtained a copy of his orders, Lee moved quickly to concentrate his scattered forces. Longstreet's divisions were recalled from Hagerstown and sent to reinforce the Confederates blocking the passes through South Mountain. There on September 14, D. H. Hill's division fought a delaying action at Turner's Gap (1) against two full Federal corps under Major General Ambrose Burnside. Three miles to the south at Crampton's Gap (2), Lafayette McLaws's division deployed across the valley in an attempt to bluff Federal Major General William B. Franklin into believing that Jackson's entire corps was nearby. These Thermopylae-like actions prevented Franklin from relieving the beleaguered Federal garrison at Harpers Ferry, and won time for Lee who was in hasty retreat toward the fords across the Potomac near Sharpsburg, Maryland.

While these skirmishes were being fought, Jackson was surrounding Harpers Ferry, which surrendered the next day (September 15). Once encircled, the Federals in Harpers Ferry were in a hopeless situation, for the little village was situated at the juncture of the Shenandoah and Potomac Rivers and dominated on three sides by high ground. Having occupied this high ground and placed artillery there, Jackson had the town at his mercy.

Jackson sent word to Lee of the Union capitulation and of his intention to leave A.P. Hill behind to "mop up" at Harpers Ferry, and start north immediately with four divisions. Lee received Jackson's message at Sharpsburg, and decided to turn and fight. It was a risky decision. The Potomac River was at his back, and until Jackson joined him, he had only about 19,000 men to hold off McClellan's 80,000. This time, however, Lee's confidence in McClellan's timidity was justified. Jackson arrived at Sharpsburg on the afternoon of the 16th only hours before the first Federal units appeared on the high ground across Antietam Creek. Even with Jackson's four divisions, however, Lee could field only about 40,000 men, half McClellan's strength. Moreover, Lee's men had no time to prepare any significant field fortifications; they would have to meet the Union attack in the open.

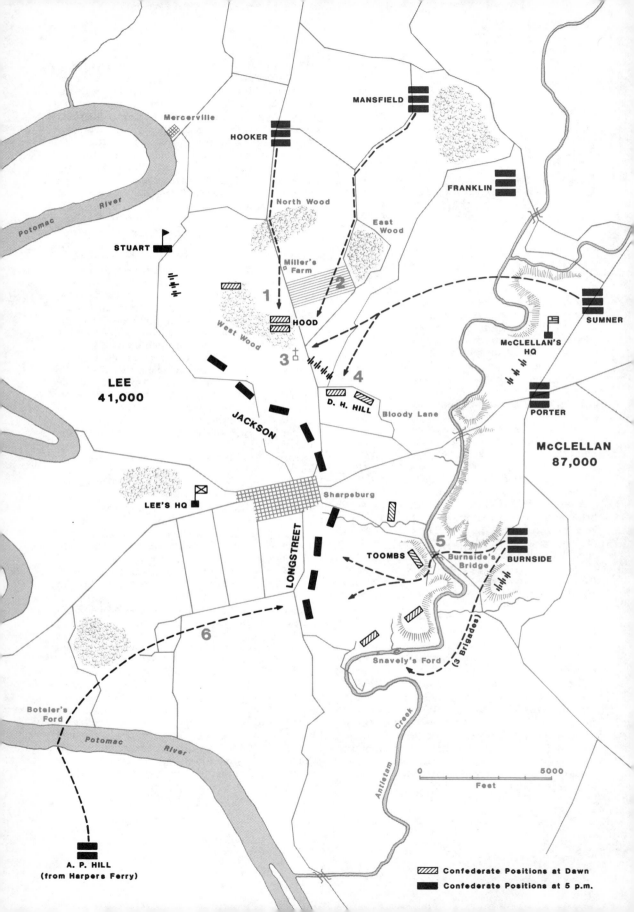

MERCERVILLE

HOOKER

MANSFIELD

FRANKLIN

North Wood

East Wood

Potomac River

STUART

Miller's Farm

1

2

West Wood

HOOD

3

4

SUMNER

McCLELLAN'S HQ

LEE 41,000

JACKSON

D. H. HILL

Bloody Lane

PORTER

McCLELLAN 87,000

LEE'S HQ

Sharpeburg

LONGSTREET

TOOMBS

5

Burnside's Bridge

BURNSIDE

6

(3 Brigades)

Snavely's Ford

Boteler's Ford

Potomac River

Antietam Creek

0   5000
Feet

A. P. HILL
(from Harpers Ferry)

▨ Confederate Positions at Dawn
■ Confederate Positions at 5 p.m.

MAP 19

Antietam (Sharpsburg)

September 17, 1862

Consciously or unconsciously, McClellan's plan of attack against Lee's army at Sharpsburg was a model of Napoleonic tactics. He would attack the Confederate left, and then the right, hoping to force Lee to weaken his center. Then at the climax of the battle he would send his reserves (Porter's corps) smashing through the center. The weakness of this plan was that with it McClellan threw away his greatest advantage—numerical superiority. The Union army was more than twice the size of Lee's and a coordinated assault would likely have overwhelmed the unentrenched and outnumbered defenders. But McClellan committed his corps piecemeal, winning local victories but unable in the end to destroy the enemy.

The Union First Corps, commanded by Major General Joseph ("Fighting Joe") Hooker, delivered the initial attack at dawn, driving Jackson's brigades through the West Woods (1). But Confederate Major General John B. Hood counterattacked and the Confederate line held. The Twelfth Corps of Major General Joseph Mansfield attacked next at about 7:30 A.M., charging through Miller's cornfield (2) where some of the heaviest fighting of the entire war took place. In this early-morning fighting, both Union corps commanders were hit—Hooker fell wounded, and Mansfield was killed outright. Nevertheless, the Union troops fought their way forward and captured the Dunker Church (3) at about 9:00 A.M. The Confederates were already in a precarious position, barely able to hold off the furious but uncoordinated Union attacks.

The third Union attack at mid-morning was executed by Major General Edwin V. Sumner's Second Corps. One division, led by Sumner himself, entered the fight at the Dunker Church, while the other two fell upon D.H. Hill's division, which was defending a sunken road that soon earned the sobriquet "Bloody Lane" (4). Union soldiers took heavy losses, but finally secured a lodgement and drove out the Confederates. A fresh Union assault at this moment might have carried the field. But it never came. McClellan continued to hold Porter's troops in reserve and the hard-pressed Confederates on the left and center were granted a reprieve as the battle shifted to the south.

On the Confederate right (the Union left), the shallow Antietam Creek separated the two armies. Though there were several fords where troops might have waded across, the Union commander, Major General Ambrose Burnside, concentrated his attacks on the stone bridge that would ever after bear his name (5). Two Georgia regiments commanded by Brigadier General Robert Toombs had taken up positions in an abandoned stone quarry on a bluff overlooking the bridge. Throughout the morning Burnside launched half-hearted attacks on the bridge, allowing a few hundred Confederates to stymie an entire Union corps. Finally at about 1:00 P.M. Union troops carried the bridge and clambered up the bluffs to gain the level ground. But even now Burnside delayed, taking time to bring up reinforcements before launching a general advance at about 3:00. Within an hour he had driven Longstreet's men back to the outskirts of Sharpsburg. But at this critical moment, as if following the script of some melodrama, the leading elements of A.P. Hill's division marched onto the field, at the end of a seventeen-mile forced march from Harpers Ferry (6). Their counterattack halted the Union advance and ended the battle.

That night both armies slept lightly, expecting a renewal of the action the next day. McClellan had used only about half of his available strength and still had Franklin's and Porter's corps in reserve. Lee's army, on the other hand, was in a serious if not desperate situation. Many of his officers urged him to withdraw south of the Potomac under cover of night. But, motivated perhaps by some sense of personal honor, Lee chose to hold his ground. The next morning both armies remained in place, each side expecting the other to make a move. That night, believing that honor had been served, Lee withdrew his army across the Potomac.

McClellan believed he had won a great victory, and even Lincoln saw it as enough of a triumph to justify his announcement of the Emancipation Proclamation. Indeed, McClellan had driven Lee from Maryland, and despite his having been the attacking force, he had inflicted significant casualties on Lee's army (estimates range from a low of 10,000 to a high of nearly 14,000, as compared with Federal casualties of 12,400) in the war's single bloodiest day. Even so, more significant was what he had *not* done—he had not smashed Lee's army. Neither McClellan nor anyone else would again have such an opportunity to win a decisive victory over Lee in the open field.

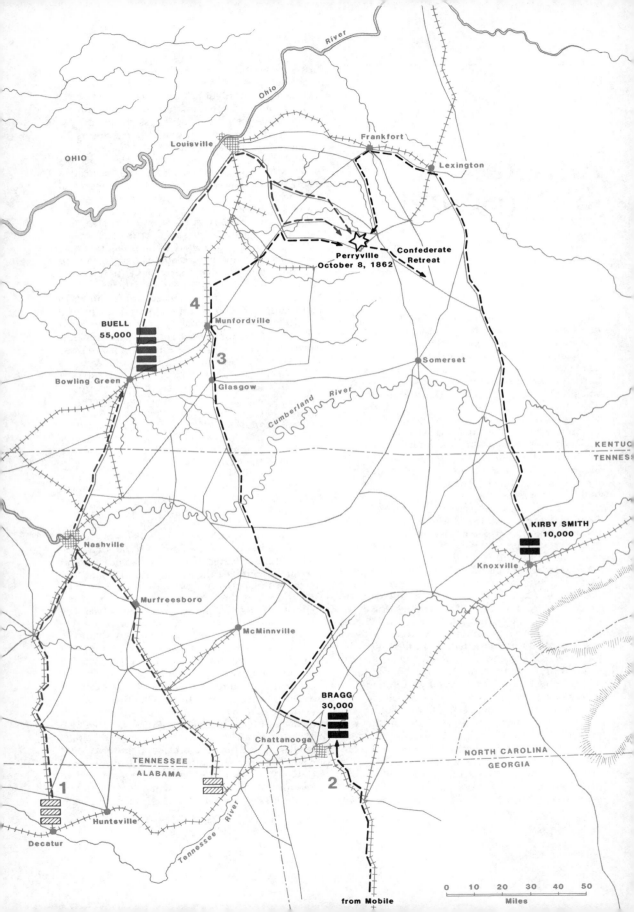

OHIO

Ohio River

Louisville

Frankfort

Lexington

Perryville
October 8, 1862

Confederate
Retreat

4

BUELL
55,000

Munfordville

3

Bowling Green

Glasgow

Somerset

Cumberland River

KENTUC
TENNESS

Nashville

KIRBY SMITH
10,000

Knoxville

Murfreesboro

McMinnville

BRAGG
30,000

Chattanooga

NORTH CAROLINA

GEORGIA

2

TENNESSEE

ALABAMA

1

Huntsville

Tennessee River

Decatur

0   10   20   30   40   50
Miles

from Mobile

MAP 20

Confederate Invasion in the West (Perryville)

July-October, 1862

While Lee was conducting his short-lived invasion of Maryland, Confederate forces in the West also embarked on an "invasion" by advancing into central Kentucky, a state which the South claimed (the Confederate flag bore stars for both Kentucky and Missouri), but which they had not occupied since the onset of hostilities. This southern offensive was in part the result of changes in the command structure of each side. After the Battle of Shiloh (*see* Map 8), Halleck had directed a glacier-like advance toward Corinth, which Beauregard evacuated on May 29. Disappointed by Beauregard's failure to halt Halleck's inexorable advance, Jefferson Davis replaced him with Major General Braxton Bragg, an unimaginative and quarrelsome individual who nevertheless possessed Davis's confidence. At roughly the same time, Lincoln called Halleck to Washington to assume overall command of the Union armies, and as a result the Federals reverted to a divided command in the West: Grant taking charge of Union forces west of the Tennessee River, and Buell assuming command of the reconstituted Army of the Ohio charged with an advance on Chattanooga.

Buell's army of about 31,000 men moved very deliberately and by mid-July, after forty days on the march, had advanced only as far as Decatur, Alabama (1). Meanwhile Bragg decided to take advantage of Buell's hesitancy. Leaving Generals Earl Van Dorn and Sterling Price behind to watch Grant, Bragg shipped 35,000 of his own forces south to Mobile by rail, then northeast to Atlanta, and finally to Chattanooga (2), where he arrived in late July (*see* railroad network in Map 2). This roundabout maneuver marked the first impor-

tant strategic use of a national railroad network and caught Buell quite off guard.

While in Chattanooga, Bragg planned a coordinated advance in conjunction with Edward Kirby Smith's forces at Knoxville. Together they would whip Buell's army, then march west to take care of Grant. After resting his men in Chattanooga for a month, Bragg launched a northward movement that forced Buell to fall back toward Nashville to concentrate his scattered forces and protect his communications. For two weeks Bragg and Buell kept parallel courses. Buell completed his concentration at Bowling Green on September 14 (the day of the Battle of South Mountain) as Bragg's forces marched through Glasgow (3).

When Bragg entered Munfordville (4), where he captured the Federal garrison of 4,000, he cut Buell's rail connections to Louisville. The Confederate commander thought this move might provoke Buell into attacking him, but instead Buell moved north to Louisville where he prepared to defend the city from an expected Confederate attack. The attack did not come, however, and Buell was finally prodded into a forward movement on October 1 by the threat of being removed from command. The Confederates meanwhile had concentrated around Perryville and it was there on October 7 that Buell encountered them.

Bragg was absent from his army at the time of the battle, having traveled to the state capital of Frankfort to witness the inauguration of a Confederate governor. Nevertheless, on hearing of Buell's approach, he ordered Major General Leonidas Polk, his second-in-command, to attack. The initial Confederate assault on October 8 enjoyed brief success, but a Union counterattack drove the outnumbered rebels from the field. The battle brought little credit to either commander. Bragg had underestimated Union strength, while Buell played almost no part in the battle at all and failed to initiate a pursuit of the retreating Confederates. For this final failure, Buell was replaced in command by William S. Rosecrans.

Though the Confederates had inflicted heavier losses on Buell's army at Perryville than they had suffered themselves (4,200 to 3,400), the offensive was a failure. Bragg fell back all the way to Chattanooga where he had begun the campaign six weeks before. His men had marched over 500 miles in those six weeks but achieved no victories or lasting advantages for their trouble. Though Bragg's problems had resulted in part from the lack of any centralized command authority, much of the blame for the failure of the campaign belonged to Bragg himself, whose orders were so erratic that his own subordinates had come to distrust their instructions. For his part, Buell had proved himself utterly incapable of high-command responsibilty. All in all, the result was a lost opportunity for both sides.

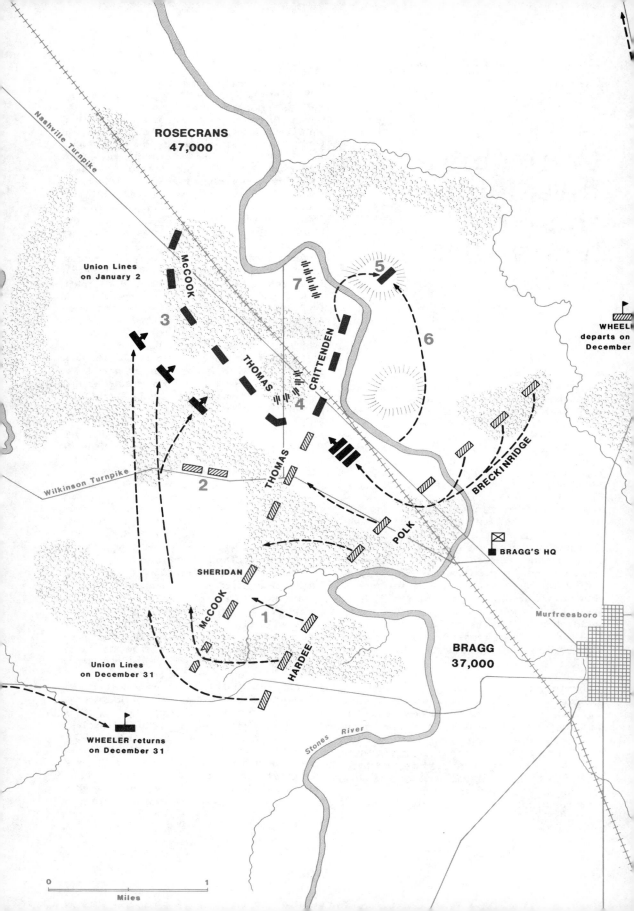

ROSECRANS
47,000

Nashville Turnpike

Union Lines
on January 2

McCOOK

3

THOMAS

2

Wilkinson Turnpike

CRITTENDEN

7

5

6

WHEEL
departs on
December

BRECKINRIDGE

THOMAS

POLK

BRAGG'S HQ

SHERIDAN

McCOOK

1

Murfreesboro

HARDEE

BRAGG
37,000

Union Lines
on December 31

WHEELER returns
on December 31

Stones   River

0   1

Miles

MAP 21

Stones River (Murfreesboro)

December 31, 1862-January 2, 1863

After the collapse of his invasion of Kentucky, Bragg traveled to Richmond to confer with President Davis. Bragg had been the target of severe criticism—some of it from his own lieutenants—for his handling of the Perryville campaign. Sensitive to the criticism but unwilling to sack Bragg, Davis appointed Joseph E. Johnston, now recovered from the wound he had received at Fair Oaks, to overall command in the West, with authority over Bragg's Army of Tennessee and John C. Pemberton's Army of Mississippi. But Johnston was not a favorite of Davis and the Confederate President traveled to Tennessee in December to assess the situation for himself. His visit convinced him that Bragg's army was secure, and Davis decided to send 10,000 of Bragg's men to Pemberton at Vicksburg. Reduced by this transfer to slightly under 35,000 men (excluding cavalry), Bragg faced a Union army of about 47,000 at Nashville under Major General William S. Rosecrans, who had replaced the hapless Buell.

For his part Rosecrans was under a great deal of pressure from Washington to launch an offensive; Major General Halleck wired him that unless he moved soon he would be replaced. Rosecrans refused to be bullied and replied, in essence, that he would advance when he was ready. Nevertheless, the day after Christmas he had his army on the move southward. His advance was slowed by the necessity to fend off Confederate cavalry under Brigadier General Joseph Wheeler who harassed his lines of supply, but in four days the Federal army had reached the outskirts of Murfreesboro.

Bragg chose to make his stand just north of the city in relatively open country dotted with patches of red cedar and divided by the meandering, easily fordable Stones River. There were no particular geographic advantages to his position, but Bragg did not intend to remain on the defensive in any case.

During the night of December 30, both commanders planned attacks. Rosecrans planned to hit Breckinridge's corps while Bragg planned to send Hardee's corps against the Federal right. If the attacks had been launched simultaneously, the result might have been likened to a revolving door. But Rosecrans had directed his attack to begin at 7:00 A.M. and Hardee's brigades stepped out at first light. In consequence, the attack on Breckinridge never materialized, and the Confederates seized and held the initiative.

The first two Federal divisions—those on the extreme right wing—collapsed almost immediately (1). But the third division, commanded by Major General Philip Sheridan, not only held fast, but counterattacked and established a secondary line along the Wilkinson Turnpike (2). This position Sheridan held until his men ran out of ammunition when they were forced to retreat along with the rest of McCook's shattered command to the Nashville Pike (3).

By 10:00 A.M. the whole Federal right wing had been folded back on itself. To administer the *coup de grace*, Bragg called Breckinridge's brigades across the river and threw them against the "hinge" of the Federal line near a cluster of trees called the Round Forest, but referred to by the men on both sides as "Hell's Half Acre" (4). Here the Federal brigade of William B. Hazen, supported by Federal artillery, held fast against a series of costly Confederate attacks.

When night fell on New Year's Eve, it was plain that Bragg had won a victory, but it was just as plain that the victory was incomplete. Indeed, the Confederate position was precarious. Bragg's forces were still badly outnumbered and his best units had been seriously weakened by the day's fighting.

The first day of 1863 was a quiet one north of Murfreesboro; neither side seemed particularly anxious to renew the slaughter. On January 2, however, Rosecrans sent a division from Crittenten's corps to occupy some high ground east of Stones River (5). Observing this move, Bragg resolved to retake the hill. Though Breckinridge protested against the attack, he followed orders and launched about 4,500 men against the Union position (6). The Confederates took the hill, but massed fire from fifty-eight Federal guns across the river (7) made their position untenable and they had to retreat.

This failure seemed to convince Bragg of the wisdom of what his subordinates had already suggested: there was nothing more the Army of Tennessee could gain on this battlefield. The next night the Confederates retreated southward, having suffered 12,000 casualties, nearly a third of those engaged. The Federal army lost 13,000 and Rosecrans, happy to have survived, did not pursue.

PART THREE

Confederate High Tide

The first six months of 1863 witnessed a string of impressive Confederate military victories, creating a feeling of euphoria in the South and of despair in the North. Lee's Army of Northern Virginia won convincing triumphs over Federal armies at Fredericksburg (December, 1862) and Chancellorsville (May, 1863) and then embarked on an invasion of Northern territory that threatened Washington, Baltimore, and even Philadelphia. But Southern euphoria was shattered abruptly in early July, with the twin Confederate defeats at Gettysburg and Vicksburg that subsequently seemed to mark the turning point of the war. Historians have often pointed to the failure of Pickett's desperate and dramatic charge at Gettysburg as the "high-water mark" of the Confederacy. But what the Confederate victories at Fredericksburg and Chancellorsville concealed was that the Southern experiment in independence had already moved into its ebb tide.

A balance sheet of the war compiled at the beginning of 1863 would have suggested a fairly even struggle. After all, except for small Federal enclaves in west Tennessee, northern Arkansas, the Carolina coast, and the city of New Orleans, the Confederacy still controlled most of the territory it claimed. But such a balance sheet would be deceiving, for the Confederacy was simply not capable of sustaining a long war on a massive scale. Even in its greatest victories, the South was being bled to death. At Fredericksburg and Chancellorsville, the Army of Northern Virginia inflicted nearly 29,000 casualties on the Federal armies, while suffering only 18,000 in return. Expressed as a percentage of the forces engaged, however, the Southern losses were proportionally greater, 30 percent to 26 per-

cent. Moreover, the Confederacy had a limited manpower pool from which to make up such losses. The North, by contrast, seemed to many Southerners like the mythical Hydra that grew two new heads each time one was cut off. Simply stated, the South could not afford such victories, brilliant as they were.

In addition to the loss of manpower in the ranks,

General Braxton Bragg commanded the Confederate Army of Tennessee from Perryville through Missionary Ridge. A particular favorite of President Jefferson Davis, Bragg failed as a commander because of a casual attitude about military intelligence, and a resulting tendency to change his orders, characteristics that cost him the trust and confidence of his subordinates. (Cook Collection, Valentine Museum)

Confederate Brigadier General Lewis Armistead leads the charge against Cushing's Battery at Gettysburg. A moment later Armistead fell mortally wounded. (NA)

Lieutenant General Thomas J. ("Stonewall") Jackson was Lee's strong right arm until he was mortally wounded at Chancellorsville at the moment of his greatest triumph. (NA)

Lieutenant General James Longstreet, "Old Pete" or "Old Peter" to the troops, was commander of the Confederate First Corps. He became indispensable to Lee after Jackson's death at Chancellorsville, but his performance at Gettysburg, where he opposed Lee's tactics, has been controversial ever since. (Cook Collection, Valentine Museum)

Major General Ambrose Burnside succeeded McClellan in command of the Army of the Potomac. He offered a bold front with his bluff manner and elaborate side whiskers, but his own inner doubts were more than justified by the results of his brief tenure in command of the Union army. (NA)

the Confederacy in 1863 began to feel the effects of a serious drain on its officer corps. The sense of personal honor cherished by many Southerners frequently led them to expose themselves unnecessarily to enemy fire for the benefit of morale. The result was a disproportionate loss of life at the brigade and division levels. The death of Stonewall Jackson after the Battle of Chancellorsville in May was only the most serious of a long list of casualties that deprived the Southern armies of many of their most promising leaders. Every brigade commander participating in Pickett's charge was killed or wounded. Lee would find it difficult to replace them.

Of course, there was always the hope of foreign intervention. One reason Lee sought a decisive engagement in the North during July was the hope that such a victory would convince Britain or France, or both, to take a more active role in the war. But Lincoln's issuance of the Emancipation Proclamation the previous September had cooled British ardor, and Napoleon III would not make a move without Britain. The only real hope for the Confederacy was that the Yankees would simply tire of the war and let the South go.

At the beginning of 1863 such an outcome seemed possible. McClellan's dismissal was an open ad-

Major General Joseph Hooker was a vain and assertive commander who got off to a good start, but lost his nerve at a critical moment. A punctuation error in an official communication gave him his nickname: "Fighting Joe Hooker." (LC)

Major General George Gordon Meade became the third Union commander in six months just prior to the Battle of Gettysburg. Lincoln is supposed to have remarked that as a Pennsylvanian, Meade would probably fight well on his own dung hill. Ordinarily taciturn, he was prone to fits of temper that earned him the nickname "Old Snapping Turtle." (NA)

mission of defeat by the administration in Washington. Lincoln had given the mercurial general two chances and had finally decided that he was unacceptable. In his place Lincoln appointed the dashing and elaborately whiskered Ambrose Burnside. The choice was based not on Lincoln's confidence in Burnside, but simply on Burnside's seniority and position. His military performance to date had been satisfactory, though some had criticized his tardiness in getting across the bridge subsequently named for him at Antietam. Burnside's principal shortcoming was that his bluff and hearty manner concealed an inner self-doubt. His insecurity manifested itself in a stubborn inflexibility and defensiveness about his decisions. That inflexibility would spell disaster for him and his army in his first campaign.

After Burnside's star faded, Joseph Hooker—Fighting Joe—became the new commander. As Burnside's whiskers had made a contribution to the American vernacular, so did Hooker's policy of allowing "camp followers" into the soldiers' bivouacs contribute to the lore of the world's oldest profession. Hooker fared little better than Burnside, and in late June, on the eve of the greatest battle ever fought in the Western Hemisphere he was replaced by George Gordon Meade. Meanwhile, as

Lincoln experimented with new commanders for the Army, the long-suffering men in the ranks stoically did their duty. By the end of 1863 it was they, and not their indifferent commanders, who had sapped the strength of the Confederacy.

The waning of Confederate hopes was most apparent in the West where the hard-hitting team of Grant and Sherman besieged the Confederate fortress of Vicksburg. The brilliance of Lee's victories along the Rappahannock and his invasion of Pennsylvania in July drew popular attention away from the fact that Grant's dogged siege of Vicksburg was about to divide the Confederacy in half. Ironically, Vicksburg's final capitulation, inevitable since May, came the day after the failure of Pickett's charge at Gettysburg, thus making the shock of defeat all the more telling.

By the end of 1863 the Federal blockade was closing Confederate ports, the Mississippi River was in Union hands, Confederate hopes for foreign recognition were fading, and the Southern economy was increasingly fragile. Even to contemporaries, it must have seemed that the Confederacy was at ebb tide. But Lee's army in Virginia was still as dangerous as ever, and news of a Confederate victory at Chickamauga in northern Georgia renewed Southern hopes that Confederate arms might yet triumph.

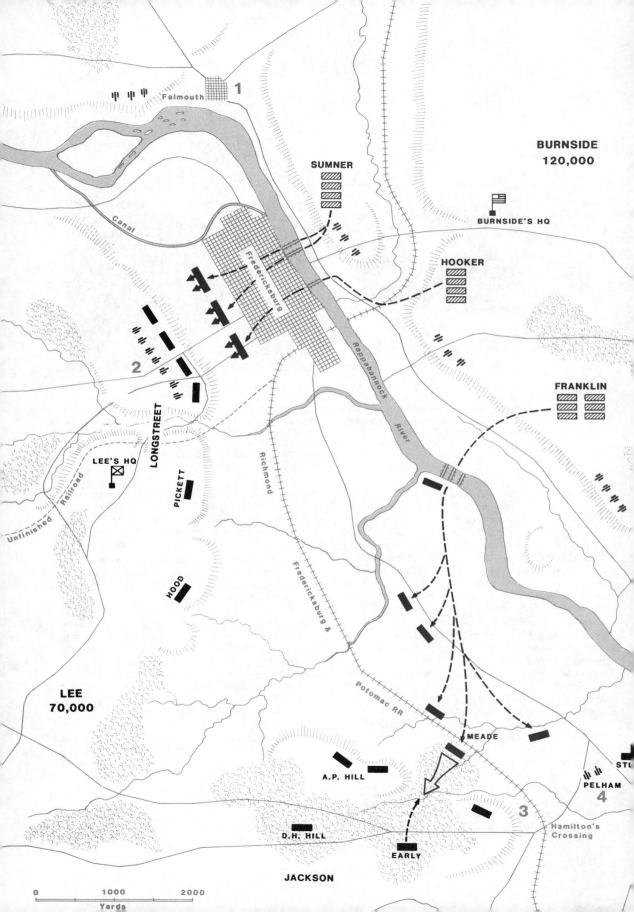

BURNSIDE
120,000

Falmouth

1

SUMNER

BURNSIDE'S HQ

Canal

Fredericksburg

HOOKER

Rappahannock River

2

FRANKLIN

LONGSTREET

Richmond

LEE'S HQ

Unfinished Railroad

PICKETT

Fredericksburg &

HOOD

LEE
70,000

MEADE

STU

Potomac RR

PELHAM

4

A.P. HILL

3

Hamilton's Crossing

D.H. HILL

EARLY

JACKSON

0	1000	2000

Yards

MAP 22

Fredericksburg

December 13, 1862

Ambrose Burnside never intended to have to fight his way across the Rappahannock River at Fredericksburg. His entire strategic scheme was predicated on getting his 120,000-man army across the river and onto the high ground beyond before Lee could get there to contest the crossing. Indeed, when the lead elements of the Army of the Potomac arrived on the north bank of the river on November 17, there were only about 500 Confederate soldiers in Fredericksburg. Lee's army was more than a day's march away at Culpeper and Jackson's corps was off in the Shenandoah Valley. All Burnside's men had to do was cross the river and seize the heights beyond.

Of course, all the bridges had been destroyed by the Confederates, but Burnside had anticipated this and had arranged with General Halleck to have pontoon trains meet him at Falmouth (1). But the promised bridging equipment did not arrive until November 22 and by then the heights beyond Fredericksburg were swarming with Lee's veterans who were busily digging in on Marye's Heights (2). The culprit in this logistic snafu was not Burnside but Halleck. The General in chief had opposed Burnside's plan to cross the Rappahannock at Fredericksburg and as a result had made no serious effort to ensure that the appropriate bridging equipment was available.

At this point, Burnside would have been well advised to call off his planned attack. But the man who had battered his way across Burnside's Bridge was not so easily deterred. Instead he devised a new plan to launch two simultaneous attacks on the Confederate positions: one against Jackson's corps and one directly across the river and up the gentle slope of Marye's Heights. He ordered that three pontoon bridges be laid directly across the river to the city, and three more about two miles downstream, halfway between the city and Hamilton's Crossing, where Jackson's corps was bivouacked among the tree-covered hills south of the city (3).

It took the Federal engineers nearly two weeks to complete the six bridges. In part this was because Confederate sharpshooters harassed the bridge-builders from the buildings along the river's edge. Burnside had to order several companies of volunteers across the river in boats to chase the snipers away. Finally in early December the bridges were ready and the long columns of the Army of the Potomac filed across. During the fog-enshrouded morning hours of December 13, the blue columns formed up outside the city and went forward.

The attack on Marye's Heights might have called to mind the comment of the Frenchman who witnessed the charge of the Light Brigade: it was magnificent, but it was not war. The Federal soldiers advanced up the slope and were slaughtered: first by the Confederate artillery, and then, if they survived long enough to get within range, by the six ranks of Confederate infantry standing in a sunken road behind a stone wall. Throughout the long afternoon, rank upon rank of blue-coated soldiers advanced up the hill, only to be broken by the sheet of fire from the crest. Though over ten thousand men fell in the effort, none came closer to that stone wall than 100 feet. Watching from the heights Lee commented: "It is well that war is so terrible; men would love it too much."

Three miles to the south, the 50,000-man corps of Major General William B. Franklin tentatively measured the strength of Jackson's position. Franklin plainly misunderstood his assignment. Though he had clear numerical superiority over Jackson, he allowed his advance to be held up by harassing fire from Stuart's cavalry and in particular by a two-gun battery commanded by Major John Pelham (4). Then when he did attack, he sent one lone division under Major General George Gordon Meade across the railroad and into the treeline. Incredibly, it struck precisely at a gap in the rebel line and drove uncontested into the Confederate rear. A South Carolina regiment was surprised and nearly captured intact with its arms stacked. But Meade's assault was unsupported and a Confederate counterattack soon drove the Yankees back down the hill and the opportunity was lost.

Meanwhile the suicidal Federal assaults on Marye's Heights continued. Not until nightfall did Burnside finally decide that the game was up and called off the attack. Twelve thousand Federals had fallen during the day, most of them on the slopes of Marye's Heights. Lee's army, by contrast, suffered only 5,000 casualties. Assessing the results of the day's action, a Federal newspaper correspondent reported to his readers: "It can hardly be in human nature for men to show more valor, or generals to manifest less judgement." The next day a visitor to Burnside's tent found the commanding general pacing back and forth with his head bowed muttering, "Those men. Those men."

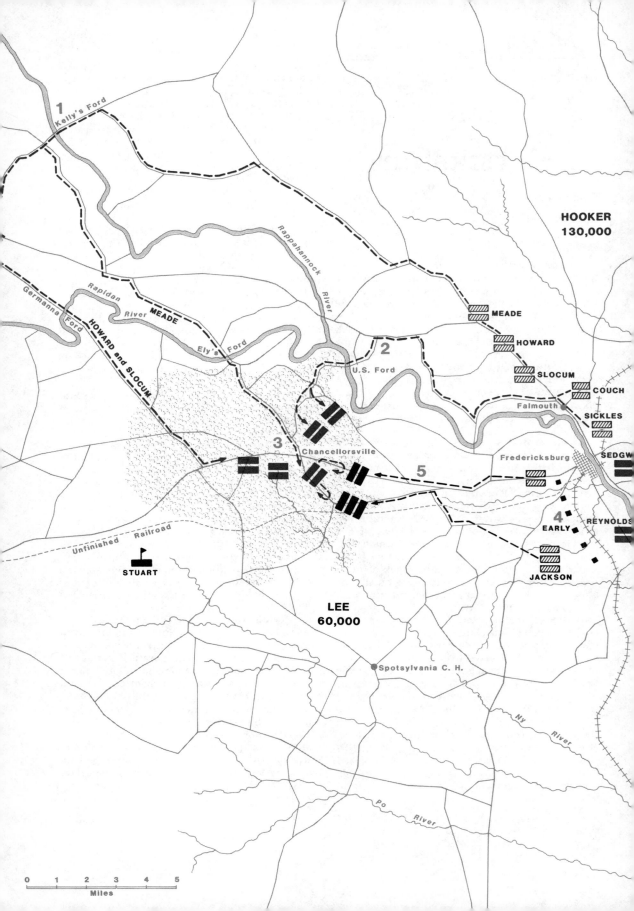

1

Kelly's Ford

HOOKER
130,000

Rappahannock River

MEADE

Rapidan River

Germanna Ford

HOWARD and SLOCUM

Ely's Ford

MEADE

2

U.S. Ford

HOWARD

SLOCUM

COUCH

Falmouth

SICKLES

SEDGW

3

Chancellorsville

Fredericksburg

5

Unfinished Railroad

STUART

4

EARLY

REYNOLDS

JACKSON

LEE
60,000

Spotsylvania C. H.

Ny River

Po River

0 1 2 3 4 5
Miles

MAP 23

Chancellorsville, I

April 26-May 1, 1863

Burnside's tenure as commander of the Army of the Potomac lasted only eighty-one days. Following the fiasco at Fredericksburg, he made one more attempt to launch an offensive across the Rappahannock River when he ordered a night march upstream in an effort to get around Lee's flank. It went well enough at the start, but then it began to rain, a heavy winter rain that turned the dirt roads into quagmires. The guns sank to their axles and threatened to disappear altogether. To inspire the men, Burnside authorized the issue of a whiskey ration, which raised spirits but hardly contributed to efficiency. The Confederate pickets were treated to the sight of drunken Union soldiers wallowing in mud and even engaging in some extracurricular fisticuffs with one another. After a day and a night of battling the mud, Burnside gave up and ordered the army to return to its camp near Falmouth. More than anything else, this infamous "mud march" eroded the army's confidence in its commander. As a consequence, Burnside was replaced by Major General Joseph Hooker—called "Fighting Joe" by his admirers—on January 25, 1863. Hooker had been in the forefront of Burnside's detractors during the latter's brief period of command. Now in command himself, Hooker resolved first to restore the army's fighting spirit, and then to avoid Burnside's folly of a frontal attack by outflanking "Bobby Lee" to the west.

Through the late winter and early spring, Hooker concentrated on improving morale, establishing an efficient army intelligence system, and reorganizing the Federal cavalry. So preoccupied did Hooker seem with these efforts that Lee decided to send Longstreet with part of his corps to the Carolinas to counter Federal threats in that theater. His decision reduced his army's strength to about 60,000 while Hooker's army was growing to more than twice that. Lee, however, believed that his strong defensive position at Fredericksburg compensated for his inferiority in numbers.

Hooker had no intention of attacking directly across the river. Instead he planned a grand flanking movement that he was certain would force Lee to give up his strong position at Fredericksburg and accept battle in the open country south and west of the city. Hooker began his movement on April 26. First he dispatched Brigadier General George Stoneman with an entire corps of Federal cavalry to disrupt Lee's rail communications with Richmond and draw the Confederate cavalry southward. Then he sent three full corps of infantry—about half of his army—on a long march toward Kelly's Ford (1) some twenty miles upriver from Falmouth. He calculated that the remaining half of his army was still strong enough to repel any Confederate offensives across the river, should Lee be so foolish as to attempt them. When the advance Federal units "uncovered" the fords nearer to Fredericksburg, Hooker sent two more corps across the river at U.S. Ford (2) to join them. In four days, five of the seven Federal corps were concentrated around the crossroads settlement of Chancellorsville (3).

Hooker hoped that the thick forests of the area known as "the Wilderness" would mask his move from Lee until it was too late. But Lee was kept informed of Hooker's movements by reports from Stuart, who had refused to follow Stoneman's raid southward. Lee recognized that his position was serious. He could choose one of four alternatives. He could retreat, which was undoubtedly what Hooker expected him to do; he could stay at Fredericksburg and attempt something against the 47,000 Union soldiers still facing him there; he could divide his army in half and attempt to fight on two fronts; or he could leave a weak screening force at Fredericksburg and take the bulk of his army to the west to face Hooker. The last alternative carried the greatest risk but also the greatest possibility for a decisive victory if successful. Lee considered the second alternative briefly, but in the end he left a single reinforced division under Major General Jubal Early at Fredericksburg (4) and took the rest of his army off toward Chancellorsville (5).

At Chancellorsville, Hooker spent the morning of May 1 consolidating his position. Not until the afternoon did he put his five corps in motion eastward along the Orange Plank Road and the Orange Turnpike. His men had advanced only a short distance, however, and were still well within the boundaries of the Wilderness when they ran into rebel skirmishers from Lee's army. At this point Hooker lost his nerve. Instead of pushing forward to gain the open country, he recalled the advance—despite the protests of his senior corps commanders—and pulled back to his positions around Chancellorsville to await Lee's attack. His decision left the initiative to Lee and, as he would discover, that was most unwise.

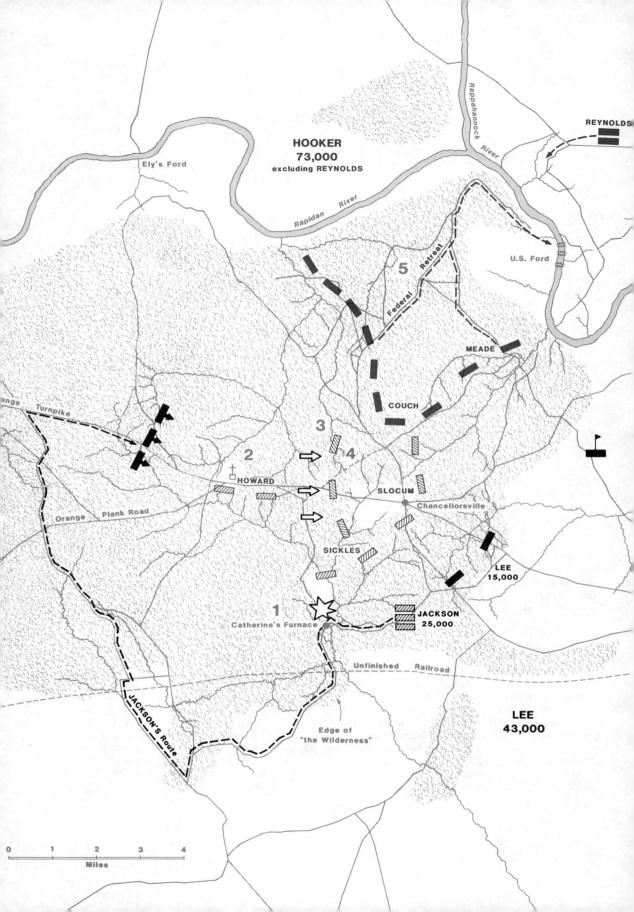

REYNOLDS

HOOKER
73,000
excluding REYNOLDS

Ely's Ford

Rappahannock River

Rapidan River

U.S. Ford

5

Federal Retreat

MEADE

COUCH

3

Orange Turnpike

2

4

HOWARD

SLOCUM

Chancellorsville

Orange Plank Road

LEE
15,000

SICKLES

1

JACKSON
25,000

Catherine's Furnace

Unfinished Railroad

JACKSON'S Route

LEE
43,000

Edge of
"the Wilderness"

0   1   2   3   4
Miles

MAP 24

Chancellorsville, II

May 2-4, 1863

Hooker's decision to remain on the defensive within the Wilderness offered Lee a chance to turn disaster into opportunity. Though outnumbered almost two to one, he determined to divide his forces yet again and dispatch Jackson with the greater part of the army—some 25,000 men—on a long march around Hooker's right flank. Of all Lee's battlefield decisions this was the most audacious, for it sent Jackson across the front of a superior enemy on narrow forest roads whose routes were only imperfectly known, and left Lee with only about 15,000 men to contain Hooker's five full corps.

Jackson began his move at 10:00 A.M. on May 2. Early in the march the grey column had to cross a piece of open ground near Catherine's Furnace (1) within sight of the men of Major General Daniel Sickle's Third Corps. A sharp skirmish ensued as Jackson's rear guard held off a series of Federal probes. Naturally, news of the Confederate movement soon reached Hooker, but the Union commander chose to believe that this was evidence that the rebels were in retreat. If Hooker had pushed forward at this moment, Lee's army surely would have been overwhelmed. But, confident that things were going exactly as he had imagined they would, Hooker remained where he was.

At about 3:00 P.M. Jackson's lead brigades crossed the Orange Plank Road. He considered attacking along this thoroughfare, but determined that the further north he launched his attack, the more decisive it would be. He was aware that he was stretching his luck, but the devout Jackson believed more in fate than in luck anyway, and he decided to push ahead and attack along the Orange Turnpike.

At 5:00 P.M. the mostly German soldiers of Major General Oliver O. Howard's Eleventh Corps were sitting around their campfires cooking dinner in a clearing near the Wilderness Church (2). Out of the supposedly impenetrable forest to the west came the sound of bugles. Scores of animals—deer and rabbits—bounded out of the woods, flushed from cover by the advance of 25,000 men. Then the eerie

high-pitched sound of the "rebel yell" reached the Federals' ears and they ran for their rifles neatly stacked nearby. Too late. Jackson's men were on them before they could form line of battle. Their panic was contagious and Howard's entire corps dissolved before the rebel onslaught. Riding among his men, Jackson urged them on, crying "Press them! Press them!" So precipitate was the Federal retreat that Sickles's men found themselves in a collapsing pocket and were threatened with encirclement. Finally at about 8:00 P.M. the Union army succeeded in forming a secondary line (3).

The sun had been down for more than an hour now (it set at 6:48 P.M.) but a nearly full moon made night operations just possible. Desperately eager to achieve a decisive victory before the Federals recovered from their initial shock, Jackson rode ahead with his staff to explore a secondary road (4) that he hoped would make it possible for his brigades to pinch off the Federal salient. As Jackson returned from this reconnaissance, a Confederate picket fired at the horsemen in the woods. A scattered volley rang out. Jackson was hit twice: in the left arm and the right hand. The wounds were painful but did not appear to be life-threatening. Nevertheless, command of the Second Corps had to be passed first to A.P. Hill, and then, when Hill was wounded by a shell fragment, to Jeb Stuart. But the night attack Jackson had sought was abandoned. The battle died away in isolated skirmishes in the forest.

The next morning Hooker pulled his forces back into a defensive arc protecting his line of communications across the Rappanhannock at U.S. Ford. At midday, news reached both armies that Early's detached division had been overwhelmed by Sedgwick's corps on the heights above Fredericksburg and Sedgwick was now marching on Chancellorsville from the east. Leaving Stuart to watch Hooker, Lee marched back toward Fredericksburg to deal with Sedgwick. Their forces met on May 4 at the Battle of Salem Church. Though the fight was indecisive, Sedgwick chose to retreat that night back across the Rappahannock.

That same night, Hooker, too, decided to re-cross the river (5). Another Federal offensive had come to grief south of the Rappahannock. The Federals had suffered 16,800 casualties to the Confederates' 13,000 but more importantly they had been badly handled by an army only half as large. At the critical moments Lee had demonstrated audacity and nerve; Hooker, after a good start, had lost his momentum and then the initiative and altogether failed to live up to his nickname. But the Confederate victory was a costly one, for "Stonewall" Jackson, after a temporary recovery following the amputation of his left arm, contracted an infection and fever, and died on May 10. Lee had lost his "strong right arm."

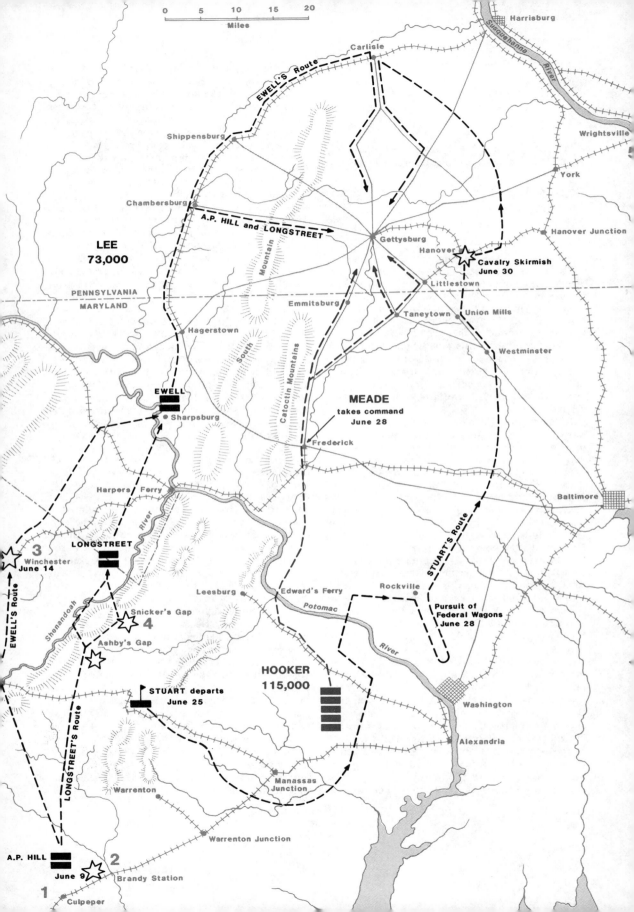

0 5 10 15 20
Miles

Harrisburg

Susquehanna River

EWELL'S Route

Carlisle

Shippensburg

Wrightsville

Chambersburg

A.P. HILL and LONGSTREET

York

Hanover Junction

LEE
73,000

Gettysburg

Hanover

Cavalry Skirmish
June 30

PENNSYLVANIA

MARYLAND

Littlestown

South Mountain

Catoctin Mountains

Emmitsburg

Taneytown

Union Mills

Hagerstown

MEADE
takes command
June 28

Westminster

EWELL

Sharpsburg

Frederick

Harpers Ferry

River

Baltimore

STUART'S Route

3

Winchester
June 14

LONGSTREET

Shenandoah River

Snicker's Gap

4

Ashby's Gap

Leesburg

Edward's Ferry

Potomac

Rockville

Pursuit of
Federal Wagons
June 28

EWELL'S Route

River

STUART departs
June 25

HOOKER
115,000

Washington

Alexandria

LONGSTREET'S Route

Manassas
Junction

Warrenton

A.P. HILL

June 9

2

Brandy Station

Warrenton Junction

1

Culpeper

MAP 25

Lee's Second Invasion

June, 1863

Having missed the action at Chancellorsville to participate in a fruitless siege at Suffolk, Longstreet returned to the Army of Northern Virginia in late May. His two divisions boosted Lee's strength to over 70,000 men—its greatest since the Seven Days a year earlier. Jackson's death forced Lee to reorganize his enlarged army. Longstreet retained command of the First Corps; Richard S. "Dick" Ewell, whom the troops called "Old Bald Head," was given the Second Corps, and A.P. Hill was promoted and given command of the new Third Corps.

Determined to try once again to take the war to the North, Lee shifted his base westward upriver from the Wilderness to Culpeper on the Orange and Alexandria Railroad (1). From there Stuart's cavalry—nearly 10,000 men—would screen the army's movement into the Shenandoah Valley, the invasion highway. Stuart held a massive review of his cavalry division at Brandy Station just north of Culpeper on June 5. So impressed was he with the results that he repeated it two days later for Lee. But news of the performance also reached the ears of Federal Major General Alfred Pleasanton who took about 11,000 troopers of his own to Brandy Station on June 9. Surprised by the Federal initiative, Stuart's men were hard-pressed before recovering sufficiently to drive off the Federals in the largest cavalry action of the war (2). Still, Stuart's pride had been hurt, and Stuart's determination to redeem that pride would play and important role in the coming campaign.

A week after the clash at Brandy Station, Lee started his infantry corps northward. Ewell's corps moved first, passing through Chester Gap on its way toward Winchester. On June 14 it fell upon a Federal division of about 5,000 at Winchester (3), and inflicted a crushing defeat, taking almost the whole division prisoner. As Ewell marched on toward Sharpsburg, Longstreet moved northward east of the mountains toward Ashby's Gap and Snicker's Gap (4). On June 17 the disposition of Lee's army was approximately as shown at left.

Fully aware now of Lee's intentions, Hooker rec-

ommended to Washington an immediate attack on Hill and a rapid descent on Richmond. President Lincoln rejected his proposal, arguing that "Lee's army, and not Richmond, is your true objective." Somewhat grudgingly, Hooker started north, keeping his army between Lee and the Federal capital.

Longstreet's corps hovered in the vicinity of the passes into the Valley until it became clear that Hooker was heading north. Meanwhile A.P. Hill's men leapfrogged past Longstreet and followed Ewell across the Potomac. During this week Stuart's cavalry had been busy fending off Federal probes. His job nearly finished, Stuart requested permission to conduct a raid to plunder the Federal rear. Through Longstreet, Lee gave conditional approval. But Lee's orders warned that when Hooker crossed into Maryland, Stuart must rejoin the army.

With about half of his cavalry division, Stuart departed on June 25, determined to ride around the Federals as he had before the Seven Days and following Sharpsburg. But because Hooker himself was also on the move, Stuart had to ride a considerable distance to get around him. Though he accomplished great deeds on his raid—throwing a scare into Washington and capturing 125 fully loaded Federal wagons—he left Lee to grope his way northward into Pennsylvania without Stuart's regular intelligence reports to provide him with clear knowledge of the enemy dispositions.

Leading the Confederate advance, Ewell's men had already marched through Chambersburg. From there he sent one division under Major General Jubal Early eastward to Gettysburg and took the rest of his command north to Carlisle. Early's men met only scattered militia units and pushed through Gettysburg on toward York and finally to Wrightsville on the Susquehanna River (5). (NOTE: For clarity the movements of this division are not indicated on the map at left. Early rejoined Ewell on June 30 north of Gettysburg.)

Hooker meanwhile had gotten into another dispute with his superiors—Lincoln, Stanton, and Halleck—this time over the Harpers Ferry garrison, and had threatened to resign. The issue was not as important as the result. Already displeased by Hooker's performance to date, Lincoln surprised Hooker by calling his bluff and accepting his resignation. When the Federal army reached the vicinity of Frederick, a messenger informed Major General George Gordon Meade that he was to succeed to the command of the Army. Meade was not a brilliant strategist, but his great virtue was that he did not think that he was one. He continued to move the army northward on parallel roads that converged on the small college town of Gettysburg.

Lee learned of the Federal change of command—and the proximity of the Army of the Potomac—on June 28. He immediately ordered his corps commanders to concentrate either at Cashtown or the more centrally located community of Gettysburg.

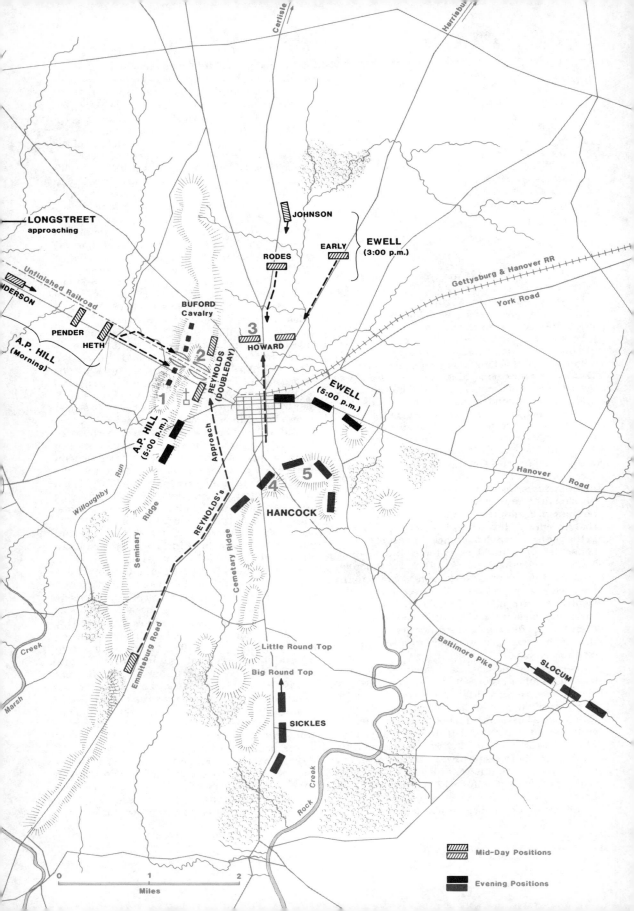

Carlisle

Harrisbu

LONGSTREET
approaching

JOHNSON

EARLY

EWELL
(3:00 p.m.)

RODES

Gettysburg & Hanover RR

York Road

Unfinished Railroad

NDERSON

BUFORD
Cavalry

3

PENDER   HEET

HOWARD

A.P. HILL
(Morning)

2

REYNOLDS
(DOUBLEDAY)

EWELL
(5:00 p.m.)

1

A.P. HILL
(5:00 P.m.)

5

Hanover   Road

REYNOLDS's

4

Approach

HANCOCK

Willoughby Run

Seminary Ridge

Cemetery Ridge

Baltimore Pike

SLOCUM

Little Round Top

Creek

Big Round Top

Emmitsburg Road

SICKLES

Marsh

Rock Creek

Mid-Day Positions

Evening Positions

0   1   2

Miles

MAP 26

Gettysburg: The First Day

July 1, 1863

Two Federal cavalry brigades under Major General John Buford, riding in advance of the main body, entered Gettysburg from the south on June 30, 1863. Buford examined the ground north and west of the town and decided that the gentle tree-covered ridge, which was dominated by the white cupola of a Lutheran seminary, was worth defending. Though Meade had not ordered him to fight for Gettysburg, Buford had his men dismount and take up positions just in front of the ridge on a rise known as McPherson's Ridge (1) after a local farmer. He knew that dismounted cavalry could not stop a determined infantry assault, but he hoped to hold on until he received support from Major General John Reynolds's infantry corps, the lead unit of Meade's main body. Initial contact between the two armies took place that afternoon, when a foraging Confederate brigade in search of shoes became aware of the presence of Buford's cavalry. This news was soon carried to Confederate Major General "Harry" Heth who commanded the lead division of A.P. Hill's Corps west of Gettysburg.

The next morning Heth had his division on the road by 5:00 A.M., intending to brush aside the blue troopers in his path. Arriving outside the town at about 8:00, he deployed two brigades and sent them across Willoughby Run and up the ridge. Buford's troopers fought hard and casualties were heavy on both sides. Some Confederates who advanced along an unfinished railway bed found themselves trapped in a deep cut and vulnerable to heavy fire on both flanks (2). Then, after nearly two hours of combat, the lead elements of Reynolds's infantry corps arrived on the ridge. Reynolds himself rode to the front to assess the situation, and was killed almost instantly by a rebel sharpshooter. The Confederates had not expected to encounter the hardened veterans of the Army of the Potomac, and after another hour of close combat, they pulled back, leaving the ridge in Federal hands.

Lee arrived on the field at about 2:00 P.M. while Heth was reassessing his situation. The army commander was disturbed to find Federal infantry at Gettysburg—in what strength he did not know. He was on the verge of calling off the action altogether when the lead elements of Ewell's Corps coming south from Carlisle struck the Federal right flank in precisely the spot Lee would have selected, had he planned it (3). He hadn't. But he was quick to recognize an opportunity and he issued orders for a general advance.

On the Federal side, Reynolds's death put Abner Doubleday (who had fired the first Federal gun at Fort Sumter) in command of the First Corps. He in turn was superseded by O. O. Howard when that officer brought his Eleventh Corps into line on Doubleday's right. Howard's men, like their commander, were still suffering from their humiliation at Chancellorsville, and when Ewell's Valley veterans smashed into their front, it was an uneven contest. The Federals broke and fled, fending off the pursuing rebels as best they could while withdrawing through the town and onto the slightly higher ground of Cemetery Hill just to the south (4).

For those interested in the "might have beens" of history, there is little doubt that, had Ewell pushed his attack in the twilight of that July 1, the Federals would have been driven from their new positions. But, Lee had cautioned all of his corps commanders not to bring on a full battle until the army was concentrated and, Longstreet's corps was still approaching along the Chambersburg Pike. Ewell's subordinates urged him to attack anyway, arguing that Lee surely did not mean that Ewell should let such a priceless opportunity as this slip away. Tradition has it that Major General Isaac Trimble pointed toward Cemetery Hill toward which the Federal fugitives were streaming and cried "Give me a brigade and I will take that hill." If Trimble did make such a plea, Ewell did not accede.

At about the time this perhaps apocryphal exchange was taking place, Federal Major General Winfield Scott Hancock was attempting to bring some organization out of the chaos on Cemetery Hill. Meade had sent Hancock ahead of his corps to take command of the defense, and though his authority was disputed by Howard (who was senior), Hancock by midnight had made the Federal position relatively secure.

That night Lee visited Ewell to discuss the next day's operations. Lee suggested that Ewell might be able to turn the Federal right flank. But "Old Bald Head" replied that the Union positions were too strong. Lee therefore decided that Ewell should make a "demonstration" against Culp's Hill (5) the next day and, if opportunity presented, he should turn it into an attack. The main Confederate effort, however, would be made on the Confederate right by the fresh troops of Longstreet's corps.

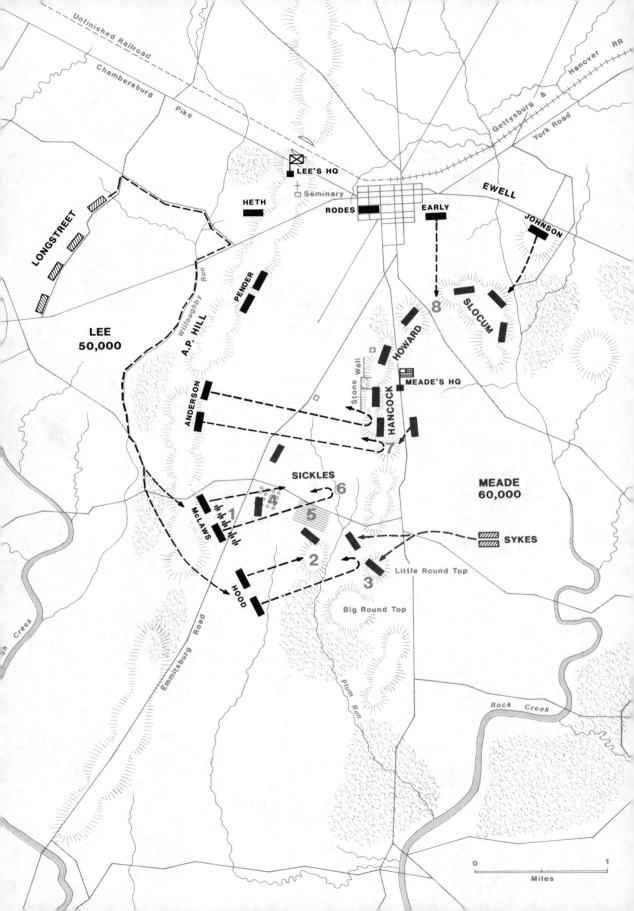

Untinished Railroad

Chambersburg   Pike

Gettysburg & Hanover RR

York Road

LONGSTREET

Willoughby Run

LEE
50,000

A.P. HILL

HETH

Seminary

LEE'S HQ

RODES

EWELL

EARLY

JOHNSON

SLOCUM

8

PENDER

ANDERSON

HOWARD

Stone Wall

MEADE'S HQ

HANCOCK

7

SICKLES

6

4

5

MEADE
60,000

McLAWS

1

2

SYKES

3

Little Round Top

HOOD

Big Round Top

Emmitsburg Road

Creek

Plum Run

Rock Creek

0   1

Miles

MAP 27

Gettysburg: The Second Day

July 2, 1863

When dawn broke over Gettysburg on July 2, the two armies faced each other on parallel ridges across an open plain. Both armies had been reinforced overnight. Longstreet had arrived with two of his divisions—those of McLaws and Hood—which brought Confederate strength up to about 50,000. Only Pickett's division, still en route, and Stuart's cavalry were missing. (July 2 found Stuart moving northward, east of Gettysburg, toward Carlisle.) But Longstreet's arrival did not improve Lee's odds, for three Union corps had also arrived during the night and a fourth was on the way so that The Federal army now numbered at least 60,000. Lee planned to attack nevertheless.

Because Meade's attention would necessarily be focused northward where Ewell's corps was in plain view of the Federals on Culp's Hill, Lee planned to strike from the south. Seeing no blue uniforms as yet on the Round Tops, Lee ordered Longstreet to attack "en echelon" up the Emmitsburg Road, presuming that such a maneuver would strike the Federals in flank and rear. Though Lee intended to begin this movement in the morning, it was 11:00 A.M. before he issued the orders. The most serious delay, however, was due to Longstreet. "Old Peter" was convinced that the Confederate army should slip past Meade's left and take up positions in his rear thus forcing the Federals to assume the tactical offensive. Lee's practice of providing only general guidance to his lieutenants worked here to the South's disadvantage; Lee needed either to issue peremptory orders, or to take command himself. But he did neither and Longstreet delayed his preparations for the attack, perhaps hoping that Lee would call it off. Even after Longstreet began to move, it took several hours to march the troops southward, screened from Federal view by Seminary Ridge, to their assigned positions.

Upon reaching those positions, Hood and McLaws were dismayed to find a full Federal corps deployed directly across their planned line of attack. Federal Major General Daniel Sickles had decided independently to advance his corps to the Emmitsburg Road from Cemetery Ridge and in doing so had created an exposed salient that now became the target of the Confederate attack.

Lee's orders called for an attack "en echelon," meaning sequentially from right to left. Preceded by a bombardment from Longstreet's massed artillery (1), Hood's division went first at about 4:00 P.M. attacking into the hell of the "Devil's Den" (2), a rock-strewn jumble of boulders where the fighting was hand-to-hand. Several regiments swept past this rocky eminence and challenged the Federals who only moments before had occupied Little Round Top. Here the 20th Maine regiment withstood three charges by the men of Hood's division and then counterattacked just as the Confederates were withdrawing, sweeping them off the hill (3). The rebels fell back to the Devil's Den, where they were still within musket range of Little Round Top, and from there they carried on a desultory but deadly exchange of fire with the bluecoats across Plum Run.

At about this time (5:00 P.M.), Longstreet unleashed McLaws's division. It swept over the Federal defenders of the Peach Orchard (4) and pushed on into the adjacent wheatfield (5) where the fighting was again hand-to-hand. Though McLaws's men had the better of this struggle, Confederate losses in the wheatfield so weakened the division that its attack stalled on the banks of Plum Run (6).

Now Anderson's division attacked. Hancock, who had charge of the Federal center, had weakened his section of the line to support Sickles, and toward that weakened center Anderson's three brigades came at a run. One brigade actually topped the crest of the ridge and for one moment looked down upon the Federal rear. Desperate, Hancock ordered the First Minnesota regiment, just arriving on the field from Cemetery Hill, to counterattack. It did, and though it suffered 82 percent casualties in the effort, it slowed the Confederate assault long enough to allow Hancock to establish a new defensive line (7). The new line held, and Anderson's men began the long retreat back across the valley.

On the other end of the long curving line of battle, Ewell had waited all day to deliver his attack, which was to begin when he heard the guns of Longstreet's advance. One division assaulted Culp's Hill and another the "saddle" between Culp's Hill and Cemetery Hill (8). Both attacks met with initial success. It looked for a moment as though the "opportunity" Lee sought might be present. In the growing darkness, Early's division actually broke through the Federal line, but unsupported and faced with Federal counterattacks, it had to withdraw.

July 2 had been a bloody day—each side losing about 10,000 men. Lee had not broken the Federal line, but he had come close three times. Moreover, Meade was aware of how close he had come. That night the Union commander called a staff meeting to discuss a possible retreat. His corps commanders voted to stay where they were. After the meeting Meade expressed his opinion that having attacked both the left and the right, Lee would next attack the Federal center. He was right.

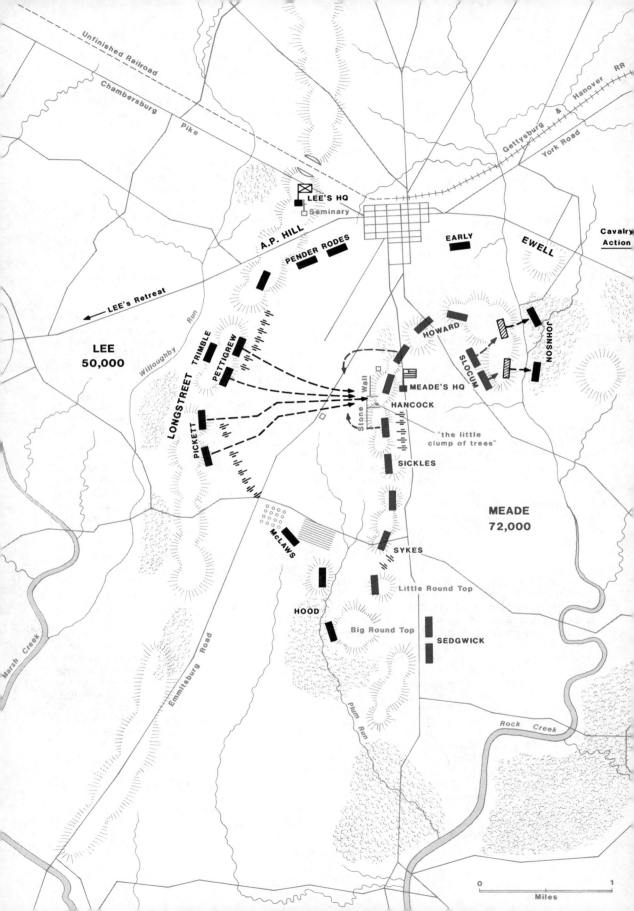

MAP 28

Gettysburg: The Third Day

July 3, 1863

Though the armies at Gettysburg had suffered heavily in the first two days of battle, continuing reinforcements kept the two sides at or above their strength of July 2. For the Confederates, Major General George Pickett's division had arrived at twilight on July 2 and later that evening a bedraggled Jeb Stuart finally reported himself at Lee's headquarters. For once Lee allowed anger into his voice in greeting his cavalry chief, but he soon softened and together they planned how best to use the cavalry in the offensive which Lee was already planning for the next day. The centerpiece of those plans was Pickett's fresh division of Virginians with whom Lee hoped to pierce the Federal center. On the Union side of the field, Sedgewick's corps—the largest in the army—arrived during the night, raising Federal strength to about 72,000. Despite Meade's earlier premonition that Lee would attack the center, the Union commander placed Sedgwick on the left behind the Round Tops.

The first action of July 3, however, took place not on the left or the center, but on Culp's Hill, where Slocum attacked at 4:00 A.M. to regain the southern spur of the hill. The battle swayed back and forth until about 10:30 A.M., when the Confederates were forced to retreat across Rock Creek.

Meanwhile, on Seminary Ridge Lee was explaining his battle plan to a protesting Longstreet. The latter tried every argument short of outright refusal to dissuade his chief, but to no avail. Longstreet's mood contrasted markedly with that of Pickett, who fairly bubbled at the prospect. Pickett would command his own three brigades, plus two detached from Anderson's division. To Pickett's left, four of the wounded Heth's brigades were placed under the command of Johnson Pettigrew, and behind him, two of Dorsey Pender's brigades were placed under the command of Isaac Trimble. All together there would be some 12,500 men—an impressive force but, as Longstreet noted, a bit smaller than the force that had struck the Federal line the day before. Lee reasoned, however, that those attacks had not been coordinated and this time the men would all go in together, preceded by an artillery barrage from no less than 140 Confederate cannons.

The bombardment began at 1:00 P.M. The cannonade sent the Federals along the center of the line scrambling for safety, but also drew counter-battery fire from the Union guns. For an hour the thunder of the exchange filled the air, and smoke from the guns filled the valley between the armies with a heavy white cloud. Shortly after 2:00, the Federal gunners slacked their fire to delude the Confederates into believing they had been put out of action. The ruse worked, and at about 3:00, with the guns of both sides silent now, the Confederate infantry stepped out of the woods atop Seminary Ridge and dressed ranks for the assault.

There were eleven brigades in the attack, and the colors of forty-two regiments hung limply in the sultry air. Within an hour, thirty of those flags would be in Federal hands as trophies of war. A few officers gave short speeches. Pickett himself shouted to his men to remember that they were from Virginia and he led them off across the mile-wide field toward the "little clump of trees" in the center of the Federal line that Lee had pointed out to Longstreet as the attack's objective. They marched at a walk—one hundred yards a minute. Halfway across, Pickett's division executed a smart left oblique, as if it were on the parade ground, to close the gap between the advancing divisions. As they advanced, enfilading artillery fire from both Cemetery Hill and Little Round Top struck them in the flanks. When they reached the Emmitsburg Road, Federal batteries on Cemetery Ridge opened up with canister blasting huge holes in the lines. Officers and color-bearers were singled out for special attention by the Federal infantry behind the stone wall that ran across the front of the little clump of trees. It seemed incredible that anything could live on that field, but onward they came.

With a desperate yell the rebels charged. Over the wall came Brigadier General Lewis Armistead, his hat on his sword point as a guide to the 300 or so men who followed him. Armistead charged the Federal battery of Colonel Alonzo Cushing who lay dead among his guns. In a rush, Armistead reached the guns, the traditional "high water mark" of Confederate fortunes, and fell mortally wounded.

The attack had failed. Indeed it had been shattered. As the remnants came streaming back, Lee went out to meet them and to prepare them for the expected Federal counterattack. Of the 12,500 men who set out across the field, fully 7,500 failed to return. Of Pickett's 5,000 men, only 800 reported for duty the next day. Though Lee and Longstreet both expected Meade to follow up his victory, the Union commander was content with what had been accomplished. "We have done well enough," he said.

Federal casualties for the three days totaled 23,000; the Confederates 28,000. At about noon on July 4—the 86th anniversary of American Independence—as the two exhausted armies watched each other across that blood-soaked valley, it began to rain. That night, Lee began his retreat to Virginia.

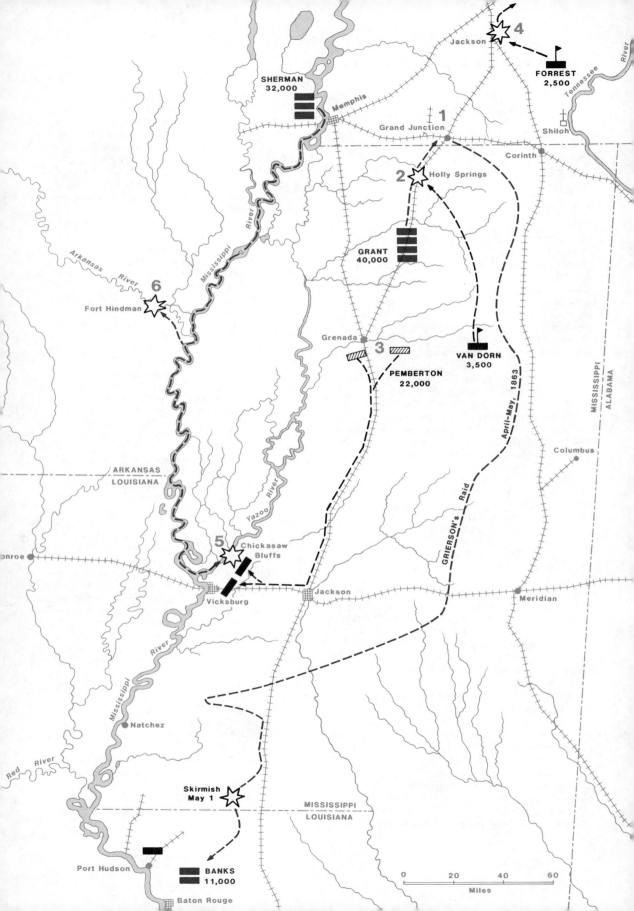

MAP 29

Vicksburg, I

December, 1862-June, 1863

Though most contemporaries (and most historians) focused their attention on the dramatic clash at Gettysburg, in the West events of at least equal significance were simultaneously moving toward a climax. In Mississippi the Federal team of Grant and Sherman had clamped the key city of Vicksburg under a tight siege and on the very day that Lee began his withdrawal from Seminary Ridge, the remnant of the emaciated Vicksburg garrison marched out of the city and stacked arms in formal surrender. With its surrender, the Confederacy was sundered in two.

The sequence of events that culminated in that surrender began in October 1862 when Grant became commander of the Department of Tennessee. At about the same time, Jefferson Davis appointed Lieutenant General John C. Pemberton, the only Northern-born Confederate officer to attain three-star rank, as the new commander of the Army of Mississippi. Earl Van Dorn, the former commander, took over Pemberton's cavalry division.

Grant had more than twice as many troops available as Pemberton; when he began to move south in November from his base at Grand Junction (1), he fielded an army of nearly 40,000 as compared to Pemberton's 22,000. On his way south, Grant established a major supply base at Holly Springs (2) and then moved on across the Tallahatchie River. Pemberton fell back to Grenada (3) and called for reinforcements. It was at this point, in late December, that Jefferson Davis visited the Western theater and ordered Bragg to send a 10,000-man division to Pemberton from Murfreesboro. But before these reinforcements arrived, Pemberton's position was dramatically altered by the exploits of the man he had replaced as army commander.

At dawn on December 20, Van Dorn led about 3,500 Confederate troopers into Holly Springs at a gallop. The 1,500 Federal defenders surrendered almost immediately. Van Dorn's troopers helped themselves to what they could carry and set fire to the rest. Over one and a half million dollars worth of supplies, food, and ammunition was put to the torch. Moreover, about eighty miles to the northeast, Nathan Bedford Forrest was duplicating Van Dorn's feat at Jackson, Tennessee (4), on Grant's supply route to Columbus, Kentucky. Forrest not only destroyed the Federal supplies at Jackson, but also ripped up over sixty miles of track and pulled down the telegraph lines as well. Grant reported that these raids "cut me off from supplies, so that further advance by this route is perfectly impracticable." The next day he began to retrace his steps to Grand Junction.

Meanwhile other events, seemingly unconnected with the military campaigns in Mississippi, would cause Grant to modify his plan of operations. Unknown to Grant, Illinois Democratic politician John A. McClernand had visited President Lincoln in September and presented him with a plan and a problem. The plan was an offer by McClernand to raise an army—on his own—from the Midwestern states, and to use that army to capture Vicksburg. The problem was that there was no way Lincoln could agree to this proposal without destroying the command system in the West, and there was no way he could reject it without alienating McClernand, who was a powerful political force in that part of the country. Besides, if nothing else, McClernand's scheme might raise some new levies for the army. Lincoln therefore agreed and sent a happy McClernand off to raise an army. Not until December did Grant learn about this curious arrangement and when he did, he queried Lincoln about it. The President reassured Grant that he was the theater commander and could do with troops in his department what he deemed best. What Grant deemed best in December 1862 was that Sherman should add McClernand's recruits to his own command at Memphis and take them downriver for an assault on Vicksburg before McClernand arrived.

Sherman headed south on December 20 (the same day as Van Dorn's raid) and on December 27 he assaulted Chickasaw Bluffs (5) just north of Vicksburg in a fruitless effort that resulted in nearly 1,800 Federal casualties, while inflicting only 187. What Sherman did not know when he launched this attack was that Van Dorn's raid had forced Grant to retreat and that Pemberton had quickly shipped his army back to Vicksburg in time to repel the new threat. Sherman was nevertheless ready to try again, but on the last day of the year McClernand arrived (with a new wife in tow) and superseded him in command.

McClernand's first operation was a success. His expedition to Fort Hindman (6) led not only to the fort's surrender, but to the capture of 5,000 Confederates. But both Sherman and Navy Captain David Dixon Porter had become so disgusted with McClernand's overbearing manner and pompous military pronouncements that they begged Grant to come to Vicksburg and take command personally. Grant showed up in late January and assessed the situation for himself. What he saw of it, and of McClernand, convinced him that Sherman and Porter were right. Despite McClernand's protest, Grant concentrated his forces on the river for a campaign against the city from the west which he would direct personally.

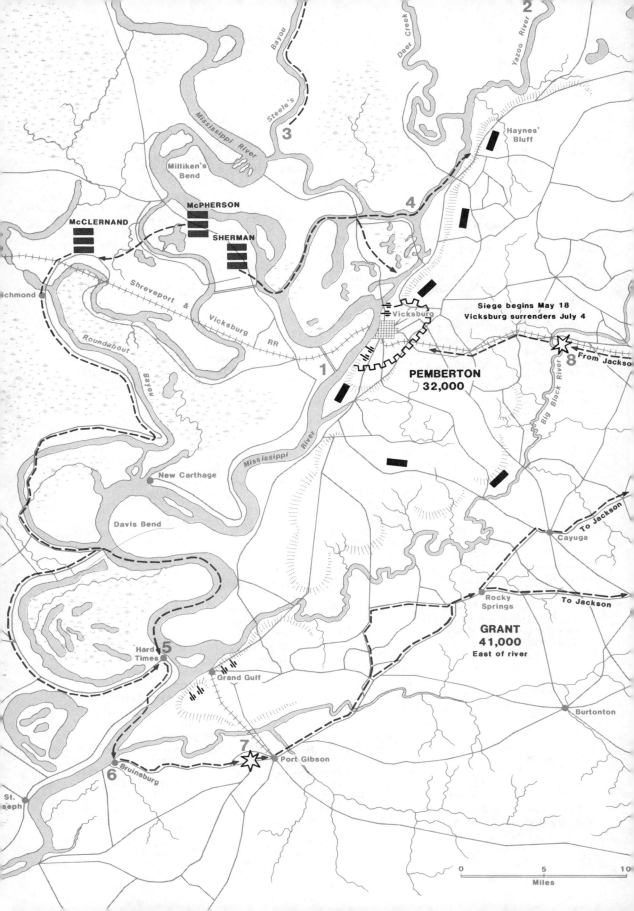

Bayou

Steele's

3

Deer Creek

Yazoo River

2

Haynes'
Bluff

Mississippi River

Milliken's
Bend

4

McPHERSON

McCLERNAND

SHERMAN

Siege begins May 18
Vicksburg surrenders July 4

Vicksburg

Shreveport &

1

8

From Jackso

Richmond

Vicksburg RR

PEMBERTON
32,000

Roundabout

Mississippi River

New Carthage

Big Black River

Bayou

Davis Bend

To Jackson

Cayuga

Rocky
Springs

To Jackson

GRANT
41,000
East of river

Burtonton

Hard
Times

5

Grand Gulf

6

Bruinsburg

7

Port Gibson

St.
seph

0   5   10
Miles

MAP 30

Vicksburg, II

January-July, 1863

Between them, Van Dorn and McClernand had committed Grant to an attack on Vicksburg from the river. Even though he still believed that the best approach was from the east, Grant knew that any retrograde movement now such as a retreat upriver to Memphis would be perceived as an admission of failure and would become grist for the mills of anti-administration newspapers. Grant therefore resigned himself to a campaign against Vicksburg from his base at Milliken's Bend. He organized his 60,000-man army into three corps of about equal size, commanded by McClernand, Sherman, and James B. McPherson, and set to work to devise a plan of attack.

Grant's principal problems from the outset had to do with the environment: mud, rain, swamp, and disease. Living conditions were abominable and the army's morale suffered accordingly. Grant kept his men busy primarily by setting them to work expanding an abandoned canal across the DeSoto peninsula across from Vicksburg (1). This was a project in which Lincoln had a particular interest, and Grant was ever-sensitive to the President's interests. In February and March Grant authorized three separate attempts to avoid a direct assault against the heights north of Vicksburg, all of which involved finding a water route to Vicksburg's back door, and none of which bore fruit. McPherson's corps was charged with investigating the lakes and bayous west of the river (not shown on the map) while other detachments explored the upper reaches of the Yazoo River (2) and Steele's Bayou (3).

Not until April did Grant begin his final and successful campaign. He had believed from the beginning that Vicksburg could be taken only from the east. The problem was how to get there. What he proposed to Porter on April 2 was that the Admiral run his entire fleet past the city while the army sought an overland route around the swamps and bayous to the west. At New Carthage or Hard Times Landing the two forces would rendezvous and Porter would ferry the men across the river. It was simple. But it was also risky, for if the maneuver failed for any reason, there was no going back.

Porter might run past the Vicksburg batteries going downstream without sustaining serious damage, but would not be able to return with the same expectations against the 5-knot current.

Choosing a dark night, Porter made his move on April 16. Alert sentries on the bluffs fired warning shots and daring volunteers from Vicksburg crossed the river in small boats to light bonfires on the western shore which silhouetted the Union gunboats on the inky river. For over an hour the rebel gunners shelled the passing armada, but except for one transport and a few barges, the vessels got through unscathed.

Now it was the army's turn. McClernand's corps took the lead in the march along the old levees bordering Roundabout Bayou. The roads were poor and progress was slow. To draw rebel attention from this maneuver, Grant made use of two diversions: one by Sherman against the bluffs north of the city (4), and one by Brigadier General William Grierson who led a cavalry raid the length of the state of Mississippi from Grand Junction to Baton Rouge (see Map 29). While Confederate attention was fixed on these threats to the north and east, some 43,000 Federal troops gathered at Hard Times Landing (5) for the jump across the river.

The original plan called for Porter's fleet to reduce the Confederate batteries at Grand Gulf where the troops would then land. This proved more difficult than expected, however, for Grand Gulf was nearly as tough a nut to crack as Vicksburg. As a result Grant on April 30 landed his men at Bruinsburg, ten miles downriver (6). Advancing inland, Union forces easily brushed aside a small detachment of Confederates outside Port Gibson (7) on May 1, thus outflanking Grand Gulf and forcing its evacuation.

For the next two weeks, Grant abandoned his lines of communication and marched his forces east toward the Mississippi state capital of Jackson which he captured on May 14. Then he turned westward, advancing on Vicksburg along the route of the Vicksburg and Jackson Railroad. Pemberton tried to stop him at Champion's Hill (off the map to the east) on May 16, and at the crossing of the Big Black River (8) the next day. But Grant had superior numbers and he made no mistakes. Failing to halt Grant's advance, Pemberton fell back inside his prepared defenses and, though Grant tried twice to fight his way in (on May 19 and May 22), from that point on the campaign became a siege.

The siege lasted forty-eight days, during each of which the Federals shelled the city and waited for hunger to conquer the enemy. By July the remaining population was in danger of literally starving to death. On July 3 Pemberton asked Grant for terms and the next day, while Lee began his retreat from Gettysburg, Pemberton's men marched out of the city and stacked arms in formal surrender.

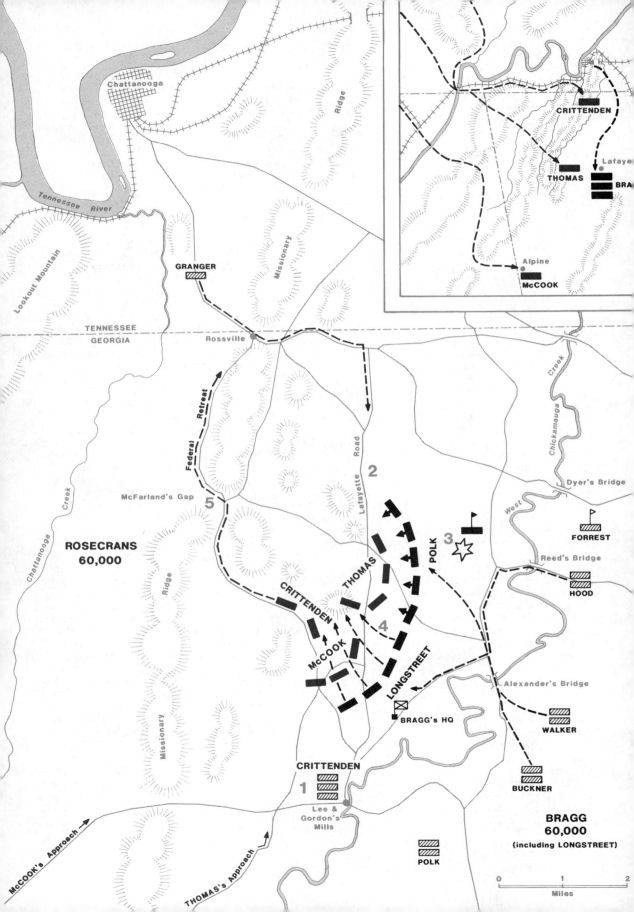

Chattanooga

Tennessee River

Lookout Mountain

Ridge

Missionary

GRANGER

TENNESSEE
GEORGIA

Rossville

CRITTENDEN

THOMAS

Lafaye

McCOOK

Alpine

BRA

Creek

Chattanooga

Creek

Federal   Retreat

McFarland's Gap

ROSECRANS
60,000

Ridge

Missionary

2

Lafayette Road

5

CRITTENDEN

THOMAS

POLK

3

West

Dyer's Bridge

FORREST

Reed's Bridge

HOOD

McCOOK

4

LONGSTREET

BRAGG's HQ

Alexander's Bridge

WALKER

CRITTENDEN

1

Lee &
Gordon's Mills

POLK

BUCKNER

BRAGG
60,000
(including LONGSTREET)

McCOOK's Approach

THOMAS's Approach

0   1   2
Miles

MAP 31

Chickamauga

September 19-20, 1863

In late June while the siege of Vicksburg was reaching its climax and Lee was marching into Pennsylvania, Major General William S. Rosecrans put into motion the Army of the Cumberland that had been resting near Murfreesboro since January. Rosecrans moved west and south around the left flank of Bragg's Army of Tennessee, forcing the Confederates to fall back to Chattanooga. Then after "resting" for another six weeks, Rosecrans again moved around Bragg's flank and crossed the Tennessee River west of Chattanooga in August. As a result, Bragg evacuated the city and retired southward about twenty-five miles to Lafayette, Georgia. Believing that his adversary was in headlong flight, Rosecrans flung his three corps in pursuit and by the first week of September the Federal army was spread out over a 40-mile front, as shown in the inset map at left.

Bragg, however, was not in retreat. Indeed he had been reinforced by the 9,000-man army of Major General Simon Bolivar Buckner from east Tennessee, and by small detachments sent from Johnston's army in Mississippi. Still more reinforcements were on their way from Lee's Army of Northern Virginia: the divisions of Hood and McLaws under the command of Longstreet. With their arrival—expected momentarily—Bragg would have numerical parity, and given the dispositions of Rosecrans's army, he would be in a position to destroy his enemy in detail, beginning with Thomas's corps only a few miles to the west. Not since McClellan was handed a copy of Lee's orders during the Antietam campaign had such an opportunity been offered a commander.

That the opportunity was not seized was largely due to the poor command relationship that had grown up in the Army of Tennessee since Murfreesboro. The army's corps commanders had grown wary of Bragg's frequent and occasionally contradictory instructions. On September 11, and again on the 13th, Bragg's lieutenants hesitated and asked for clarification upon receiving orders to attack, allowing Thomas to withdraw from his exposed position to the passes through Missionary Ridge.

Having failed to trap Thomas, Bragg decided to move northward and attack Crittenden's corps of about 14,000 men at Lee and Gordon's Mills on the west bank of Chickamauga Creek (1). Even though McLaws's division was still en route, Bragg had a better than two-to-one superiority in numbers. Inexplicably, Bragg waited five days before attacking and in the interim the corps of Thomas and McCook marched north to join Crittenden. Thomas's men in particular achieved feats of marching that the martyred Stonewall Jackson would have admired: the men tramped onward even at night, with bonfires to light the way. By the morning of September 19, Rosecrans had concentrated his army along the Lafayette Road (2) north of Lee and Gordon's Mills. That road was the prize for which the armies contested, since possession of it by the Confederates would cut off Rosecrans from Chattanooga and leave him open to destruction.

The battle opened quite by accident at mid-morning when Forrest's cavalry division, fighting dismounted, ran unexpectedly into a brigade from Thomas's recently arrived corps (3). Both sides fed in reinforcements until a full-blown battle was in progress. Thomas's men, drawn up in a curved line guarding the Lafayette Road, bore the brunt of the Confederate attacks. Though the Federals were driven back more than a mile from the initial point of contact, the arrival of McCook's corps enabled them to retain control of the Lafayette Road.

That night Longstreet arrived in the Confederate camp and Bragg immediately reorganized his army into two wings: the left under Longstreet, and the right under Major General Leonidas Polk. Bragg's plan for the next day, September 20, called for Polk's wing to roll the Federal left away from the Lafayette Road and then for Longstreet to apply the finishing stroke. The battle started late, but Polk's attack made good progress and Rosecrans detached a brigade from his right to reinforce the left. This movement, however, left a yawning gap in the Federal right and through this gap poured Longstreet's five divisions (4). McCook's command crumpled immediately. The men of both McCook's and Crittenden's corps began to retreat for McFarland's Gap (5) and the corps commanders and Rosecrans himself went with them. Only Thomas's corps, which had had the worst of it all day, stood firm, earning their commander the nickname "Rock of Chickamauga." Despite terrific pressure from three sides, Thomas's men held on until nightfall, when they conducted an unmolested retreat through McFarland's Gap and back to Rossville near the Tennessee border.

Longstreet was eager to pursue, but Bragg could not be convinced. Impatient with Bragg's timidity, Longstreet complained then and later that the Army of Tennessee lost the fruits of victory because of weak generalship. The cost was high enough: 18,000 Confederates and 16,000 Federals. For such a "butcher's bill," Bragg had won little besides possession of the battlefield, and with it, the right to call Chickamauga a victory.

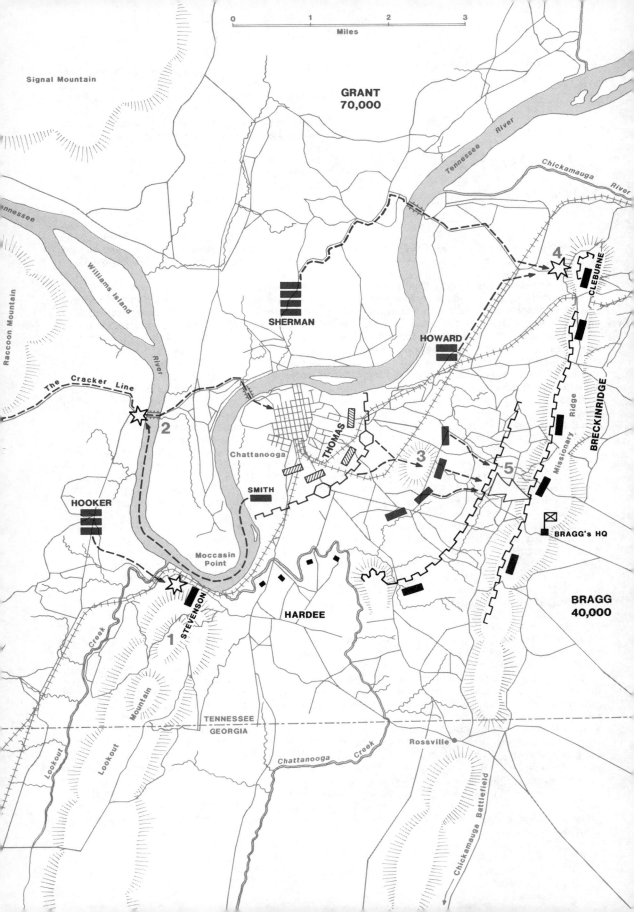

Signal Mountain

Miles
0   1   2   3

GRANT
70,000

Tennessee River

Chickamauga River

Williams Island

Raccoon Mountain

SHERMAN

HOWARD

4
CLEBURNE

The Cracker Line

2

Chattanooga

THOMAS

SMITH

HOOKER

Moccasin Point

3

5

Missionary Ridge

BRECKINRIDGE

BRAGG's HQ

STEVENSON

1

HARDEE

BRAGG
40,000

Creek

Lookout Mountain

Lookout

TENNESSEE
GEORGIA

Chattanooga Creek

Rossville

Chickamauga Battlefield

MAP 32

The Battles for Chattanooga

November 23-25, 1863

Following his headlong flight from the battlefield at Chickamauga, Rosecrans withdrew to Chattanooga and awaited a Confederate assault. But matters were soon taken out of his hands, for in Washington Lincoln and Halleck made two important decisions that affected the future of the siege and of the whole war. The first was to send Joe Hooker with a corps from the Army of the Potomac to Chattanooga. The second was to place U.S. Grant in overall command in the West. Grant's new commission gave him authority to retain Rosecrans or replace him, as he saw fit. Assuming from such orders that Rosecrans was not in high favor in Washington, Grant wired Chattanooga and ordered Thomas to take command.

Grant arrived in the city on October 23, and found Federal forces in a near-desperate situation. Thomas's army was physically secure in the city, but with Confederate forces on Lookout Mountain (1), the Federals were cut off from supplies via the Tennessee River. Opening a secure supply route, then, became Grant's first priority. A scheme to achieve this was offered by Thomas's chief of staff, Brigadier General W.F. "Baldy" Smith, who suggested an amphibious attack on the rebels holding Brown's Ferry (2). Grant liked the idea and approved it immediately. In the pre-dawn darkness of October 27, Smith and about 3,500 men drifted silently past the Confederate position on Lookout Mountain and charged ashore at Brown's Ferry just before dawn. After chasing off rebel pickets, the bluecoats erected a pontoon bridge and opened up the line of supply that the soldiers immediately dubbed "the cracker line."

Having solved the supply problem, Grant next made plans to raise the rebel siege. The means to do so were now at hand. On the day Smith's men captured Brown's Ferry, Hooker arrived with the lead elements of his corps of 16,000, and Sherman was en route with another 20,000. When they arrived, Grant would be able to field more than 70,000 men. At the same time, Bragg's forces, which had numbered upwards of 65,000 when the siege began, were down to 40,000. The principal reason for the decline was that Longstreet, with a corps of 15,000, had been dispatched to Knoxville. Old Peter was sent on this mission largely because he had made his strong disapproval of Bragg so clear. When Jefferson Davis visited the army in mid-October, he tried to heal the dissension in the army by proposing that Longstreet be sent on this independent foray. Thus it was that in November, when Grant began his campaign to drive off the rebel army, Longstreet was several hundred miles away in east Tennessee.

Grant's plan was a simple one: Hooker and Thomas would make strong demonstrations against the rebel left and center, and then Sherman with four divisions would attack the northern end of Missionary Ridge and sweep down its length, rolling up the rebel line. Preliminary to this main attack, Grant instructed Thomas to move his forces out of the Chattanooga trenches to Orchard Knob (3), about halfway between the two armies. In part this was to test the determination of the rebel defenders who were rumored to be preparing to evacuate. Thomas's men complied with alacrity, seizing the knob on November 23.

The next day Hooker attacked Confederate Major General Carter L. Stevenson's division on the slopes of Lookout Mountain. The ordinary "fog of war" was augumented in this attack by a thick heavy mist that hung over the mountain all day. Heavily outnumbered as they were, Stevenson's men could hold up Hooker only a short while and after nightfall they evacuated the mountain altogether and fell back to Missionary Ridge.

The stage was now set for Sherman's entrance, and he attacked at dawn on the 25th (4). But he found the going much tougher than anticipated. His four divisions could make no progress against the one division of Major General Patrick R. Cleburne. Even when Howard's two divisions joined in the attack, the Federals could make no dent in the rebel line. Grant began to worry that, if reinforced from the center, Cleburne might actually go over to the offensive. To forestall such a move, Grant asked Thomas at about 3:30 P.M. to send his men against the rebel rifle pits at the base of the ridge.

Thomas gave the signal and 25,000 men went forward from Orchard Knob. They burst through the first line of defense at the foot of the ridge but then, spontaneously and without orders, began to ascend the ridge itself (5). At first Union officers tried to stop them, but, caught up in the spirit of the assault, they soon joined in and it became almost a race for the top, men scrambling hand over hand up the face of the ridge. Incredibly, they reached the crest, pierced the Confederate center, and threw Bragg's entire army into confused retreat. Bragg himself barely escaped capture, though over 4,000 of his men were less lucky. All together, the Confederates lost some 6,700 in all categories, as compared to 5,800 Federal losses. They had also lost Chattanooga. Most of all, however, they had lost the initiative. They never got it back.

PART FOUR

Total War

The particular poignancy of the American Civil War is the fact that it was both the last of the old-style wars and the first of the modern total wars. In the war's early months it occasionally resembled scenes from Sir Walter Scott's novels, replete with chivalric gestures by romantics on both sides. But the war soon underwent dramatic changes, finally becoming less a duel between armies than a struggle between societies.

This metamorphosis worked to the advantage of the Federals, who possessed vastly superior economic and industrial resources. Moreover, by 1864 the North was finally able to bring its superior manpower resources to bear. The Federal draft was not very efficient or equitable—often new immigrants were marched straight from the piers to the barracks— but it kept the Union armies supplied with replacements for the horrible losses suffered in the spring campaigns. On February 1, 1864 Lincoln issued a draft call for 500,000 more men—twice as many as in all the Confederate armies combined.

The new warfare tested the strength of each side's economy, transportation network, and industrial plant, any and all of which became accepted military targets. Because the sale of cotton overseas was one of the few ways the Confederacy could acquire foreign exchange, Federal cavalry raiders regularly burned cotton bales wherever they were found. Because railroads carried men and supplies for the armies, they were frequently the target of raids by both sides. (Indeed, by 1864 a standard method of railroad destruction had emerged: the rails were pried up and the ties collected into piles and set ablaze; then the rails would be heated over

The ruins of Richmond after the Confederate evacuation in April 1865 stand as eloquent testimony to the emergence of total warfare. The city was set afire by the Confederates who sought to deny to its captors the small comforts left in the war-torn southern capital. (NA)

the fire until the iron glowed red. At that point the rail would be wrapped around a nearby tree or telegraph pole and allowed to cool.) Because factories and forges produced munitions of war, these too became military targets. Finally, because armies could not fight unless they were fed, even food became a military target. In the midst of all this destruction, the line between acceptable and unacceptable violence became increasingly blurred.

William Tecumseh Sherman was described by one of his soldiers as "the most American-looking man I ever saw; tall and lank, not very erect, with hair like thatch, which he rubs up with his hands, a rusty beard trimmed close, a wrinkled face, sharp, prominent red nose, small, bright eyes, coarse red hands; black felt hat slouched over the eyes, dirty dickey with the points wilted down, black old-fashioned stock, brown field officer's coat with high collar and no shoulder straps, muddy trousers and one spur. He carries his hands in his pockets, is very awkward in his gait and motions, talks continually and with immense rapidity." (NA)

Ulysses S. Grant, a stolid, taciturn, but eminently pragmatic commander, gained command of all Union armies in February, 1864 and presided over the conquest of the South. (NA)

Benjamin F. Butler, was indispensable to the Lincoln administration early in the war because of his political connections (he was a former Democratic Congressman from Massachusetts), but after his manifest failures in 1864, and the Republican election victories in November, Lincoln sacked him—to Gran 's great relief. (NA)

The man most closely associated with this new type of warfare was William Tecumseh Sherman, whose name still evokes strong emotional response in much of the South. More clearly than others, Sherman recognized that for the Union to win the war, the will of the South had to be broken. Sherman's march to the sea (see Map 41) was tragic, but no more tragic than the war as a whole and in many ways it was the inevitable culmination of the violence begun in 1861. Likewise, the Federals' depredations in the Shenandoah Valley (which Confederate Jubal Early considered so conscienceless as to warrant his exacting an indemnity from Hagerstown and Frederick during his invasion of Maryland in 1864) constituted a sound military move, for they deprived Lee's besieged army in Petersburg of the food it needed to prolong the war. The new Federal team of Grant, Sherman, and Philip Sheridan (who oversaw the final devastation of the Valley in 1864) argued that any action that served to shorten the war was humane and therefore justified.

The tactics employed by both sides also changed. In 1862 it had struck many soldiers on both sides that fighting from behind breastworks was unmanly. Lee had become the object of some scorn as the "King of Spades" for ordering the army to prepare defensive entrenchments around Richmond in the summer of that year. But by 1864, much of northern Virginia was crisscrossed by entrenchments thrown up by the armies of both sides. Whenever the armies stopped even for a night, the men began to dig: first rifle pits, then parapets for the guns, and finally slashes and lunettes to create interlocking fields of fire. Either army was capable of turning an empty field into a sophisticated fortification in less than 48 hours. After a week, the lines had assumed a form that would have been familiar to soldiers on the western front of World War I. During this final phase of the war, there would be only two grand assaults in the tradition of Fredericksburg or Gettysburg: one in the West at Franklin, and one in the East at Cold Harbor. In both cases the attackers suffered casualties too terrible to justify the modest gains they achieved.

Another major change greatly affecting the struggle was the appointment on March 1, 1864 of Ulysses S. Grant to the position of general-in-chief of all Union armies. He was also assigned the newly revived rank of lieutenant general, heretofore held only by George Washington. Grant's determination, and his ability to see the whole picture clearly, would infuse the eastern armies with a new sense of purpose. Less than two months after receiving his new commission, Grant crossed the Rapidan and began a campaign that lasted, with few interruptions, until the end of the war nearly a year later. Though the battles would have different names— Wilderness, Spotsylvania, Cold Harbor—in fact they were all one fight. Having set his teeth into Lee,

Entrenchments like these around Petersburg dominated the new style of warfare that doomed the smaller Confederate armies to a war of attrition. (LC)

Grant did not let him go, regardless of how much Lee mauled him. Grant's army—actually Meade's army, but under Grant's orders—suffered horrible casualties, earning Grant the title "butcher" from critics. But he never lost the initiative, finally bringing Lee to bay at the small crossroads community of Appomattox Court House.

While Grant pinned Lee's army at Petersburg, Sherman annihilated the Confederacy's western armies and the South's war-making capability. Sherman's grinding offensive in the West captured Atlanta, destroyed the Confederate Army of Tennessee, ravaged Georgia, and cut a brutal swath through the Carolinas. When General Joseph Johnston's army capitualted at Durham Station, it was an even more pitiful remnant than Lee's tattered veterans at Appomattox.

For Southern armies the winter of 1863-64 was a hard one, but the winter of 1864-65 would be even harder. The Federal blockade was tightening and inflation was soaring; a barrel of flour cost over a thousand Confederate dollars by 1865 and a rebel soldier's dinner would often consist of a single biscuit or sweet potato. Nevertheless, Lee's army in Virginia remained unconquered, both in fact and in spirit, and as always the South could claim to be winning as long as it remained unconquered. Even in 1864, Southerners believed themselves unconquerable. But their romantic idealism could not survive in a war that would be decided by superior manpower, resources, and organization.

General John Bell Hood was a classic example of the Peter Principle: he was a gallant and fearless Brigade and Division Commander under Lee in Virginia, and a competent if not thoroughly loyal Corps Commander under J.E. Johnston in Georgia, but as an Army commander in 1864 he was a complete disaster. (LC)

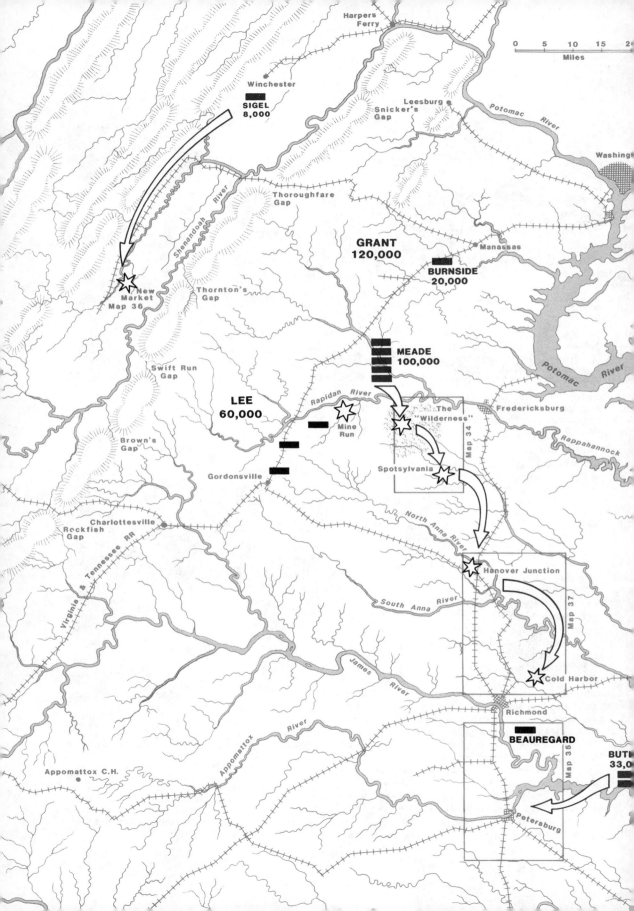

MAP 33

Grant's Strategic Plan

Spring, 1864

Lieutenant General Ulysses S. Grant quietly arrived in Washington on March 8, 1864. With his fourteen-year old son, Fred, he checked in at Willard's Hotel, and that night went to one of the President's weekly White House receptions, there meeting Lincoln for the first time. Amid the bustle of the Presidential reception there was little opportunity for meaningful conversation, but the next day when the two men talked about the war and Grant was formally invested with his new responsibilities, Grant discovered that the President had no specific orders for his new general-in-chief. Both men seemed to understand what was needed: Lincoln would keep the river of recruits and supplies flowing, and Grant would use them to go after Lee.

Of course Union generals had "gone after Lee" before and come out of the experience much chastened. But Grant had two advantages his predecessors had lacked. The first was that the disparity in numerical and industrial strength between the two sides was greater in the spring of 1864 than at any previous time. Grant sought to lengthen the odds even more by reducing the number of Union soldiers assigned to garrison duty, and swelling the ranks of the field armies. By drawing on the Washington garrison, and assuming operational control of Burnside's command, which was technically independent of the Army of the Potomac, Grant could field a reorganized army of over 120,000 combat effectives. By contrast, Lee could muster only about half as many, his returns for March showing a total of 61,953 of all arms.

The second advantage Grant had over his predecessors was that, as general-in-chief, he could coordinate the efforts of all the Federal armies and thus bring maximum pressure to bear on the enemy. Of course, Lincoln, through Halleck, had attempted such coordination in the past, but commanders had always found reasons to postpone or cancel ordered offensives, thus frustrating all such efforts. To prevent a repetition of such difficulties, Grant placed his most trusted subordinate, Major General William Tecumseh Sherman, in overall command in the West, with orders to "go after" Joe Johnston's army (*see* Map 38). Meanwhile, Grant

set off by train on March 10 to join Meade's Army of the Potomac, thus ensuring that Meade went after Lee at the same time and with the same determination. Of course, other subordinates were not as reliable, and Grant had his share of frustrations attempting to coordinate campaigns along the Red River and the Atlantic coast; but he made certain that the two principal armies were wielded with firm hands.

When Grant left Washington for the front, he fully intended to relieve Meade as commander of the Army of the Potomac. Meade's tentative advance across the Rapidan the previous November had been stymied along the banks of Mine Run (*see* map), and since then the army had remained passive. Grant concluded from this that Meade did not have the stuff for offensive operations. But after talking to the "Old Snapping Turtle," Grant decided that Meade would do after all—especially since Grant intended to travel with the army in any case, like an admiral aboard his flagship, and Meade would therefore be subject to Grant's orders at all times. "Lee's army will be your objective point," Grant told him. "Wherever Lee goes, there you will go also."

In addition to planning a direct confrontation with Lee, Grant ordered Major Generals Franz Sigel in the Shenandoah Valley and Benjamin Butler on the Yorktown Peninsula to launch simultaneous offensives of their own, as shown at left. They were almost certainly not the men Grant would have selected for command, had he based his choices on talent alone. But both men had important political constituencies: Butler had been a prominent Democratic politician before the war, and Sigel was a highly visible German national in an army that relied heavily on German and Irish recruits. Perhaps their lack of military prowess would not matter; neither man faced strong opposition. If Grant could keep the Army of Northern Virginia fully occupied, Lee would be unable to detach men to meet these threats to his Valley "breadbasket" and to his capital. It might even be possible for Butler to occupy Richmond while Lee was defending the Rapidan River crossings. In the eastern theater, as in his national strategy, the key to Grant's plan was a coordinated offensive.

Map 32 shows the approximate positions of the forces in the field on May 1, 1864. The next four maps portray the results of the five weeks of nearly constant combat that followed, perhaps the most crucial period of the war. At the end of it Lee's army, much reduced by battlefield casualties, was pinned inside its fortifications around Richmond and Petersburg, and so weakened as to be incapable of further offensive operations. Neither Sigel nor Butler, as it turned out, was much help in the campaign, but Grant's determination—or, as his enemies said, his lack of regard for human life—ensured that the Federals kept the initiative throughout these crucial forty days.

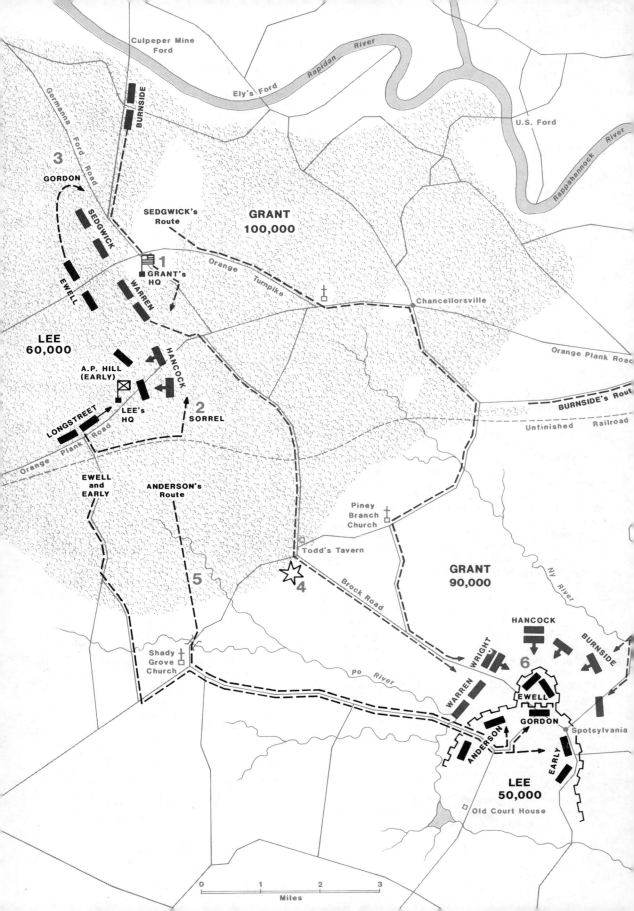

Culpeper Mine Ford

Rapidan River

Ely's Ford

U.S. Ford

Rappahannock River

BURNSIDE

Germanna Ford Road

3

GORDON

SEDGWICK

EWELL

SEDGWICK's Route

**GRANT
100,000**

1

GRANT's HQ

WARREN

Orange Turnpike

Chancellorsville

Orange Plank Road

BURNSIDE's Rout

Unfinished   Railroad

**LEE
60,000**

A.P. HILL
(EARLY)

HANCOCK

LEE's HQ

2

SORREL

LONGSTREET

Orange Plank Road

EWELL
and
EARLY

ANDERSON's Route

Piney Branch Church

Todd's Tavern

5

4

Brock Road

**GRANT
90,000**

Ny River

Shady Grove Church

Po River

HANCOCK

BURNSIDE

WRIGHT

WARREN

6

EWELL

GORDON

ANDERSON

Spotsylvania

EARLY

**LEE
50,000**

Old Court House

0   1   2   3

Miles

MAP 34

The Wilderness and Spotsylvania

May 4-20, 1864

On May 4 the Army of the Potomac crossed the Rapidan River and moved into a thick forest of mixed cedar and pine known locally as "the Wilderness." Outnumbered nearly two-to-one, Lee was determined to strike at the Federal army while it was within the confines of the Wilderness and preferably while it was still on the march. Approaching from the west on the Orange Turnpike and the Orange Plank Road, the corps of Dick Ewell and A.P. Hill struck Grant's army on May 5 with first contact being made not far from the Wilderness Tavern (1). Despite some initial success, Lee's two corps soon discovered that they had bitten off a bit too much. The Federals counterattacked all along the line and the Confederates had to fall back and erect breastworks. The Federals pushed hard; but without coordination, which was impossible in the heavy undergrowth, the impact of their superior numbers was minimized. The combination of deepening twilight, drifting smoke from a hundred thousand rifles, and thick underbrush resulted in a battle in which no man could see. Soldiers fired at muzzle flashes in the smoke and darkness. The muskets frequently set the dry underbrush aflame, and soon a dozen small forest fires added to the hell-like atmosphere. Wounded men, unable to get out of the way of the fires, burned to death, their anguished screams piercing the darkness.

The battle continued the next day. Hancock's corps drove A.P. Hill's men back more than a mile to a small clearing where Lee had established his headquarters. Only just in time did Longstreet's corps come up on the Orange Plank Road to stave off disaster. Lee met the arriving troops and tried to lead them personally into battle, but the men refused to budge until Lee had gone to the rear. Then they pitched into Hancock's forces and threw them back. Longstreet pressed his temporary advantage and nearly achieved a breakthrough when a flank attack by Colonel G. Moxley Sorrel hit the exposed Federal left flank (2). But in the confusion of maneuvering in the dense woods, two Confederate units ran into one another and opened fire, seriously wounding Longstreet. Many men in the Southern army must have remembered that Jackson had been fatally wounded by his own men in these same woods, exactly a year before.

On the other end of the five-mile-long front, Confederate Brigadier General John B. Gordon hit the Federal right flank and threatened to roll up the Union line altogether (3). But Gordon's attack came too late in the day, and not enough hours of daylight remained to exploit the advantage. Nevertheless, the Army of the Potomac had been very roughly handled. The Federals had lost 17,600 men in the two days' fighting and inflicted only 8,000 casualties in return. Both Federal flanks had been turned. It was one of Lee's greatest victories.

But it did not end with a Federal retreat. Grant simply refused to accept defeat. Both armies remained in place on May 7 and at 8:30 that night Warren's corps left its breastworks and, screened by Hancock's corps, marched not north but south, toward the crossroads of Spotsylvania Court House. Lee had suspected that Grant would attempt such a move, and a cavalry skirmish near Todd's Tavern (4) confirmed his suspicions. He ordered Richard Anderson, who had succeeded command of the First Corps, to march south to meet it (5). At about the same time, A.P. Hill's sudden illness required Lee to turn the Third Corps over to Jubal Early. Anderson and Early found themselves in a virtual race for the crossroads, a race the Confederates won, but just barely. Jeb Stuart's troopers were giving ground to the lead elements of Warren's corps when Anderson's men arrived at about 8:00 A.M. (May 8), in time to shore up the collapsing line. As reinforcements came up for both sides, the battle widened and intensified.

For the next week the two armies contested the crossroads in some of the fiercest fighting of the war. Grant showed every sign of a willingness to slug it out until the issue was decided. To Lincoln he wrote: "I propose to fight it out on this line if it takes all summer." The critical battle occurred on May 12 when Grant sent nearly 60,000 men against a jutting salient in the rebel line that both sides called "the Mule Shoe" (6). Hancock's corps burst through the lines and charged into the salient, only to encounter John B. Gordon's reserve division which counterattacked and regained possession of the Mule Shoe. But even when they were pushed out of the salient, the Federals clung to the outside wall of the rebel works and the two sides fought muzzle-to-muzzle through the night. The Mule Shoe thus earned a new nickname: the Bloody Angle.

Heavy rains on May 13-16 slowed the bloodletting, but Grant renewed his attacks on the 18th. Finally satisfied that Lee's lines were too strong for continued frontal assaults, Grant began an easterly move on the 20th. For two weeks the armies had been in nearly constant contact and in those two weeks, Grant had lost 36,000 men while inflicting only half as many casualties on Lee. Expressed as a percentage of those engaged, however, the losses were identical—30 percent on each side. More importantly, Grant would be able to replace his losses, and Lee would not.

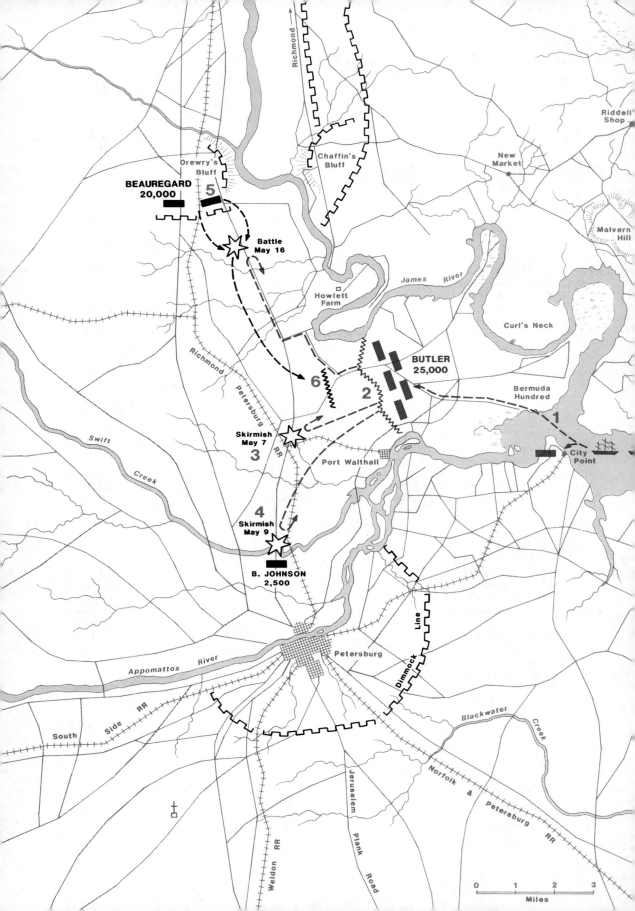

Richmond

Riddell
Shop

Chaffin's
Bluff

New
Market

Drewry's
Bluff

BEAUREGARD
20,000

5

Malvern
Hill

Battle
May 16

James River

Howlett
Farm

Curl's Neck

6

BUTLER
25,000

2

Bermuda
Hundred

1

Skirmish
May 7

3

Port Walthall

City
Point

Swift

Creek

4

Skirmish
May 9

B. JOHNSON
2,500

Richmond
Petersburg

RR

Appomattox River

Petersburg

Dimmock
Line

Blackwater
Creek

South   Side   RR

Weldon RR

Jerusalem
Plank
Road

Norfolk
&
Petersburg
RR

0   1   2   3

Miles

MAP 35

Butler's Advance

May 5-16, 1864

On May 5, the day Lee pitched into Grant's army in the Wilderness, Major General Benjamin F. Butler was putting ashore the first of some 30,000 Federal soldiers at the plantation landing of Bermuda Hundred, near the confluence of the James and Appomattox Rivers, south of Richmond (1). Embarked on some 200 vessels and escorted by Navy ironclads, the "Army of the James," as Butler styled it, had ascended the river the night before and was now disembarking at Richmond's back door. Butler detached one division at City Point, and the next day he had five divisions marching westward toward the vital Richmond and Petersburg Railroad. At the base of the peninsula formed by the James and Appomattox Rivers, however, they stopped and began to entrench (2). Only when his men had completed a continuous line of fortifications across the base of the peninsula did Butler send out a brigade to reconnoiter the railroad. After skirmishing with rebel pickets, the brigade returned to report that there were, indeed, Confederate soldiers south of Richmond.

But not many. The only enemy forces in Butler's path that day were 750 men scraped together by Major General George Pickett and a "division" of perhaps another 2,500 under Major General Bushrod Johnson. Nevertheless, when Butler sent out four full brigades (about 8,000 men) on May 7 to seize the railroad, they encountered fierce resistance from Johnson's men near Walthall Junction (3). Apparently not inclined to press the issue, the Federals broke off the fight and returned to their entrenchments.

The next day (May 8) Butler himself arrived at the front and announced his determination to take the bulk of the army forward, lay firm hands on the vital railroad, and seize Petersburg in the process. On May 9 when the army advanced, it was discovered that Walthall Junction had been abandoned by all but a handfull of rebel skirmishers and that Johnson's men were drawn up behind the unfordable Swift Creek (4). After looking over the situation, Butler's two corps commanders, professional officers hand-picked by Grant to ensure that Butler had the benefit of their expertise, announced that Petersburg could not be taken from the north. The

army should return to the peninsula, bridge the Appomattox, and attack the city from the east. Butler was furious: why then had the army come this way to begin with? In a huff, he ordered the whole army back to its entrenchments. Three times, in ever-increasing strength, the army had sortied from the peninsula, each time to skirmish with a numerically smaller opponent and turn back.

Rejecting the advice to move south of the James, Butler determined instead to leave Petersburg unmolested and go after the real prize—Richmond itself. On May 12 the Federal army ventured forth again, this time turning north. In two days it advanced barely five miles and then halted in front of Fort Darling, a line of heavy field fortifications on Drewry's Bluff (5). Behind those fortifications were nearly 20,000 Confederate soldiers. In the time granted by the Federal false starts, Major General P. G. T. Beauregard had managed to gather a force nearly as large as Butler's and while Butler and his subordinates debated what to do, Beauregard planned an offensive of his own.

His plan called for an attack upon Butler's army from the south by Confederate forces defending Swift Creek now under the command of W. H. C. Whiting, while Beauregard's own force assaulted Butler from the north. But Whiting never got underway and at last, on May 16, Beauregard decided to attack anyway. A sharp battle ensued, the Federals initially getting the worst of it and then rallying. Each side lost about 4,000 men, but at the end Butler decided once more to return to his entrenchments near Port Walthall. Beauregard followed, and when the Federals were secure in their lines, he began to erect a parallel set of entrenchments a mile or so west of the Federal position (6). When completed, this "Howlett Line" (named after a nearby farm) would make it possible for a single division to bottle up Butler's entire army. Beauregard could then dispatch badly needed reinforcements to Lee's army at Spotsylvania.

Though Butler was satisfied that he had achieved all that could reasonably be expected, he had bungled the entire campaign and bungled it badly. Beauregard's men joked that they were the wardens of the largest prisoner-of-war camp in the Confederacy, and for all practical purposes they were right. Butler's two corps were trapped in the cul-de-sac of the Bermuda Hundred, pinned in by troops one-quarter their strength. Grant himself commented that Butler was as useful there as if he were "in a bottle strongly corked."

The news of Butler's fate was a great disappointment to Grant, who at about the same time learned that the third arm of his planned triple offensive, Sigel's push into the Shenandoah Valley, had also come to grief at the Battle of New Market on May 15.

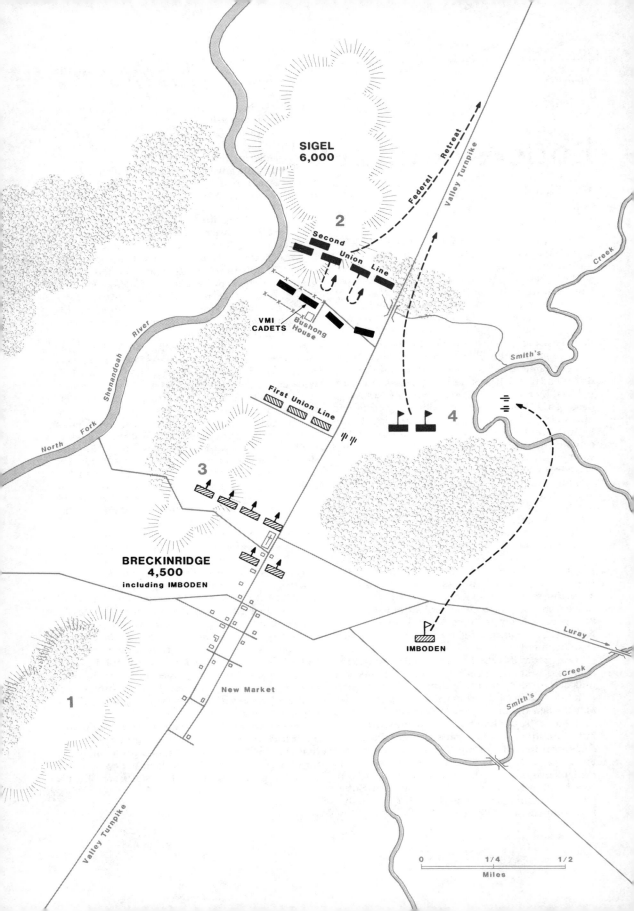

SIGEL
6,000

2

Second Union Line

Federal Retreat

Valley Turnpike

Creek

VMI CADETS

Bushong House

Smith's

First Union Line

4

Shenandoah River

North Fork

3

BRECKINRIDGE
4,500
including IMBODEN

Luray

IMBODEN

New Market

Smith's

Creek

1

Valley Turnpike

0   1/4   1/2
Miles

MAP 36

New Market

May 15, 1864

The day before Beauregard turned back Butler's halting advance toward Richmond at Drewry's Bluff, the third arm of Grant's planned triple offensive—Sigel's push up the Shenandoah Valley—came to grief at the Battle of New Market.

With nearly 8,000 men, Sigel began a cautious advance southward from Martinsburg, West Virginia on April 29. The Confederates had little to stop him. Confederate Brigadier General John D. Imboden had about 1,500 cavalry, and much further south Major General John C. Breckinridge had two small brigades of infantry, perhaps 2,500 men. Lee let both men know that he could send no help; Grant was across the Rapidan and Lee needed every soldier he had.

Sigel's immediate objective was Staunton on the Virginia Central Railroad. But harried by Imboden's troopers, his progress was slow, and Breckinridge got there first arriving on May 8 while Sigel was still at Winchester nearly 100 miles to the north. At Staunton, the Confederate commander received a message from the Superintendent of the Virginia Military Institute, Major General Francis H. Smith, offering the service of the Corps of Cadets, 250 boys aged 14 to 18. Outnumbered as he was, Breckinridge felt the crisis was sufficiently grave to justify accepting the offer.

Despite his numerical inferiority, Breckinridge chose not to stay on the defensive at Staunton, but to press ahead to meet Sigel as far north as possible. Dawn on May 15th found both armies in the vicinity of New Market, forty miles north of Staunton at the junction of the Valley Pike and the Luray Road that led to Thornton's Gap in the Blue Ridge (see Map 33). Breckinridge occupied Shirley's Hill (1), a gentle rise south of town, while Sigel occupied the town itself and the high ground north of it known as Bushong's Hill (2) after the farmer whose home became the focus of the battle.

Breckinridge hoped to entice Sigel to attack him, but the Federal commander declined to oblige, and Breckinridge therefore assumed the offensive himself. At mid–morning he sent forward a line of skirmishers who encountered light Federal resistance and pushed the enemy back through the town, over Manor's Hill (3), and toward the forward slope of Bushong's Hill.

Imboden's cavalry, meanwhile, sought an opportunity to enfilade the Federal left. Skirting a thick patch of woods, the rebel troopers crossed Smith's Creek, and opened fire on the Federal cavalry, driving the blue troopers from their position (4). Imboden's initiative did not lead to anything decisive, however, because by crossing Smith's Creek, he had effectively cut himself off from the main battle for Bushong's Hill.

On the other side of the field, Sigel had arranged his infantry in two lines. His plan was for the first line to take the starch out of the attacking rebels, and then for the second line to administer the *coup de grâce*. The rebel infantry assault easily drove through the first line of Federal defenders, but found the going much tougher against Sigel's second line. Their momentum was halted near the Bushong house; they wavered and began to fall back. Two of the gray regiments were roughly handled and their decimation left a gaping hole in the center of the Confederate line. This was the moment when Sigel should have delivered his counterattack, but characteristically, he hesitated, and his hesitation gave Breckinridge time to re-form his line. He brought his reserves forward, among them the Corps of Cadets from V.M.I. "Put the boys in," he told his ordnance officer, "and may God forgive me for the order." Though Breckinridge had intended to keep them out of the fight if possible, the young cadets now found themselves at the center of the Confederate line just as the Federal infantry came charging down the hill.

But the Federal assault was undermanned. Sigel sent only three regiments, some 1,500 men, against the rebel line. The Confederates held, the Federals began to retreat, and, buoyed by the sight of the retreating enemy, the rebels rose up to attack again. With a cheer they surged forward, the V.M.I. contingent in the forefront. Their charge was slowed by the wet ground—it had rained all day on the 14th and was raining still. Many of the cadets lost their shoes in the thick mud, but they continued the advance. This time their momentum carried them up and over the hill and the battle was won.

The Federals retreated in good order. Sigel's rear guard halted temporarily at Rudes' Hill two miles to the north, but running low on ammunition and throughly demoralized, the Federals retreated across the Shenandoah River and burned the bridge behind them.

News of the Federal disaster reached Grant at about the same time that he learned of the results of Butler's fiasco. He know then that there would be no concurrent Federal advance on Lee's back door. Indeed, with the Valley secure, Breckinridge was able to take 2,500 reinforcements to Lee at Hanover Junction in time for his next contest with Grant.

GRANT
100,000

WARREN

WRIGHT

BURNSIDE

HANCOCK

A.P. HILL ANDERSON

Hanover Junction

EWELL

1

LEE
50,000

North Anna River

Little River

South

Anna

River

0 1 2 3 4 5
Miles

BURNSIDE and WARREN

HANCOCK and WRIGHT

Pamunkey River

Hanover
C.H.

Ashland

A.P. HILL

EWELL

and

ANDERSON

Virginia Central RR

Fredericksburg & Potomac RR

Richmond

Hanovertown **2**

3 Cavalry
Action

Haw's
Shop

4

Totopotomoy Creek

Pole Green
Church

Atlee's Station

Shady Grove
Church

Yellow Tavern

EARLY

Bethesda
Church
GRANT's HQ

BURNSIDE

WARREN

GRANT
110,000

ANDERSON

SMITH

WRIGHT

HANCOCK

Mechanicsville

LEE
60,000

Gaines'
Mill

Old
Cold
Harbor

LEE'S HQ

Richmond
Defenses

Chickahominy River

New Cold Harbor

A.P. HILL

Grapevine Bridge

Richmond

MAP 37

The North Anna Crossing and Cold Harbor

May 21-June 3, 1864

Grant abandoned the line in front of Spotsylvania—where he had promised to fight it out all summer—on May 21. He shifted his forces eastward and southward, hoping to get around Lee's right flank. Lee scurried south to get in front of him, and established a strong defensive position on the south bank of the North Anna River protecting the critical railroad intersection of Hanover Junction (1).

At mid-day on May 23 the lead elements of Grant's army appeared on the northern bank of the river and that afternoon the Federals attacked Lee's army on both flanks: Warren's corps on the Confederate left, and Hancock's on the right. Moderate success in these attacks convinced Grant that he had an opportunity to achieve a double envelopment of the rebel army. But Lee was very pleased with the developing situation, for by arranging his three corps in an inverted "V" with the apex anchored on the river, his forces acted as a wedge to split the Army of the Potomac into two halves with the river between them, leaving each half open to a concentrated counterattack. That such a counterattack did not come off was due to a sudden cautiousness by Grant, who recognized almost too late the potential disaster inherent in the situation, and to the illness which kept Lee confined to his cot most of the day.

After pondering Lee's entrenched position for three days, Grant again moved the Army of the Potomac east and south, marching on parallel roads to another crossing of the Pamunkey River fifteen miles downstream near Hanovertown (2). Lee made the appropriate countermove south through Atlee's Station to a new position along the banks of Totopotomoy Creek, where he arrived on May 29. From there he sent two cavalry brigades, under his nephew Fitzhugh Lee and Wade Hampton, north to reconnoiter the Federal situation. This reconnaissance led to a major cavalry action near a small crossroads community called Haw's Shop (3).

On May 30, Grant tested Lee's lines along the Totopotomoy (4) in an indecisive skirmish that cost each side about 2,000 casualties and convinced Grant to move around Lee's flank yet again. Lee presumed that Grant would head for the critical road junction of Old Cold Harbor about a mile east of the site of the 1862 Battle of Gaines' Mill, and he sent Fitz's cavalry to hold the junction until infantry could arrive. Grant, too, sent his cavalry ahead to seize the crossroads, and the two mounted forces clashed there on May 31. Sheridan had the better of the cavalry action, but the Confederate infantry got there in time to succor the gray troopers and hold the good ground. Bolstered by 15,000 reinforcements from Richmond and Petersburg, Lee intended to launch an offensive against Grant's army while it was still on the move. But the attack never got underway, due to poor leadership at the brigade and division levels. With Jackson dead and Longstreet still convalescing from the wound he received in the Wilderness, the Army of Northern Virginia lacked experienced senior leaders, and Lee, still sick with intestinal cramps, was unable to assume the full burden himself.

The result of all the maneuvering, then, was another stalemate. Both sides dug in along a seven-mile front extending from the Totopotomoy to the Chickahominy. This stalemate was particularly disappointing to Grant, for another southeasterly move might mire the army in the swamps of the Chickahominy, where McClellan had come to grief two years before. Grant therefore planned a frontal assault against Lee's ragged veterans before they had a chance to prepare elaborate fortifications like those he had faced at Spotsylvania.

A preliminary Federal attack on June 1 drove in some exposed Confederate units and Grant spent June 2, a day of heavy rains, preparing for an assault the next morning. Grant felt confident of success, but the men in the ranks knew better. Many spent the hours before the attack writing letters home and some even pinned their names and addresses to their coats so that their bodies could be identified afterward.

At dawn on June 3 they attacked—60,000 of them, half of Grant's army. They charged into a lead hailstorm, assailed by musketry not only in front but on their flanks, the rebels having arranged their lines to create interlocking fields of fire. The grand attack lasted just eight minutes, and in that eight minutes, nearly eight thousand Union soldiers fell—one thousand per minute, better than sixteen per second. It was the bloodiest charge of the war, bloodier even than Pickett's charge at Gettysburg. The men in blue who leapt from their trenches to cross no-man's-land knew it would be that way, but they went anyway. A diary pulled from the pocket of one dead Union soldier told the story of the final measure of their devotion. The last entry read: "June 3. Cold Harbor. I was killed."

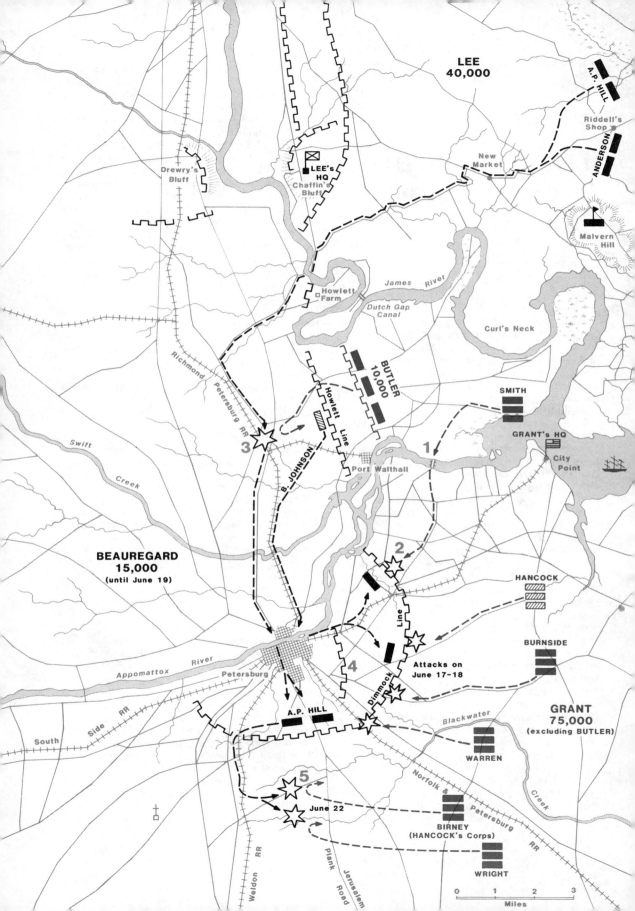

LEE
40,000

A.P. HILL

Riddell's
Shop

ANDERSON

New
Market

Malvern
Hill

Drewry's
Bluff

LEE's
HQ
Chaffin's
Bluff

James   River

Howlett
Farm

Dutch Gap
Canal

Curl's Neck

Richmond

Petersburg RR

Howlett
Line

BUTLER
10,000

SMITH

GRANT's HQ

City
Point

1

Swift

Creek

3

B. JOHNSON

Port Walthall

2

HANCOCK

BEAUREGARD
15,000
(until June 19)

Line

BURNSIDE

4

Dimmock

Attacks on
June 17-18

Appomattox   River

Petersburg

A.P. HILL

South   Side   RR

Blackwater

GRANT
75,000
(excluding BUTLER)

WARREN

Norfolk &

5

June 22

Petersburg

RR

Creek

BIRNEY
(HANCOCK's Corps)

Weldon RR

Plank   Road

WRIGHT

0   1   2   3

Miles

MAP 38

The Siege of Petersburg

June, 1864

Cold Harbor having demonstrated once more the difficulty of smashing *through* Lee's army, Grant yet again sought a way *around* it. Rather than attempt to slide across Lee's front onto the Yorktown peninsula, the scene of McClellan's defeats in 1862, he planned a more grandiose flanking movement: he would cross the James River and operate against Petersburg from the east and south.

The first unit to move was the 18,000-man corps of Major General W. F. "Baldy" Smith, which embarked on army transport vessels at White House Landing on June 13. After a daylight cruise down the Pamunkey and a night ascent of the James, it landed at Bermuda Hundred the next day. On the 15th, Smith's engineers laid a pontoon bridge across the Appomattox at Point of Rocks (1) and by that afternoon the lead elements were approaching the "Dimmock Line" laid out in 1862 by Confederate Captain Charles H. Dimmock in response to McClellan's peninsular campaign. Ten miles long, twenty feet thick, and fronted by a dry moat and entanglements, it was really more a large fort than a line of field works, and after their recent experience at Cold Harbor, Smith's men were not eager to test these lines. But in fact there were only about 2,000 Confederates south of the Appomattox River, making the odds about nine to one in favor of the attackers. As a result, when Smith's men assaulted the line at 7 P.M., they easily drove off the outnumbered defenders and occupied over a mile of the Confederate entrenchments (2).

The next seventy-two hours were critical, for during those hours the door to Petersburg—and thus Richmond—stood open. It is possible that Smith's men could have seized the city unaided, but knowing that three more Union corps (those of Hancock, Burnside, and Warren) were due to arrive that night, Smith decided to wait for them. When the sun came up on June 16, fully 75,000 Federal soldiers were in position to assault Petersburg from the east.

Beauregard, meanwhile, had been sending out desperate pleas for help. Major General Robert F. Hoke arrived first with a 5,000-man division, and Bushrod Johnson having left a few pickets behind to watch over the Howlett Line brought another 3,000. Pulling Johnson's "cork" from the bottle of Bermuda Hundred released Butler's Army of the James, but fortunately for the Confederates, a division of Anderson's corps arrived at Walthall Junction in time to drive them back (3). All these reinforcements raised Beauregard's total to about 15,000, but he faced an army five times as large and, moreover, an army that occupied a mile of his own fortifications.

On June 17 and 18 the Federal army launched a series of attacks against the Dimmock Line, but poor staff work resulted in uncoordinated attacks, and all that the Federals could accomplish was the occupation of another mile or so of Confederate trenches. Nevertheless, Beauregard's position was precarious and he ordered the construction of a shorter defensive line two miles closer to the city (4). On the 18th the lead elements of A.P. Hill's corps marched into the city with the news that the rest of Lee's army was on the way. When the Federal army renewed its attack on the 19th, the bluecoats were startled to discover that the Dimmock Line was abandoned and that the new line was manned by Lee's veterans.

For four days the back door to Richmond had stood not only unlocked but ajar. Poor coordination of vastly superior Union forces had given the rebels the time they needed to scrape together sufficient forces to slam the door shut. Grant tried one more time to kick it open. On June 22 he sent Wright's newly arrived corps and Hancock's corps (now under the command of David B. Birney) to cut the Weldon Railroad south of Petersburg. On their way west, the two Union corps lost contact with one another and A.P. Hill attacked first one and then the other, driving both back across the Jerusalem Plank Road (5).

From this point on, Union operations against Petersburg resembled the kind of trench warfare that would characterize fighting on the Western Front in World War I. Eventually the bulk of Grant's army, its numbers rising to well above 100,000, occupied a set of field works paralleling the modified Dimmock Line. Over the next ten months, Grant's forces slowly extended these lines westward, stretching the thinning ranks of the Confederate army and threatening the vital southern rail lines into the city. Given the disparity in numerical strength, time was clearly Grant's ally, and Grant knew it. So did Lee. To regain his flexibility of movement, the Southern commander pinned his hopes on Jubal Early. If Early could win a convincing victory in the Valley and mount a legitimate threat to Washington, it might force Grant to loosen his grip on Petersburg in order to protect the Federal capital. It all depended now on "Old Jube."

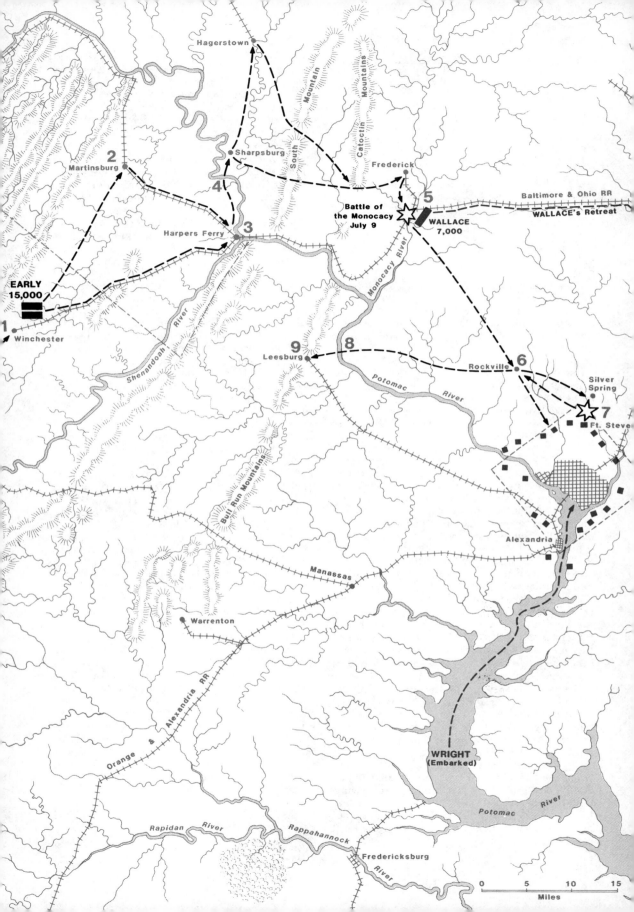

Hagerstown

South Mountain

Catoctin Mountains

Sharpsburg

Frederick

Martinsburg

2

4

Harpers Ferry

3

Battle of
the Monocacy
July 9

5

Baltimore & Ohio RR

WALLACE 7,000

WALLACE's Retreat

Shenandoah River

Monocacy River

**EARLY
15,000**

1
Winchester

Leesburg

9

8

Potomac River

Rockville

6

Silver
Spring

7

Ft. Steve

Bull Run Mountains

Manassas

Warrenton

Orange & Alexandria RR

Alexandria

**WRIGHT
(Embarked)**

Rapidan River

Rappahannock River

Fredericksburg

Potomac River

0   5   10   15

Miles

MAP 39

Early's Raid

June 14-July 14, 1864

With about 9,000 men Early left Cold Harbor on June 13, the same day Grant began his move toward Petersburg. He headed west for Lynchburg, Virginia, where he linked up with a small Confederate army under the command of Major General John C. Breckinridge. Together their forces did not quite equal the strength of the advancing Federal force of 18,000 under Major General David Hunter. But Hunter professed to believe that he was heavily outnumbered, and withdrew westward through the passes of the Blue Ridge into West Virginia, virtually taking himself and his army off the strategic map.

After a short pursuit of Hunter, Early set his small army on the road north toward Winchester (1), where he arrived on July 2. There he divided his army, sending half of it north to Martinsburg (2) and the other half ahead to Harper's Ferry (3) in an attempt to trap Sigel's 5,000-man force. Sigel withdrew to Maryland Heights and Early chose not to molest him there, satisfied to plunder the vast Federal stores in Harpers Ferry. Well fed (and well shod, thanks to a shipment of shoes from Richmond), Early's men splashed across the Potomac at Boteler's Ford (4) near the Antietam (or Sharpsburg) battlefield.

From Sharpsburg, Early sent a brigade of cavalry north to Hagerstown with orders to exact $200,000 from the citizens there on the threat of burning the town's business district. Though this act was labeled extortion by the Northern press, Early considered the payment an indemnity for the damage done by Federal forces in the Shenandoah Valley. Perhaps embarrassed by his mission, the commander of the cavalry brigade asked for only $20,000, which the citizens quickly produced. At Frederick, however, where Early led the main body, Old Jube demanded and received the full $200,000.

Early's rapid advance was having the desired effect in Washington. Halleck sent urgent messages to Grant at City Point, Virginia who responded by dispatching one 5,000-man division on July 6, and then Wright's full corps on July 9, as Early was holding Frederick for ransom. Until those troops arrived, however, the only Federals between Early and Washington were about 2,000 men of all arms scraped together by Major General Lew Wallace, who had not exercised an important field command since he had led a division at Shiloh. (Wallace is probably best remembered

today as the author of *Ben Hur.*) On his own authority, fearing that Halleck would forbid it, Wallace took his "army" to the banks of the Monocacy River just east of Frederick (5), from which place he could cover the roads to both Baltimore and Washington. The first contingent of 5,000 men from Grant's army joined Wallace there on July 8. And so, when Early got his army on the road on July 9 for the 40-mile march to Washington, he found 7,000 men, more than half of them veterans, blocking his path.

A Confederate flank attack across an unmarked ford to the south of Wallace's position turned the Federal flank and made the Battle of the Monocacy an easy Confederate victory. Wallace lost 1,800 men, most of them captured, and fled with the remnants toward Baltimore. But the battle had cost Early a day's march.

Early had his men on the road well before dawn the next morning and by nightfall they had reached the vicinity of Rockville (6). There, Early divided his forces again, sending the cavalry straight ahead toward the Federal capital, and directing the infantry to Silver Spring, just outside the District line. At about 1 P.M. the siege guns from the fortifications surrounding Washington began trying their range against the advancing rebel army, and a half-hour later Early stood inside the District of Columbia examining the earthworks of Fort Stevens (7), one of the several dozen major forts guarding the city. Confederate sharpshooters deployed and began picking off the home-guard forces manning the works. (Though Early could not have known it, one of those silhouettes on the ramparts belonged to Abraham Lincoln.) But Early knew that an attack that night was impossible, for his men were too tired.

Even as Early watched, however, the blue-coated veterans of Wright's corps were marching up the Seventh Street Road toward Fort Stevens, and that night it was Wright who launched an offensive, attacking after dark and pushing the rebels back several hundred yards before calling it off. Later that night Early ordered a general retreat. His mission, after all, had been to draw strength away from Grant's army and the presence of Wright's corps proved that he had done that. The Confederate army retraced its steps to Rockville and then turned south to re-cross the Potomac at White's Ford (8). The army camped near Leesburg in friendly Virginia (9) on July 14.

Early had achieved all that Lee might have hoped. He had regained the Shenandoah Valley won a victory on enemy soil, invaded the outskirts of the Federal capital, and drawn forces away from Grant. But aside from the propaganda value, which was considerable, the strategic impact of the raid was minimal. Grant's army continued to hold Lee immobile at Petersburg even without Wright, and in the West Sherman was forcing Johnston irresistibly back to Atlanta.

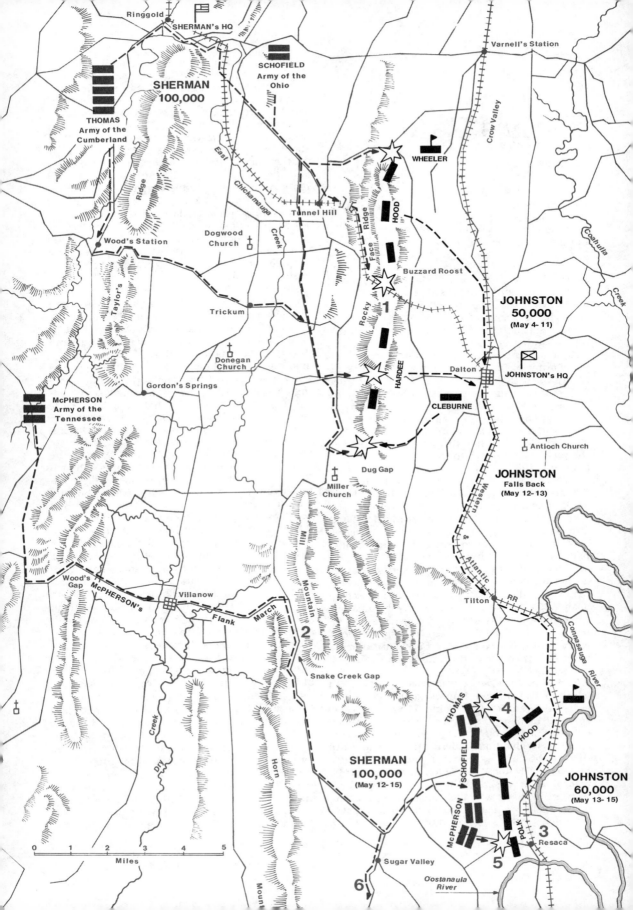

Ringgold

SHERMAN's HQ

Varnell's Station

SHERMAN
100,000

SCHOFIELD
Army of the
Ohio

Crow Valley

THOMAS
Army of the
Cumberland

WHEELER

HOOD

Ridge

East

Chickamauga

Tunnel Hill

Coahula

Creek

Wood's Station

Dogwood
Church

Face

Ridge

Buzzard Roost

JOHNSTON
50,000
(May 4– 11)

Creek

Taylor's

Trickum

Rocky

1

Donegan
Church

HARDEE

Dalton

JOHNSTON's HQ

McPHERSON
Army of the
Tennessee

Gordon's Springs

CLEBURNE

Antioch Church

JOHNSTON
Falls Back
(May 12– 13)

Dug Gap

Miller
Church

Western

Atlantic

&

Wood's Gap

McPHERSON's

Villanow

Flank

March

Mill

Mountain

Snake Creek Gap

Tilton

RR

Connasauga River

2

Creek

DIV

Horn

SHERMAN
100,000
(May 12– 15)

THOMAS

4

HOOD

SCHOFIELD

JOHNSTON
60,000
(May 13– 15)

0   1   2   3   4   5

Miles

McPHERSON

POLK

3

Resaca

Sugar Valley

5

6

Oostanaula
River

MAP 40

Dalton and Resaca

May 4-16, 1864

Aside from his own operations, the only aspect of Grant's strategic plan that achieved the success he had envisioned was Sherman's advance in northern Georgia. In that campaign, Sherman had roughly the same numerical superiority over his opponent as Grant did over Lee. Indeed, one measure of Sherman's strength was that he commanded not three *corps*, but three *armies*. George H. Thomas' Army of the Cumberland was the largest with a strength of over 60,000; James B. McPherson led the Army of the Tennessee with another 30,000; and John M. Schofield commanded the Army of the Ohio, the smallest of the three—really an enlarged corps—with a strength of about 14,000. Altogether, Sherman commanded in excess of 100,000 men. In addition, Sherman's three armies boasted 254 field guns and more than 5,000 wagons (and 800 ambulances) pulled by more than 40,000 draft animals.

To contend with this host, his Confederate opponent, Joseph E. Johnston, had two infanty corps—those of William J. Hardee and John Bell Hood—of about 20,000 men each, plus a cavalry division under 27-year-old Joseph Wheeler, which boasted some 10,000 men on paper but in reality numbered little more than half that, and 113 field guns. To compensate for his 2:1 inferiority of numbers, Johnston had the advantage of operating on the defensive in terrain where the mountain ridges and rivers cut across his enemy's line of advance. And, unlike Lee, Johnston was not anxious to assume the tactical offensive, even though President Jefferson Davis had been urging him to undertake an offensive to recover Tennessee since January. Johnston had resisted the pressure from Richmond, pleading weaknesses in supplies, draft animals, and equipment, and he and his army remained in north Georgia throughout the winter months. With the return of good weather in the spring, Johnston placed his infantry atop Rocky Face Ridge (1), west of his headquarters at Dalton, Georgia, and awaited Sherman's attack.

Sherman began his advance on May 4, the same day Grant crossed the Rapidan in Virginia. His plan was to use Thomas' army to demonstrate in front of Johnston's position, and send McPherson on a long flanking march through the unguarded Snake Creek Gap (2) to cut Johnston's line of communications at Resaca. Once McPherson was astride the Western & Atlantic Railroad to Atlanta, Johnston would be forced to abandon his position on Rocky Face Ridge and fall back to protect his supply line.

Thomas's feint successfully held Johnston's two corps in place, and Johnston did not appreciate the seriousness of McPherson's threat to his communications until it was almost too late. When Sherman heard that McPherson's column had safely passed through Snake Creek Gap, he pounded his fist into his palm and exclaimed: "I've got Joe Johnston dead!" But when McPherson arrived at Resaca on May 9, he found what appeared to be a full Confederate division there ahead of him. The gray defenders were two small brigades under Brigadier General James Cantey—about 4,000 men altogether. McPherson should have been able to smash through this small force, but because he had been told to expect only cavalry, he presumed that something had gone wrong, and he pulled back to Snake Creek Gap.

Aware at last of the peril to his flank and rear, Johnston sent two divisions southward to Resaca and prepared to follow with the rest of the army as soon as he was convinced that Resaca was indeed the Federals' principal objective. At Resaca Johnston received welcome reinforcements from Alabama—Leonidas Polk's entire Army of Mississippi—whose force comprised, in effect, a third corps (3) raising Johnston's infantry strength to 60,000. Sherman brought up the rest of his army and launched a series of assaults on Johnston's new position over a three day period (May 13-15). Neither side gained an important advantage in this fighting. Hood's corps launched a counterattack that forced the Federal left back more than a mile (4), but on the Federal right, Yankee soldiers captured the high ground near the Oostanaula River (5). Worse yet, on May 14, Johnston learned that Federal forces had crossed the Oostanaula River downstream from Resaca (6), once again threatening his railroad communications with Atlanta. The next night, the Confederates fell back again, burning the railroad bridge behind them. Losses in the fighting at Resaca were about equal: Sherman lost nearly 4,000 killed and wounded; Johnston lost about 3,500 plus another 1,400 missing, about half of whom were captured.

The actions at Rocky Face Ridge and Resaca set a pattern for the ensuing campaign. Sherman held Johnston in place with a threat to his front, then sent a smaller force on a flanking movement to turn his left, forcing him to fall back. The Confederate Army of Tennessee had held its own in the fighting, but both times the men in gray had had to fall back, giving up ground to the enemy. Eventually, the defenders would have to turn and fight or risk being outflanked all the way to Atlanta.

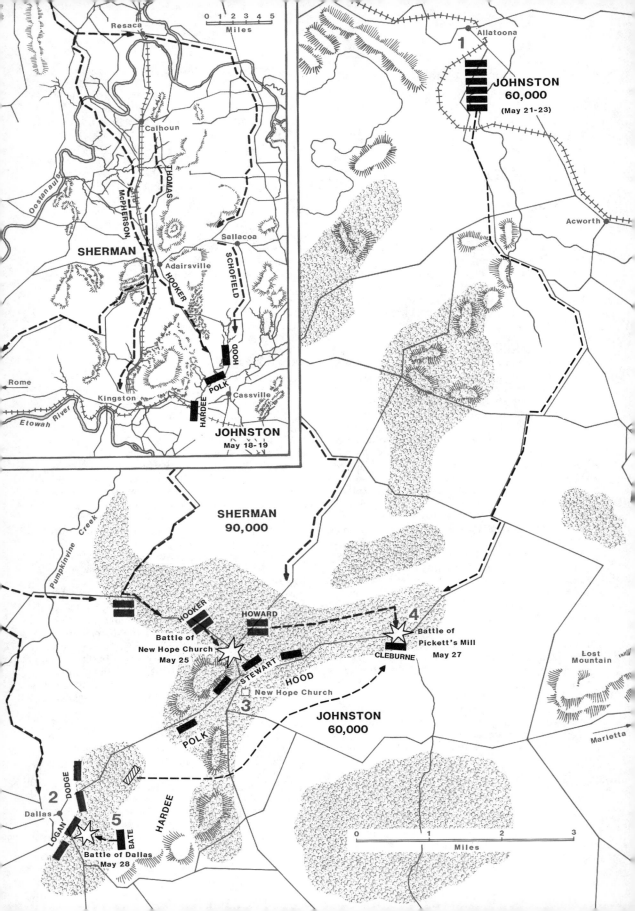

Inset map (upper left):

Resaca

0 1 2 3 4 5
Miles

Calhoun

Oostanaula

McPHERSON

THOMAS

SHERMAN

Sallacoa

Adairsville

SCHOFIELD

HOOKER

HOOD

Rome

POLK

Kingston

HARDEE

Cassville

Etowah River

JOHNSTON
May 18-19

Main map:

Allatoona

1

JOHNSTON
60,000
(May 21-23)

Acworth

Pumpkinvine Creek

SHERMAN
90,000

HOOKER

HOWARD

4

Battle of
Pickett's Mill
May 27

CLEBURNE

Battle of
New Hope Church
May 25

STEWART

HOOD

Lost
Mountain

3 New Hope Church

JOHNSTON
60,000

POLK

Marietta

DODGE

2

Dallas

LOGAN

HARDEE

5

BATE

Battle of Dallas
May 28

0 1 2 3
Miles

MAP 41

New Hope Church, Pickett's Mill, Dallas

May 25-28, 1864

From Resaca, the Confederates retreated south-ward over the Oostanaula River, through Calhoun and Adairsville, to Cassville, Georgia (see inset). Sherman divided his forces in pursuit, sending one column southwestward to Rome, and splitting most of the rest between two roads: one due south to Kingston, the other southeastward toward Cass-ville. Johnston hoped to take advantage of Sher-man's dispersal of forces to counterattack. At Cass-ville, he ordered Hardee to block the road from Kingston, and he ordered Hood to move his corps into position to ambush the Federal column proceeding directly south from Adairsville. Hood's men were in place on the morning of May 19, but almost at once his scouts reported the presence of yet another Federal force on his own flank, and Hood pulled back.

Devastated by his inability to spring the trap on Sherman, Johnston took up a new position on high ground just south of Cassville, challenging Sherman to attack him. But Hood, joined by Polk, now argued that this position, too, was untenable, and they counseled a retreat southward over the Etowah River. Johnston acceded, and once again the Army of Ten-nessee fell back. Southern morale, which had re-mained high through the battles for Rocky Face Ridge and Resaca, now began to plummet.

After crossing the Etowah River, once again burn-ing the bridge behind them, the Confederates took up very strong positions around Allatoona (1 on main map). Unwilling to attack such a strong position, Sherman executed another flanking maneuver, swinging westward to cross the Etowah well down-river, and advancing southeastward across Pump-kinvine Creek on parallel roads toward the Georgia crossroads village of Dallas (2) en route to Marietta. Learning of the Federal movement, the Confederates shifted westward as well, moving to cut them off. They met near a small Methodist meeting house called New Hope Church (3) on May 25.

Advancing almost blindly through dense forest, three Federal divisions under the command of "Fighting Joe" Hooker encountered Stewart's Division of Hood's corps, and Sherman ordered them to attack. Although the Federals had superior numbers, the Confederates had thrown up hastily-constructed field works and easily repulsed the Federal attack which was punctuated by the thunder and lightning of a driving rain storm. Increasingly in the campaign, the soldiers in the ranks had learned the value of even temporary field works, and after their repulse, Hooker's men constructed entrenchments of their own.

Sherman remained determined to break through the Confederate position, and he ordered Oliver Otis Howard with 14,000 men to slide eastward to find the Confederate right. Howard's force became some-what disoriented in the thick woods, so much so that units frequently had to rely on compass bear-ings to determine where they were going. By late afternoon, they had located what Howard thought might be the Confederate flank, and at 4:30 p.m. on May 27 he ordered an attack to initiate what came to be known as the Battle of Pickett's Mill (4). The target of this assault was Patrick Cleburne's crack division, which had recently arrived to extend the Confederate right. Cleburne's men were not fighting from cover, but they were well-placed and the Federal attack was poorly coordinated. The re-sult was much the same as at New Hope Church. Federal losses in the two fights were three times those of the Confederates (2,400 to 800).

Despite his army's success in fighting on the de-fensive—or perhaps because of it—Johnston con-sidered going over onto the offensive. On the night after the fight at Pickett's Mill, he approved Hood's request to attempt to assail the Federal left, and when that proved impossible due to a change in the Federal dispositions, he ordered William Bate's di-vision to attack the Federal right near Dallas (5) on May 28. The result was remarkably similar to Pick-ett's Mill with the attackers (the Confederates this time) being mowed down by the defenders. Confed-erate losses were near 1,000, while the Federals suf-fered fewer than 400.

Following these sharp fights in the tangled wil-derness around Dallas and New Hope Church, both sides reassessed their progress in the campaign. Sherman gave up on the idea of reaching Marietta through the wilderness, and determined to move back to the line of the Western & Atlantic. For his part, Johnston began to believe that despite its dis-appointments, the campaign was going rather well. Sherman had forced him to accept a campaign he had not planned: fighting from entrenchments and preserving his army while trading space for time. But Johnston believed that Sherman was paying disproportionately in blood for his success, and every mile the Federals advanced lengthened their pre-carious line of supply to their base in Tennessee. Johnston decided that it was all working out rather well after all. From Confederate headquarters near New Hope Church, Johnston's chief of staff wrote his family that, "If we can keep this up, we win!"

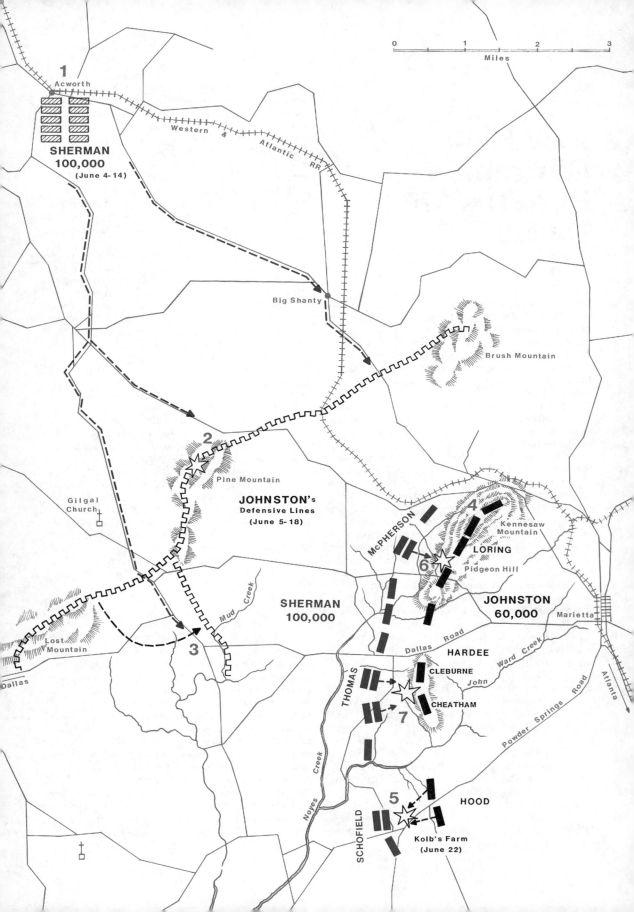

1 Acworth

SHERMAN
100,000
(June 4-14)

Western & Atlantic RR

Big Shanty

Brush Mountain

2 Pine Mountain

JOHNSTON's
Defensive Lines
(June 5-18)

Gilgal Church

Kennesaw Mountain

4

McPHERSON

LORING

6

Pidgeon Hill

JOHNSTON
60,000

Marietta

SHERMAN
100,000

Mud Creek

3

Lost Mountain

Dallas Road

Ward Creek

HARDEE

CLEBURNE

John

THOMAS

7

CHEATHAM

Powder Springs Road

Atlanta

Noyes Creek

SCHOFIELD

5

HOOD

Kolb's Farm
(June 22)

Miles
0   1   2   3

MAP 42

Kennesaw Mountain

June 27, 1864

Failing to achieve any advantage over his wily opponent in the wilderness around Dallas and New Hope Church, Sherman decided in the first week of June to return to the line of the Western & Atlantic Railroad where at least his armies could be more effectively supplied. He therefore directed his armies to march to Acworth (1), ten miles to the northeast, through a steady rain that fell on both armies, turning the roads into sloughs. Once again Johnston made the corresponding move, taking up new positions south of Acworth on a series of low hills, from Lost Mountain in the south, across the crest of Pine Mountain, to Brush Mountain.

By now, both Sherman and Johnston had begun to chafe at the indecisive character of the campaign. Johnston wrote his wife that "Sherman is so cautious that I can find no opportunity to attack him—except behind entrenchments." Sherman found Johnston's caution even more frustrating. Every time he moved, he found his ubiquitous enemy in front of him, with fresh red earth showing the location of newly-dug field works. And the Union soldiers had become chary of attacking prepared defenses. Sherman complained to Grant that, "A fresh furrow in a plowed field will stop the whole column." The Union commander even began to wonder if his troops were capable of executing a determined assault after all the weeks they had spent marching and digging. His concern was a disservice to the men in the ranks, who would soon have an opportunity to prove it.

Sherman stayed at Acworth for most of a week, building up supplies and incorporating reinforcements. Then he started south again. He found his enemy dug in across his line of advance on a wide front—some eight miles from end to end—and he immediately began probing for a weak spot. On June 14 near the center of the Confederate line at Pine Mountain (2), he espied a group of Confederate officers atop the hill looking over the defenses. At his direction, a Federal battery opened fire on the tempting target and one shell struck and killed General Polk. Most Confederate soldiers thought this was unforgivable. They hardly blinked at the slaughter of thousands of enlisted men cut down in a frontal

assault, but to target a general and kill him with artillery fire struck them as little short of murder. After the Confederates evacuated Pine Mountain, a Yankee found a note one rebel had left behind: "You damned Yankee sons of bitches have killed our old Genl. Polk."

On June 16, Johnston pulled back his left to the aptly-named Mud Creek (3) in reaction to more Federal probes, and two days after that, he withdrew again, to prepared positions on the slopes of Kennesaw Mountain (4). Seven hundred feet above the surrounding countryside, Kennesaw Mountain so dominated the terrain that one Federal soldier thought Providence must have placed it there solely as a barrier to their army. On its slopes, Johnston placed most of Polk's Corps (now commanded by William W. Loring). South of it, bracketing the Dallas Road, Johnston placed Hardee's Corps on less-imposing ground. Behind the cover of this defensive line, Johnston moved Hood's Corps to the vicinity of Kolb's Farm (5) where on June 22, Hood attacked Hooker's Corps and elements of Schofield's Army of the Ohio. Though Hood claimed a victory in this skirmish, it yielded little practical gain, and cost Hood a thousand casualties.

Johnston's line on Kennesaw Mountain was as formidable as any he had occupied in the campaign, but Sherman nevertheless decided to try to break through it. Partly this was because the rain had so ruined the roads that another flank march was impractical, but perhaps, too, he wanted to see how much fight was left in his enemy after all the marching and skirmishing since May 4. At 8:15 a.m. on June 27, Sherman sent three brigades (5,500 men) up the slopes of the southernmost shoulder of Kennesaw Mountain, called Pidgeon Hill, to test rebel defenses there (6). The firing was general, and some Federals got to within 30 yards of their objective, but this was not the Federal main effort.

Two miles south of Kennesaw Mountain, Sherman directed two infantry divisions, with two more in support, in an attack on two Confederate divisions, those of Patrick Cleburne and Frank Cheatham of Hardee's Corps. At about 9:00 a.m., a Federal cannon barked the signal and eight thousand Federals, in massed columns, emerged from the treeline in front of the rebel position, and advanced determinedly (7). Their determination, however, availed them nothing against the well-directed fire of the rebel veterans. The Confederates fired so rapidly their rifle barrels grew hot in their hands. Afterward, the Confederates recovered bodies as close as fifteen paces to their lines—but no closer. Sherman reported casualties of 2,500, but he later revised these upward to 3,000. The Confederates lost 550. Sherman's attempt to force his way *through* Johnston's army proved once again that he was better off trying to find another way *around* it.

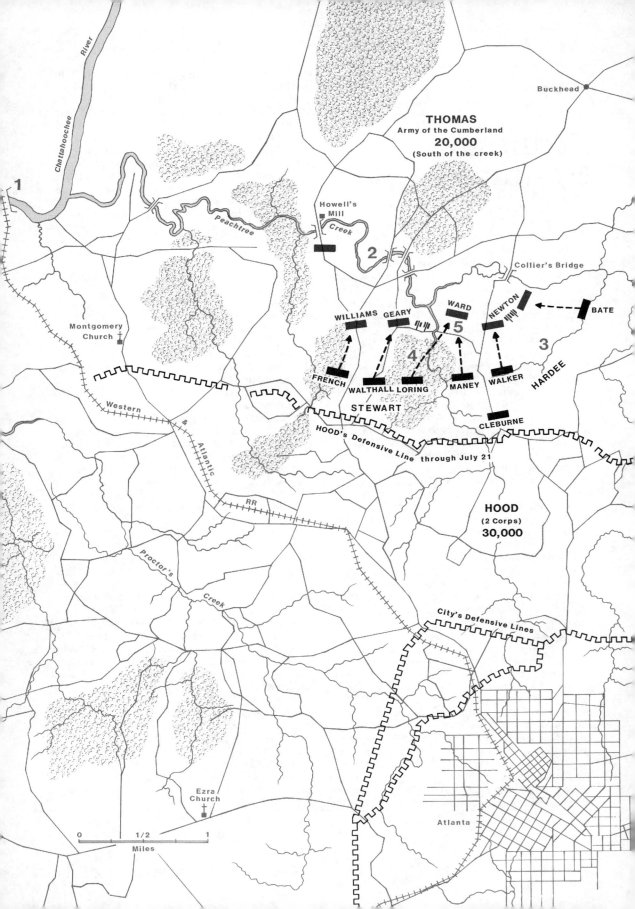

Buckhead

THOMAS
Army of the Cumberland
20,000
(South of the creek)

Howell's
Mill

Creek

2

Collier's Bridge

WILLIAMS GEARY WARD NEWTON

5

BATE

Montgomery
Church

4

3

FRENCH WALTHALL LORING MANEY WALKER HARDEE

STEWART

CLEBURNE

HOOD's Defensive Line through July 21

Western

Atlantic

&

RR

HOOD
(2 Corps)
30,000

Proctor's

Creek

City's Defensive Lines

Ezra
Church

Atlanta

0   1/2   1

Miles

Chattahoochee

River

Peachtree

MAP 43

Peachtree Creek

July 20, 1864

After his repulse at Kennesaw Mountain, Sherman once again found a way around Johnston's flank, forcing him to abandon his mountain fastness and retreat southward. As before, Johnston moved quickly to get in front of Sherman and block his advance, first at Smyrna Camp Ground six miles south of Marietta, and then in an entrenched position covering the fords over the Chattahoochee with his back to the river (1). The Chattahoochee was only half a dozen miles northwest of Atlanta, and in a very real sense, it was the last ditch. Nevertheless, when Johnston learned that elements of Sherman's army had secured a lodgement on the south bank of the river a dozen miles upstream at Roswell, he gave up that position too, and fell back to the vicinity of Atlanta. It was his last important decision in command of the army.

In Richmond, Jefferson Davis had grown increasingly anxious over Johnston's continual withdrawals. He was influenced, too, by a series of private letters which Hood had sent him that were critical of Johnston's timorousness, and which advocated the adoption of an offensive to drive Sherman from Georgia. By mid-July, Davis' patience with Johnston had run out, and on July 17 he dismissed Johnston from his command, and turned the Army of Tennessee over to John Bell Hood.

In his last conversation with Hood before he left the army to go into semi-retirement near Macon, Johnston told the army's new commander that he had planned to strike at Sherman as the Federals crossed Peachtree Creek, a small tributary of the Chattahoochee north of Atlanta (2). Hood immediately adopted the idea and wasted no time working out a plan of attack. Only two days after assuming command, he met with his corps commanders at midnight on July 19 in his headquarters just north of Atlanta to give them their orders. Only Hardee's Corps retained its original commander—indeed, Hardee was somewhat miffed at being passed over for command, for he was senior to Hood. Frank Cheatham, whose men had performed so brilliantly at Kennesaw Mountain, took over temporary command of Hood's old corps; Polk's old corps was now commanded by A. P. Stewart, who had replaced Loring when Richmond declined to confirm Loring's promotion.

Hood planned to hurl two thirds of his army—the corps of Hardee and Stewart—at Thomas' Army of the Cumberland after it crossed Peachtree Creek. Hardee's men would strike first (3), attacking *en echelon* from right to left, driving the enemy toward the northwest in order to pin the Federals into the cul-de-sac where Peachtree Creek flowed into the Chattahoochee. Stewart's corps would then join in, also from right to left (4). Cheatham, with Hood's old corps, would cover Hardee's right and protect Atlanta from a Federal *coup de main*. Hood impressing on his corps commanders the importance of a vigorous attack, pressed home. The attack would begin at one o'clock the next afternoon.

At mid-morning on July 20, however, Hood learned from Joe Wheeler, his cavalry commander, that Sherman's other two armies were pressing aggressively toward Atlanta from the northeast down the Decatur Road. Hood therefore ordered Cheatham to shift his position a mile to the southeast to block this thrust, and he ordered Hardee and Stewart to maintain contact with Cheatham by sliding eastward as well. These changes upset both the timetable and the alignment of the forces poised for attack. Not until 4:00 pm did the Confederates begin their assault. By then, the Federals south of Peachtree Creek—about 20,000 men from Hooker's and Newton's Corps—had established themselves firmly on the south back of the creek and erected field works.

Hardee's attack was disappointing. Though he had numerical superiority at the point of contact, his assault was contained due to his own incomplete understanding of Federal dispositions and a lack of coordination between Confederate brigades. On Hardee's left, Stewart's attack faced longer odds, but the terrain was more compatible to the attackers. At one point in the fight, W. W. Loring, commanding one of Stewart's divisions, broke through the Federal defenses and called for reinforcements to push the Yankees into the creek (5). But rather than commit Cleburne's Division to this attack, Hood instead dispatched it to the east in response to a plea for help from Wheeler, who reported that McPherson's entire army was advancing against his dismounted cavalry on the Decatur Road.

Hood's attempt to destroy Thomas's army failed. Moreover, by accepting the tactical offensive, he subjected his soldiers to the heavier casualties that generally befell the attacker. Federal casualties on July 20 were about 2,000; Confederate losses were nearly double that. Worse, Thomas maintained his position south of Peachtree Creek, and the Federals on the Decatur Road had advanced to within 2½ miles of Atlanta. Undeterred, Hood was making plans for another assault even before the sun had set.

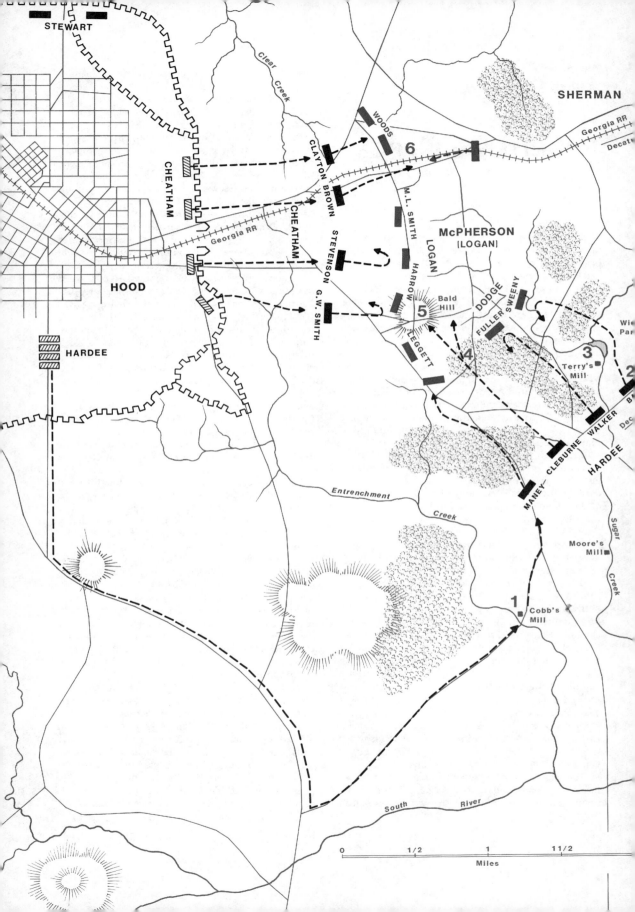

STEWART

SHERMAN

Georgia RR

Decat

Clear Creek

WOODS

CLAYTON

BROWN

6

CHEATHAM

M. L. SMITH

LOGAN

McPHERSON

(LOGAN)

CHEATHAM

Georgia RR

STEVENSON

HARROW

HOOD

G. W. SMITH

Bald Hill

DODGE

SWEENY

5

FULLER

Wi
Par

HARDEE

LEGGETT

4

3

Terry's
Mill

2

Dec

WALKER

CLEBURNE

HARDEE

Entrenchment

MANEY

Creek

Moore's
Mill

Sugar

Creek

1

Cobb's
Mill

South   River

0		1/2		1		11/2

Miles

MAP 44

The Battle of Atlanta (Bald Hill)

July 22, 1864

Although Hood was disappointed with the results of the Battle of Peachtree Creek, he was determined to retain the initiative and execute an offensive that would send Sherman's army reeling back into the hills of north Georgia. Even before the firing had ceased along Peachtree Creek, he was planning another attack, this one against McPherson's Army of the Tennessee advancing from the east along the Decatur Road. The closest available Confederate force for this assignment was Hood's own former corps, now commanded by Frank Cheatham. But Hood was unsure that Cheatham possessed the experience to execute the daring flank attack he had in mind, and so he turned once again to Hardee. Although Hardee's men had fought at Peachtree Creek, Hood did not believe that their half-hearted assault had exhausted their offensive potential.

Hood ordered Stewart and Cheatham to fall back into the defensive lines around Atlanta, Stewart facing north, and Cheatham facing east. While they held the city, Hardee's men would march southward, through the streets of Atlanta and out the McDonough Road, turning northeast onto the road to Decatur to strike McPherson in flank and rear. Although Hood envisioned that Hardee would march his force all the way to Decatur before attacking, he left the details to Hardee's discretion. When Hardee launched his attack—scheduled for dawn on July 22—Cheatham's men would rise out of their entrenchments east of Atlanta to join in the fight, thus crushing McPherson in a double envelopment.

Throughout the night of July 21-22, Hardee's men marched southward through the city, convincing many residents that the army must be evacuating. Refugees clogged the roads and slowed the movement. South of the city, Hardee's column turned eastward and by dawn it had reached Cobb's Mill (1). Since the entire corps was moving on a single road, it made up a column more than two miles long, and Hardee halted the van briefly to allow the men

to close up and get a short rest. A few miles further on, at a home belonging to a widow named Parker (2), Hardee met with his staff to consider their options. It was already well past dawn, the hour originally determined for the attack, and Decatur was still another six miles ahead. Convinced that his force must have passed the Federal left flank by now, Hardee decided to face his column northward and begin the attack. As Bate's Division had been in the van, it would form on the rebel right. Next to it would be Walker's Division, then Cleburne's, then Maney's. The attack would be conducted *en echelon*, with Bate's men going in first, followed in sequence by the remaining divisions from right to left. At noon the whole force was aligned and ready, and Hardee sent it off northward.

The terrain along the route of the attack had not been reconnoitered, and Bate's men found their way barred not only by thick underbrush, but also by a large mill pond (3), and they had to veer off to the right to go around it. Walker's men, too, were slowed by rough terrain and thick vegetation. When they did strike the Federal line, they had another unpleasant surprise. McPherson had just that morning placed the corps of Grenville Dodge on McPherson's left to guard against just such a flank attack as Hardee was attempting to execute. Thus, instead of an exposed flank, the men of Bate's and Walker's Divisions ran into an entrenched enemy front. Walker was one of the first casualties of the fight, felled by a Federal picket, although the Confederates more than evened the score when McPherson himself became a casualty, shot from his horse when he refused to heed a demand for his surrender.

Cleburne's Division had better luck, for his brigades struck a seam between two Federal corps (4). Some of Cleburne's brigades pushed northward for more than half a mile before being stopped near the foot of Bald Hill (5). By mid-afternoon, Hardee's attack had pretty much run its course, but then at about 3:30, Hood sent Cheatham's Corps into the fight. Despite furious attacks, the Confederates broke through at only one point, along the axis of the Georgia Railroad (6), but Sherman, who had arrived on the field, organized a counter-attack, and the break was contained. As night fell, the Federals continued to hold their lines east of Atlanta.

Like the Battle of Peachtree Creek, the Battle of Atlanta was a Confederate disappointment. And also like Peachtree Creek, the Confederates suffered disproportionate casualties by accepting the tactical offensive. Although difficult to determine with precision, Confederate losses in the Battle of Atlanta (or Bald Hill) were once again almost double those of the Federals, who suffered 3,800 casualties.

Hood was running out of options.

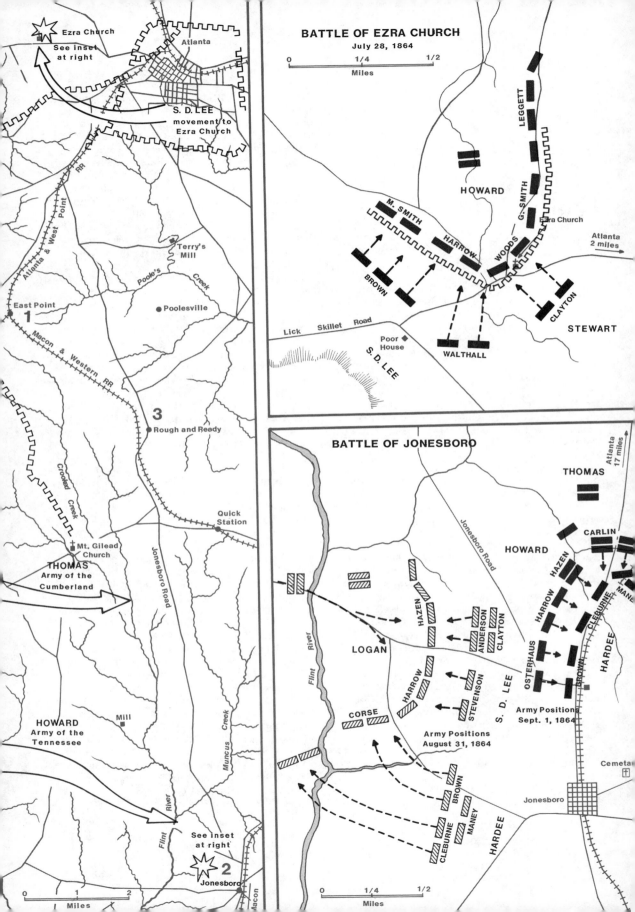

BATTLE OF EZRA CHURCH
July 28, 1864

0 1/4 1/2
Miles

Ezra Church
See inset at right

Atlanta

S. D. LEE
movement to
Ezra Church

Atlanta & West Point RR

Terry's Mill

Poole's Creek

East Point

1

Poolesville

Macon & Western RR

3

Rough and Ready

Quick Station

Crooked Creek

Mt. Gilead Church

THOMAS
Army of the
Cumberland

Jonesboro Road

HOWARD
Army of the
Tennessee

Mill

Muncus Creek

Flint River

See inset
at right

2
Jonesboro

0 1 2
Miles

Macon

LEGGETT

HOWARD

G. SMITH

M. SMITH

HARROW

WOODS

Ezra Church

Atlanta
2 miles

BROWN

CLAYTON

STEWART

Lick Skillet Road

Poor House

S. D. LEE

WALTHALL

BATTLE OF JONESBORO

THOMAS

Atlanta
17 miles

CARLIN

Jonesboro Road

HOWARD

HAZEN

HAZEN

MANEY

HARROW

CLEBURNE

ANDERSON

CLAYTON

OSTERHAUS

HARDEE

LOGAN

BROWN

STEVENSON

S. D. LEE

Army Positions
Sept. 1, 1864

HARROW

CORSE

Army Positions
August 31, 1864

Flint River

BROWN

MANEY

Cemetary

CLEBURNE

MANEY

HARDEE

Jonesboro

0 1/4 1/2
Miles

MAP 45

Ezra Church and Jonesboro

Despite his success in fending off two furious Confederate assaults in three days, Sherman was not anxious to risk his own forces attacking the rebel entrenchments around Atlanta. Instead his goal was to surround the city, cut off its railroad communications, and strangle it. In pursuit of that, he sent the Army of the Tennessee, now commanded by Oliver Otis Howard, on a circuitous march from its position east of Atlanta around to the west where it could threaten the railroad that snaked southward out of Atlanta. Since Sherman already controlled both the Western & Atlantic northward to Dalton, and the Georgia Railroad to Decatur, that railroad to the south was Hood's lifeline. Five miles south of Atlanta, the railroad split at East Point (1) with one branch continuing southwest to Montgomery, while the other led southeast to Jonesboro (2), and eventually Savannah.

When Hood learned that Howard was slipping around to the west, he dispatched Samuel D. Lee, who had succeeded Cheatham in command of Hood's old corps, to intercept him. In particular, Hood ordered Lee to occupy a critical crossroads on the vital, if oddly-named, Lick Skillet Road west of Atlanta near Ezra Church (see top map). Hood expected that Lee's men would occupy the crossroads, dig in, and force the Federals to attack. As the Federals exhausted themselves attacking Lee, Hood would send Stewart to attack the Federals in their left flank. But like both of Hood's earlier battle plans, events did not unfold as he envisioned.

Ezra Church, July 28, 1864

When the Confederates of S. D. Lee's two divisions approached the crossroads near Ezra Church, they saw that Howard's blue-coated soldiers had arrived there first and had dug in, using fence rails and even pews from the church to erect a barricade. Hood remained at his headquarters in Atlanta and was therefore unaware that the crossroads was already occupied by enemy forces. His orders required Lee "to prevent the enemy from gaining the Lick Skillet Road," and since the enemy was already on that road, Lee concluded that he was expected to take it

from them. He therefore sent his two divisions forward in frontal assaults that achieved little. Even when Stewart tried to help by sending one of his divisions (Clayton's) into the fight, it soon became evident that the Yankees could not be budged. After a long afternoon's fight, the Confederates withdrew leaving nearly 5,000 more casualties on the field, including Stewart who was wounded. With his force reduced to less than 35,000 as a result of his three offensives against Sherman, Hood had little choice now but to fall back within the defensive lines around Atlanta and surrender the initiative to Sherman.

Jonesboro, August 31-September 1, 1864

For the next two weeks, Sherman shifted his lines to the south from Ezra Church, forcing Hood to stretch his lines southward as well until the Confederate lines extended more than five miles toward the southeast beyond East Point. Hood had no hope of retaining control of the road to Montgomery, but he knew he had to cling to the road to Jonesboro for it was his last link to the rest of the Confederacy.

In August, while Union artillery terrorized the civilian population of Atlanta, Sherman devised a plan to break this crucial rail link. He ordered all three of his armies to move to the west, then swing south and east again to cut the Macon & Western Railroad between Rough and Ready (3) and Jonesboro. Howard's Army of the Tennessee took the longest route toward Jonesboro itself. Knowing he had to repel this threat or give up the city, Hood ordered most of Lee's Corps and all of Hardee's to concentrate at Jonesboro and hurl back the Federal probe.

At Jonesboro (see lower map) Hardee planned another attack *en echelon*, hoping to roll up the Federal line left to right, and he sent Lee's divisions in first, followed by his own. Cleburne's men on the Confederate left chased some Federal cavalry across the Flint River, but elsewhere the Confederates encountered stiff resistance. The Confederate onslaught stopped the Federal advance, but failed to throw the bluecoats back over the river. Nevertheless, the next day Hood recalled Lee's two divisions to Atlanta leaving Hardee with only three divisions at Jonesboro. On September 1, much of Thomas' Army of the Cumberland joined with Howard's force to concentrate on Hardee and drive him from the railroad. Hood's lifeline had been cut, and he began to evacuate the city that same night.

The next day Stanton handed Lincoln a telegram from Major General Slocum, "General Sherman has taken Atlanta." The news came just in time; the national elections were only two months away and Sherman's victory exploded the claims of the opposition party that the war had become stalemated. With Lincoln's reelection in November, Confederate hopes of final victory dimmed to a tiny flicker.

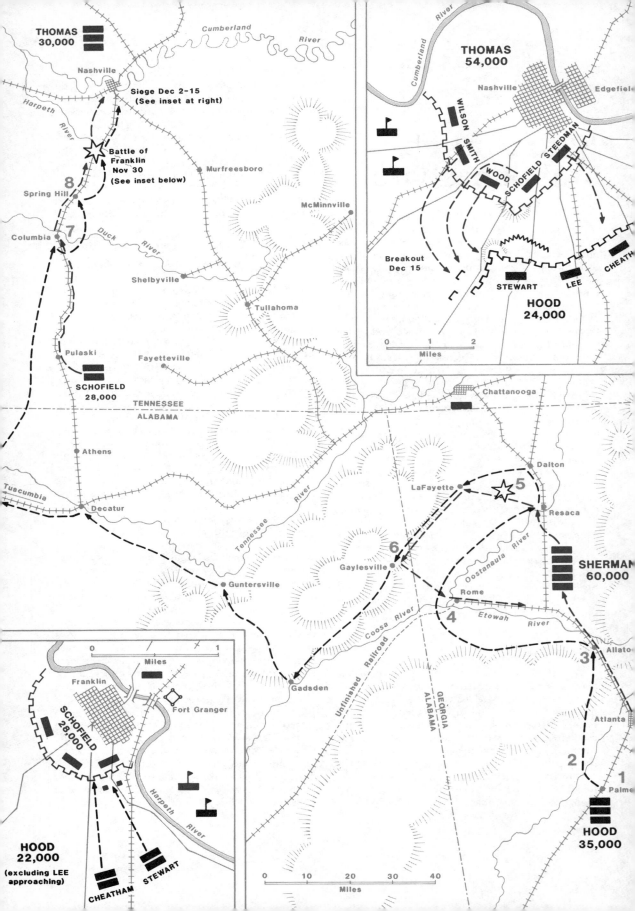

THOMAS 30,000

Cumberland River

Nashville

THOMAS 54,000

Cumberland River

Nashville

Edgefield

WILSON

SMITH

SCHOFIELD

STEEDMAN

WOOD

Siege Dec 2-15 (See inset at right)

Battle of Franklin Nov 30 (See inset below)

Breakout Dec 15

STEWART

LEE

CHEATH

HOOD 24,000

0   1   2
Miles

Murfreesboro

Harpeth River

Spring Hill

8

McMinnville

Columbia

7

Duck River

Shelbyville

Tullahoma

Fayetteville

Pulaski

SCHOFIELD 28,000

TENNESSEE

ALABAMA

Athens

Chattanooga

Tuscumbia

Decatur

Tennessee River

Dalton

LaFayette

5

Resaca

Oostanaula River

SHERMAN 60,000

Guntersville

Gaylesville

6

Rome

Etowah River

Coosa River

4

Allato

3

Gadsden

Unfinished Railroad

GEORGIA
ALABAMA

Atlanta

0   10   20   30   40
Miles

2

1

Palme

HOOD 35,000

0   1
Miles

Franklin

SCHOFIELD 28,000

Fort Granger

Harpeth River

HOOD 22,000
(excluding LEE approaching)

CHEATHAM

STEWART

MAP 46

Hood's Offensive

September-December, 1864

After abandoning Atlanta on September 1, Hood's Army of Tennessee—reduced to 35,000 effectives—retreated southward and concentrated near Palmetto (1). Hood knew that he lacked the strength to engage Sherman in a set-piece battle, but he believed that by operating against Sherman's lines of communication he could lure the Federal army northward, away from Atlanta. On September 25 Jefferson Davis visited the army at Palmetto and approved Hood's plan in principle. A few days later the Confederate army re-crossed the Chattahoochee southwest of Atlanta (2), and started north.

Hood reached the Georgia Central Railroad near Allatoona (3) on October 1 and for the next four days his men tore up tracks and cut telegraph lines. On the sixth, Hood left the line of the railroad and marched his army northwestward, avoiding Rome, which was guarded by a Federal garrison, and crossing the Coosa a few miles downstream (4) on October 10. Two days later Hood struck the railroad again near Resaca. He demanded the surrender of the city on the threat of giving no quarter if he had to storm it. But when the Federal garrison called his bluff, Hood marched away northward, gobbling up smaller Federal garrisons on his way to Dalton, where he set up his headquarters on October 13.

Hood's activity drew Sherman's attention, as planned, and the Union army moved out of Atlanta in pursuit. Hood fled westward, fighting a skirmish at Snake Creek Gap (5) on October 15 on his way to Gaylesville (6), Sherman pursued him there, but when Hood marched even further west toward Gadsden, Alabama. "Uncle Billy" decided that Hood was leading him on a wild-goose chase and he returned to Atlanta. He dispatched Thomas and Schofield to defend Tennessee and began to make offensive plans of his own (*see* Map 47).

Hood now concocted a truly desperate scheme. He would strike north through Tennessee and into Kentucky, defeat Union forces there, and then turn east along the Ohio River into Virginia, where he and Lee would cooperate to crush Grant. The scheme ignored the manpower and logistic realities of the situation, but Hood was never one for detail. He hoped that somehow an aggressive spirit would restore success to Confederate fortunes. Hood did not submit his plan to Beauregard who, as theater commander, was his nominal superior, or to Davis. He simply started his forces westward, arriving outside Decatur on October 26. Deciding that Decatur was too strongly garrisoned for him to force a crossing of the Tennessee there, Hood moved further west to Tuscumbia (off the map to the west) where the army arrived on October 30.

Though his scheme would require speed if it were to have any chance of success, Hood did not order a crossing of the river until November 18, by which time Schofield and Thomas had reached middle Tennessee to contest his "invasion." On November 26 Hood approached Columbia, Tennessee, (7) only to find his way blocked by Schofield. Hood outflanked the Federal position upstream and Schofield fell back. Hood then directed his own forces toward Spring Hill (8) where he expected to cut off Schofield's retreat. His own carelessness and sloppy staff work, however, enabled the Federals to march past the Confederate position unmolested. Characteristically, Hood blamed others for the lapse, even the men in the ranks, who he believed had forgotten how to fight.

In this angry mood, Hood started out in pursuit on November 30, and came up on Schofield's new position at Franklin that afternoon (*see* lower inset). The Federals were posted behind stout breastworks with a clear field of fire in front of them. Nevertheless Hood ordered his two corps (S. D. Lee was still coming up) to attack. Twenty thousand men, more than at Gettysburg, made the charge at about 3:30 P.M. The attack overwhelmed two outlying Federal brigades, and pursued them into the works. But the Federals counterattacked and hand-to-hand fighting went on until dark. That night, Schofield pulled out of the city, as he had intended to do all along, and continued on the road to Nashville. Hood's losses were grievous: over 6,000 men, including no less than twelve generals, six of whom were killed outright.

Hood had only about 23,000 men left after his bad-tempered assault at Franklin, but he chose to follow Schofield to Nashville where he hoped to entice the combined Union armies to attack him. The Army of Tennessee arrived outside Nashville on December 2, but they were too few to surround the city (*see* upper inset). For two weeks the Confederates suffered terribly from the weather, especially from an ice storm that hit the area on December 10. Then, on December 15, a fiercer storm broke over them when Thomas's men charged out of the city and overwhelmed Hood's left flank. Hood withdrew two miles and made another stand the next day, but the game was up. His army retreated southward through falling snow, and by the end of the year the remnants—about 18,000 ragged men of all arms—were at Tupelo, Mississippi. Though Hood put all the blame on others—his superiors, his subordinates, and most unjustly of all, the men in the ranks—he was almost solely responsible for the disaster. On January 23, still unrepentant, he was removed from the command of the army he had ruined. The war in the West was all but over.

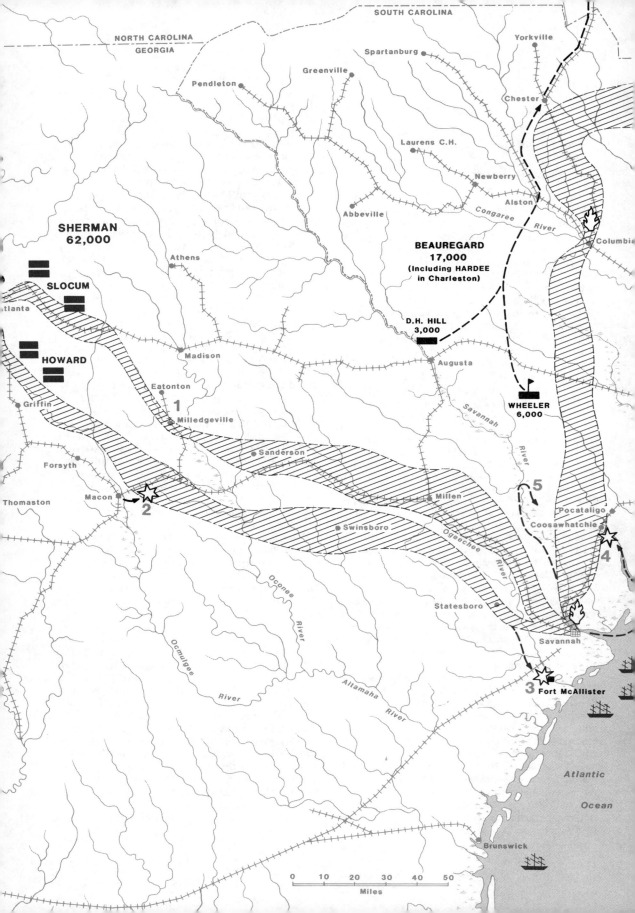

SOUTH CAROLINA

NORTH CAROLINA
GEORGIA

Yorkville

Spartanburg

Greenville

Pendleton

Chester

SHERMAN
62,000

Athens

Laurens C.H.

Newberry

Alston

Abbeville

Congaree

River

SLOCUM

BEAUREGARD
17,000
(Including HARDEE
in Charleston)

Columbia

Atlanta

HOWARD

Madison

D.H. HILL
3,000

Augusta

Wheeler
6,000

Savannah

Griffin

Eatonton

1

Milledgeville

Forsyth

Sanderson

Macon

2

Millen

Thomaston

Swinsboro

5

Pocataligo
Coosawhatchie

4

Oconee

River

Ogeechee

River

Statesboro

Savannah

Ocmulgee

River

3 Fort McAllister

Altamaha

River

Atlantic

Ocean

Brunswick

0   10   20   30   40   50

Miles

MAP 47

Sherman's March to the Sea

November 15-December 20, 1864

After abandoning his fruitless pursuit of Hood in October, Sherman retraced his steps to Atlanta, where he gave renewed consideration to a long-cherished plan to strike into the interior of the Confederacy. Up to now, any suggestion that he attempt such a foray had met with opposition from Washington and therefore from Grant, who was always sensitive to the political implications of military decisions. But Sherman's conquest of Atlanta had helped ensure a Republican victory in the November elections, and with those elections safely over, the political risks of a defeat were much reduced. Sherman therefore prepared to embark on his famous march to the sea. He reorganized the 62,000 men of his command into two wings, and placed them under the command of Major Generals Henry W. Slocum and Oliver O. Howard.

When the army left Atlanta on the night of November 15, a glow in the western sky from fires burning out of control in the city lit the way. Debate continues to this day regarding the origin of the conflagration which destroyed more than a third of the city. But while it may not have been the result of direct orders of the Federal high command, it is certain that few men in the Federal army, Sherman included, shed tears over it.

"War is hell," Sherman later reported, and as if determined to prove the truthfulness of that phrase, he issued orders to his men that while on the march they were to "forage liberally on the country." In other words, they were given, quite literally, a license to steal. Because there were no substantial bodies of enemy troops in their path, it was not necessary to keep the army concentrated, and units fanned out over broad stretches of previously unravaged countryside to "forage" more efficiently. For the next month, the Union army marked two broad swaths of destruction as it crossed the state: one wing marching through the Georgia state capital of at Milledgeville (1), and the other marching south toward Macon, then swerving east to parallel the march of the left wing.

On November 22, a few miles east of Macon (2), Georgia militia attacked a Union rear-guard detachment, the Confederates charging three times across open ground against the Federal veterans, and suffering terrible losses. After they retreated the way they had come, the Federals ventured forward to discover that the bodies left behind showed that the attack had been made by a battalion of home-guard troops—boys under sixteen and men over sixty. This pathetic and one-sided skirmish was the only "battle" fought by Sherman's men en route to Savannah. A more serious impediment to Sherman's advance was the huge and growing army of "contrabands," freed slaves who followed the blue army to ensure their own freedom. Such an encumbrance were they that Sherman tried several schemes to get rid of them, none successful.

The Federal army came within sight of Savannah on December 10. There Hardee and nearly 15,000 Confederates of all arms presented the first serious military obstacle to the Federal advance. Before assaulting the city, however, Sherman ordered a division to seize Fort McAllister (3) on the Ogeechee River in order to restore communications with the world outside Georgia via the U.S. Navy. His lines of communication thus secured, Sherman turned north to seize Savannah. Hardee's men escaped across the Savannah River, but the city itself fell on December 20 and Sherman wired Lincoln that he wished to present "as a Christmas gift, the city of Savannah."

In Richmond, Confederate authorities were distraught but powerless. On January 16 the Confederate Senate voted to make Lee general-in-chief, a deliberate slap at Davis and a desperate and futile attempt to recoup the military position. Meanwhile, as Sherman prepared to leave Savannah and move north through the Carolinas for an eventual link-up with Grant, the South could muster only about 17,000 men in the entire three-state area to oppose him. Beauregard, who had the dubious honor of this command, set up his headquarters in Columbia, uncertain as to where Sherman would go next. To keep him in suspense, Sherman feinted first toward Charleston with an amphibious attack on Coosawhatchie (4), and then toward Augusta (5). But Columbia was his real target, and his forces entered the South Carolina capital on February 17, only a few hours after Beauregard's hasty departure.

As the capital of the state that most Federals held responsible for starting the war, Columbia received even worse treatment than Atlanta or Savannah; two-thirds of the city were destroyed by fires that were whipped into blazing storms by high winds. To his credit, Sherman formed fire-fighting parties, but vengeful enlisted men re-set the fires as fast as they could be put out.

In a belated move, Davis on February 23 restored Joseph E. Johnston to the command of the remnants of Confederate forces in the Carolinas, but it was much too late and Johnston's forces were too small to prevent a junction between Sherman and Grant in any case. Such a junction would prove unnecessary, for events were moving to a climax in Petersburg as well.

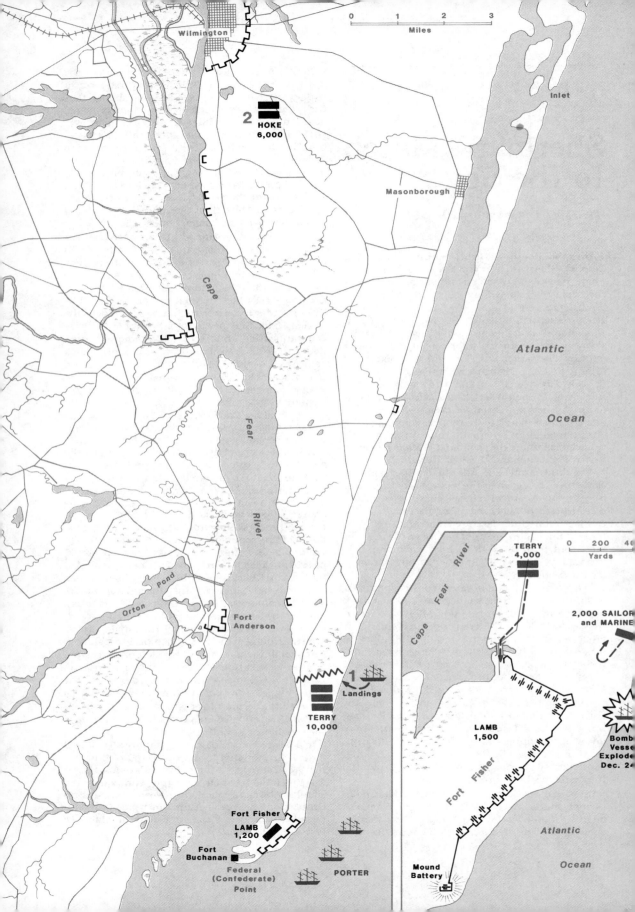

Wilmington

0 1 2 3
Miles

Inlet

2
HOKE
6,000

Masonborough

Cape

Atlantic

Fear

Ocean

River

TERRY
4,000

Cape Fear River

0 200 40
Yards

2,000 SAILOR
and MARINE

Orton
Pond

Fort
Anderson

LAMB
1,500

Fort Fisher

1
Landings

TERRY
10,000

Bomb
Vesse
Explode
Dec. 24

Fort Fisher
LAMB
1,200

Atlantic

Fort
Buchanan

Federal
(Confederate)

Point

PORTER

Ocean

Mound
Battery

MAP 48

Fort Fisher

December 13, 1864-January 15, 1865

Sherman's uncontested devastation of Georgia drastically reduced the area under effective Confederate control, and the fall of Charleston left only one major Atlantic seaport in Confederate hands. That port was Wilmington, North Carolina, on the Cape Fear River. At its wharves, blockade-runners continued to unload their cargoes of munitions, food, shoes, medicine, and other goods necessary to the continuation of the Confederate war effort. Moreover, Wilmington had direct rail connections to Petersburg and thus to Richmond. So critical was it that Lee informed the commander of the city's principal fortress, Fort Fisher, that the Army of Northern Virginia could not continue to hold Richmond if Fort Fisher were to fall.

The fall of Fort Fisher was exactly what Grant had in mind. Not only would a successful Federal seizure of Wilmington cut the Confederacy's supply lifeline, but the city could become a useful Federal base for Sherman's army grinding its irresistible way northward from Savannah. Grant therefore sent Major General Benjamin Butler and two small divisions, about 6,500 men, to Hampton Roads, where they embarked on Army transport vessels for the voyage to Fort Fisher. There Butler would cooperate with the commander of the naval blockading force, Captain David Dixon Porter, in a joint operation against the fort.

Fort Fisher was a substantial fortification, over a mile in length along the seaward side and mounting forty-seven pieces of heavy artillery. Its sand walls were more than twenty-five feet thick and impervious to even the heaviest shells. To avoid a direct attack, Butler planned to blow up the entire fort, using a vessel packed with over 200 tons of powder. He selected the USS *Louisiana* for this assignment, and a skeleton crew of volunteers guided the vessel toward the fort on the night of December 23. The ship grounded just off the fort's northeast angle (*see* inset map) and the crew set the fuses and abandoned ship. At about 1:40 A.M. on Christmas Eve, the ship exploded with a dull roar heard as far away as Beaufort, South Carolina. When the sun rose several hours later there was no sign of the *Louisiana*, but the fort appeared altogether undamaged. Indeed some of the defenders testified later that they had not even been awakened.

The failure of the bomb vessel meant that more conventional means would have to be employed. Porter began a bombardment almost immediately, and Butler detailed his second in command, Major General Godfrey Weitzel, to lead a landing party. On Christmas Day Weizel and about 2,000 men went ashore three miles north of the fort (1). This detachment advanced slowly on Fort Fisher but it soon became evident that Porter's guns had not significantly reduced the fort's firepower. Moreover, Weitzel learned that Lee had dispatched a Confederate division under Major General Robert F. Hoke to Wilmington, and that Hoke was in position to move on the Federal rear (2). When he learned of Hoke's proximity, Butler ordered his forces re-embarked and headed back to Hampton Roads, claiming that the fort could not be taken.

Porter was disgusted with Butler's timidity. More importantly, so was Grant, who asked Lincoln to relieve Butler of command and ordered Brigadier General Alfred H. Terry to lead another expedition to Fort Fisher. After Terry's arrival, Porter began a second bombardment of the fort on January 13. This time he took special care to ensure that his gunners marked specific targets rather than simply fire in the general direction of the flagpole. The Navy flung over one and a half million pounds of ordnance at the fort's parapets and knocked more than half the Confederate guns out of action. Meanwhile, Terry landed his men north of the fort and immediately set them to work digging a line of entrenchments across the peninsula to protect against a possible attack by Hoke. Then Terry turned south with just over half his men to assault the fort.

The assault took place on January 15. Porter's bombardment reached a peak at 3:00 P.M. and then suddenly stopped. Four thousand soldiers attacked along the western (river) shore, while a mixed force of 2,000 sailors and Marines attacked the northeast salient. The sailors never got closer than 300 yards. Advancing over open ground, they were easy targets for the defenders who were at last able to shoot back at their tormentors. But the attack of the bluejackets drew the defender's attention away from Terry's soldiers, who carried the ramparts near the river and were soon inside the fort. Fighting continued all afternoon and into the night, largely because of the fierce resistance by the fort's defenders under Colonel William Lamb. But the weight of numbers was irresistible, and at 10:00 P.M. the remnants of the Confederate garrison capitulated.

With the fall of Fort Fisher, Confederate forces abandoned Wilmington and it became a major Federal base. With Wilmington in Federal hands and Sherman moving north through the Carolinas, the Confederacy was clearly on its last legs. Only Lee's army at Petersburg still held on grimly. But Lee was already stretched very thin, and the loss of his supply route through Wilmington would strain him even more.

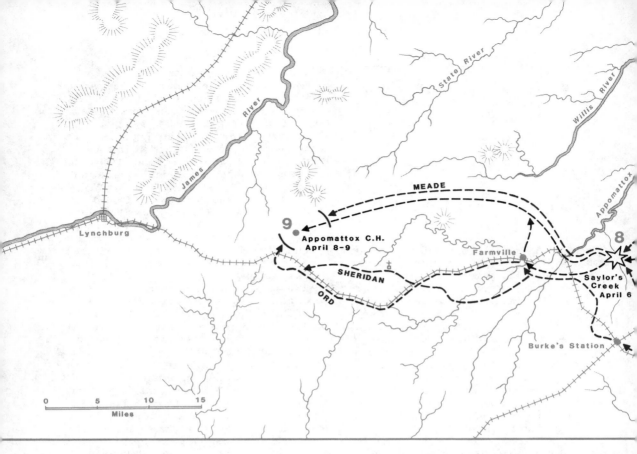

The Road to Appomattox

July, 1864-April, 1865

Grant had pinned Lee inside the Petersburg defenses in June, 1864 and the two armies had remained locked together in static combat ever since. Lee simply did not have the numbers to assume the offensive, and Grant, whose army had suffered 75,000 casualties on its march from the Rapidan to the James, was unwilling to try a frontal assault against Lee's prepared defenses. Grant's strategy, therefore, was to extend his lines westward, to cut Lee's supply line to the south, and to probe for the rebel right flank.

The most curious action of the campaign was a Federal attempt in July to blow up a section of the Confederate line, using a huge underground mine placed at the end of a 500-foot-long tunnel built by a regiment of coal miners from Pennsylvania. The mine was an engineering marvel and the explosion was spectacular, but the subsequent Union attack was a pathetic display of ineptitude. The Federals charged into the crater created by the explosion and then lost momentum. The rebels quickly recovered from the shock and counterattacked, driving the confused Federals back to their lines and inflicting 4,000 casualties.

Reverting to more conventional measures, Grant in August sent Warren and Hancock to seize the Weldon Railroad. Their advance was blunted by a Confederate counterattack on August 18 at the Battle of Globe Tavern (1) and although the Federals seized a small piece of the railroad, supplies continued to come into Petersburg along that route as Confederate wagons simply detoured around the Federal salient. In September and October, while Sherman was chasing Hood north of Atlanta, Grant again probed the limits of the rebel right flank at the Battles of Peebles Farm and Poplar Springs Church (2). And on October 27 a Federal lunge at the Southside Railroad was turned back at the Battle of Burgess Mill or Hatcher's Run (3).

These battles were not decisive, however, and in the winter months, a relative quiet settled over the no-man's-land between the two forces. Both Grant and Lee followed the news of Sheridan and Early in the Valley, of Hood's advance into Tennessee, and

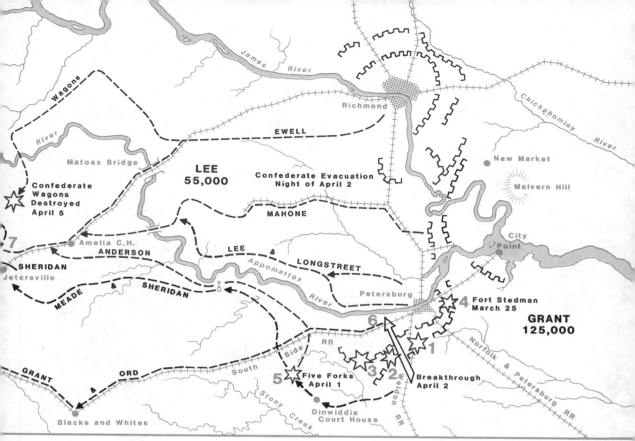

waited for news of Sherman's march through Georgia. The soldiers on both sides of the lines established informal ceasefires and traded coffee, tobacco, and news. But the winter was harder on the Confederates than on the besiegers, simply because of the relative unavailability of supplies and food. A cattle-stealing raid by Wade Hampton in September had supplied some fresh meat, but usually the fare was both sparse and poor.

With the coming of spring, both Grant and Lee knew that a decision was near. With Fort Fisher in Federal hands and only one rickety rail line still bringing a trickle of supplies into Petersburg from an ever-shrinking logistic base, Lee had only one hope left, and a slim one at that. He would try to disengage from his lines at Petersburg and attempt a junction with Johnston's army in North Carolina for an attack on Sherman. Before he could begin, however, he had to loosen Grant's grip on the city. To achieve this, he ordered John B. Gordon to attack Fort Stedman (4) and drive into the Federal rear area. Lee hoped that such a move would not only disrupt Union organization, but also draw Federal troops northward, away from the roads out of Petersburg.

Gordon's attack on March 25 was carefully planned and the rebels seized the fort itself, but Federal counterattacks contained the breakthrough and Gordon had to retreat. The attack cost Lee some 3,500 men, which by then represented 10 percent of the army's total strength. Grant surmised the purpose of Lee's stroke and countered by sending

Sheridan's cavalry, supported by Warren's infantry corps, for another try at the Confederate right. At first the Federals were stopped cold in a skirmish at Dinwiddie Court House, but then on April 1 in the Battle of Five Forks (5), the rebel right wing crumpled and Lee's position suddenly became very precarious.

Grant ordered attacks all along the line, and the next day Wright's corps broke through near Poplar Springs (6) in a battle that cost A. P. Hill his life. That night Lee began evacuating both Petersburg and Richmond. To effect a junction with Johnston, he had to reach Lynchburg ahead of Grant's pursuing legions. Five miles southwest of Amelia Court House, where the army paused on April 5, Lee found his route blocked by Sheridan's cavalry (7), and so he turned west, cutting across country.

The next day the Confederates, whose numbers now did not exceed 20,000, turned to fight off their pursuers. But the Confederate line along Saylor's Creek (8) crumbled with the first Federal attack, and nearly 8,000 tired rebel veterans were taken prisoner. With fewer than 13,000 men now, Lee pushed on to Appomattox Court House (9). There he found not only Sheridan's cavalry, but two corps of Union infantry from the Army of the James across his line of march. The game was up and Lee knew it. Though some suggested that the army disperse to carry on irregular warfare from camps in the mountains, Lee shook his head. "There is nothing left for me to do but to go and see General Grant, and I would rather die a thousand deaths."

Epilogue: Appomattox

On April 9, 1865, four years almost to the day since Beauregard's troops opened fire on Fort Sumter, Robert E. Lee met with Ulysses S. Grant in the parlor of a private home belonging to Wilmer McLean in the village of Appomattox Court House. McLean had formerly lived along the banks of Bull Run in northern Virginia, but after two great battles were fought practically in his backyard, he resolved to sell out and move away from the war to the quiet, militarily insignificant village of Appomattox Court House. When Lee's aide-de-camp went to the village on the morning of that April 9 to find a suitable site for the historic meeting, McLean was the only white civilian he could find. At first McLean suggested an empty house in town, but the aide rejected it as inappropriate. Thus, in one respect at least, the war ended where it began: at the home of Wilmer McLean.

Lee arrived at about 1:00 P.M., resplendent in his dress uniform, still erect and exuding the calmness and nobility that had made men want to follow him even to this sad end. He waited in the parlor, seated in a corner near a small marble writing table. Grant arrived at 1:30 with a dozen Union officers in tow, including Sheridan and James Ord, who had replaced Butler as the commander of the Army of the James. Lee rose to meet him and the two men shook hands. Grant had not brought a dress uniform on the pursuit from Petersburg, and he was attired in his campaign uniform and riding boots. He sat near the center of the room, his escorts standing behind him, and opened the conversation by reminding Lee that they had met once before during the Mexican War. Grant attempted some small talk,

Grant composes the surrender document in the parlor of the McLean House at Appomattox Court House on April 9, 1865. (NA)

but Lee broke in to raise the issue at hand. "I suppose, General Grant, that the object of our present meeting is fully understood. I asked to see you to ascertain upon what terms you would receive the surrender of my army."

Grant's terms were not harsh. The men would lay down their arms and receive their parole, pledging not to fight again unless and until properly exchanged. Lee nodded and asked Grant to have it put in writing. Grant called for his order book and wrote out the terms in his own hand, exempting the officers' side arms, horses, and personal baggage from the surrender.

Lee examined the document carefully, the enormity and finality of the situation weighing heavily upon him. He had one favor to ask and it came hard to his lips. What about the animals owned by individual cavalrymen and artillerists? Would the men be allowed to take their horses and mules with them? His face a mask, Grant replied that the terms as written did not allow it. "No," said Lee quietly. "I see the terms do not allow it. That is clear." There was an awkward silence in the small room. Then, perhaps recalling his conversations with Lincoln about the kind of peace he hoped to establish, Grant decided that Lee's implied request was an opportunity to make a good beginning on such a peace. "I will arrange it," he announced.

While a clean copy of the revised surrender document was prepared by an aide, Grant introduced Lee to his staff. Lee was quiet and apparently unemotional during the strained pleasantries. Shortly after 3:00 P.M. the fair copy of the surrender terms was finished and signed; Lee accepted the terms in a brief formal note, and it was over. Lee and Grant shook hands once again and the Southern commander, now a paroled prisoner of war, walked outside, mounted Traveller, and returned to tell his ragged and hungry veterans that they, too, were now paroled prisoners of war.

The war would last another week, longer in a few remote places where the news was slow in reaching the combatants. Joseph Johnston met with Sherman near Durham, North Carolina, on April 17 and the two men discussed not only the capitulation of Johnston's army, but a general surrender of all Confederate armies. John C. Breckinridge, recently made Confederate Secretary of War, attended their meeting on the 18th and gave his approval to a general instrument of surrender. But their agreement went well beyond military matters. It stipulated that new state governments would be recognized as soon as officials took an oath to the U.S. Constitution. By this time the nation was reeling under the shock of Lincoln's assassination, and those who spoke on behalf of the national government were in no hurry to re-establish the Southern state governments without some consideration of the status those states would possess. As it happened, the agreement signed by Sherman and Johnston on April 23 would subsequently be repudiated by the U.S. government. Within two months, the last Confederate units in the trans-Mississippi West laid down their arms. Under the leadership of Lincoln and Grant, the Union had waged total war and emerged with total victory.

The cost of the war in human life and misery was high indeed. Part of the Battlefield at Gettysburg. (NA)

Suggestions for Further Reading

There are a great many excellent narrative histories of the military campaigns of the Civil War. The following is not intended as a bibliography of sources, but as a list of readable narratives that describe individual campaigns in far greater detail than is possible in this short volume. In some cases the choices represent the one or two best books available from a wide selection; others are listed because they are the only narrative histories available.

A good starting point is James McPherson's *Battle Cry of Freedom* (1988), which is the best single-volume history of the war. Two longer accounts of the entire war that will provide hours of fascination and illumination for any reader— professional historian or interested amateur—are the magnificent trilogies by Bruce Catton and Shelby Foote. Catton's three volumes (*The Coming Fury*, 1961; *Terrible Swift Sword*, 1963; and *Never Call Retreat*, 1965), published during the centennial of the war, are still among the finest and most gripping narrative accounts of any war. For a closer look at the Army of the Potomac, Catton's trilogy on that subject is equally sound. While Catton betrays a mild sympathy for the Union soldiers, Foote displays a perceptible admiration for the sacrifices of the southern soldier. His three-volume *The Civil War: A Narrative* (1958-1974) eschews footnotes and borrows heavily from other histories of the war, but it is masterfully written and is an excellent survey of the war.

On a slightly more scholarly level than Foote, yet still eminently readable, are the works of Allan Nevins and Douglas Southall Freeman. Nevin's four volume *The War for the Union* (1959-1971) is military and political history at its best. Lincoln in particular comes in for extensive and sympathetic treatment. Freeman's hagiographic four-volume biography of R. E. Lee (1934-35) is a classic example of the historian's art. Freeman also wrote a three-volume account of *Lee's Lieutenants* (1942-44) which should not be overlooked.

For those interested in more detailed battle maps than the general schematic portrayals contained in this volume, the maps produced by the National Parks Service are superb and many illustrate unit dispositions down to the regimental level. The maps in Vincent Esposito, ed., *The West Point Atlas of American Wars*, vol. I: 1689-1900 are useful, as are the maps in its successor volume, Thomas E. Griess, ed., *The West Point Military History Series: Atlas for the American Civil War* (1986). The *Official Military Atlas of the Civil War*, compiled as part of the government's project to publish the official records of the war in the late nineteenth century, has been reprinted and contains hundreds of maps in full color exactly as they were prepared by the Army engineers. Unfortunately, the *Official Atlas* is virtually unorganized, and often in error. Recently, the editors of Time-Life books have published a superb volume entitled *Echoes of Glory: Illustrated Atlas of the Civil War* (1991) that contains clear and detailed maps of each campaign, and *The Civil War Battlefield Guide* (1990) published in support of the Conservation Fund for Civil War battlefields, depicts troop movements superimposed over modern road maps. Finally, many of the volumes listed below contain excellent campaign maps.

Map No.	Topic
(1)	CHARLESTON HARBOR
	E. Milby Burton, *The Siege of Charleston, 1861-1865* (1970)
	W. A. Swanburg, *First Blood: The Story of Fort Sumter* (1957)
(3-5)	FIRST BULL RUN (MANASSAS)
	William C. Davis, *Battle at Bull Run: A History of the First Major Campaign of the Civil War* (1977)
(6)	PORT ROYAL
	Bern Anderson, *By Sea and By River: A Naval History of the Civil War* (1962)
	William M. Fowler, Jr., *Under Two Flags: The American Navy in the Civil War* (1990)
(7-8)	SHILOH
	Bruce Catton, *Grant Moves South* (1960)
	Wiley Sword, *Shiloh: Bloody April* (1974)
(9)	NEW ORLEANS
	Charles L. Dufour, *The Night The War Was Lost* (1960)
	William M. Fowler, Jr., *Under Two Flags, op.cit.*
(10-12)	THE PENINSULAR CAMPAIGN & FAIR OAKS
	Stephen W. Sears, *To the Gates of Richmond: The Peninsula Campaign* (1992)
	T. Harry Williams, *Lincoln and His Generals* (1952)
(13)	JACKSON'S VALLEY CAMPAIGN
	Douglas Southall Freeman, *Lee's Lieutenants*, vol. 1, *Manassas to Malvern Hill* (1942)
	Robert G. Tanner, *Stonewall in the Valley* (1976)
(14-15)	THE SEVEN DAYS
	Clifford Dowdey, *The Seven Days: The Emergence of Lee* (1964)

See also Sears, *To the Gates of Richmond, op. cit.*

(16-17) SECOND BULL RUN (MANASSAS)
Robert K. Krick, *Stonewall Jackson at Cedar Mountain* (1990)
John J. Hennessy, *Return to Bull Run: The Campaign and Battle of Second Manassas* (1993)

(18-19) ANTIETAM (SHARPSBURG)
James V. Murfin, *The Gleam of Bayonets: The Battle of Antietam* (1965)
John M. Priest, *Antietam: The Soldiers' Battle* (1989)
Stephen W. Sears, *Landscape Turned Red: The Battle of Antietam* (1983)

(20) CONFEDERATE INVASION IN THE WEST (PERRYVILLE)
Thomas L. Connelly, *Army of the Heartland: The Army of Tennessee, 1861-1862* (1967)

(21) STONES RIVER (MURFREESBORO)
Peter Cozzens, *No Better Place to Die: The Battle of Stone's River* (1990)
James L. McDonough, *Stone's River: Bloody Winter in Tennessee* (1980)

(22) FREDERICKSBURG
Edward J. Stackpole, *The Fredericksburg Campaign* (1957)
V. E. Whan, *Fiasco at Fredericksburg* (1961)

(23-24) CHANCELLORSVILLE
Ernest B. Furgurson, *Chancellorsville, 1863: The Souls of the Brave* (1992)
Edward J. Stackpole, *Chancellorsville: Lee's Greatest Campaign* (1958)

(25-28) GETTYSBURG
Edwin B. Coddington, *The Gettysburg Campaign* (1968)
William A. Frassanito, *Gettysburg: A Journey in Time* (1975)
Craig L. Symonds, *Gettysburg: A Battlefield Atlas* (1992)

(29-30) VICKSBURG
Samuel Carter, *The Final Fortress: The Campaign for Vicksburg* (1980)
Richard Wheeler, *The Siege of Vicksburg* (1978)

(31) CHICKAMAUGA
Peter Cozzens, *The Battle of Chickamauga: This Terrible Sound* (1992)
Glenn Tucker, *Chickamauga: Bloody Battle in the West* (1961)

(32) THE BATTLES FOR CHATTANOOGA
Fairfax Downey, *Storming the Gateway: Chattanooga, 1863* (1960)
James L. McDonough, *Chattanooga: A Death Grip on the Confederacy* (1984)

(33-34) THE WILDERNESS AND SPOTSYLVANIA
William D. Matter, *If It Takes All Summer: The Battle of Spotsylvania* (1988)
Robert Garth Scott, *Into the Wilderness with the Army of the Potomac* (1985)

(35) BUTLER'S ADVANCE
William Glenn Robertson, *Back Door to Richmond: The Bermuda Hundred Campaign, April-June, 1864* (1987)
Herbert Schiller, *The Bermuda Hundred Campaign* (1988)

(36) NEW MARKET
William C. Davis, *The Battle of New Market* (1975)
Edward R. Turner, *The New Market Campaign, May 1864* (1912)

(37-38) COLD HARBOR & THE SIEGE OF PETERSBURG
Noah Andre Trudeau, *Bloody Roads South: The Wilderness to Cold Harbor, May-June, 1864* (1989)
Richard J. Somers, *Richmond Redeemed: The Siege at Petersburg* (1981)

(39) JUBAL EARLY'S RAID
Benjamin Franklin Cooling, *Jubal Early's Raid on Washington, 1864* (1989)
Frank Vandiver, *Jubal's Raid* (1960)

(40-42) THE 1864 ATLANTA CAMPAIGN
Thomas L. Connelly, *Autumn of Glory: The Army of Tenessee, 1862-1865* (1970)
Albert Castel, *Decision in the West: The Atlanta Campaign of 1864* (1992)

(43-45) THE BATTLES FOR ATLANTA
Samuel Carter, *The Siege of Atlanta, 1864* (1973)
Connelly and Castel, *op.cit.*

(46) HOOD'S OFFENSIVE
Stanley F. Horn, *The Decisive Battle of Nashville* (1956)
Richard M. McMurry, *John Bell Hood and the War for Southern Independence* (1982)
Wiley Sword, *Embrace an Angry Wind: The Confederacy's Last Hurrah, Spring Hill, Franklin, and Nashville* (1991)

(47) SHERMAN'S MARCH TO THE SEA
Burke Davis, *Sherman's March* (1980)
Joseph T. Glatthaar, *The March to the Sea and Beyond: Sherman's Troops in the Savannah and Carolinas Campaign* (1985)

(48) FORT FISHER
Rod Gragg, *Confederate Goliath: The Battle of Fort Fisher* (1991)
Rowena Reed, *Combined Operations in the Civil War* (1978)

(49) THE ROAD TO APPOMATTOX
Burke Davis, *To Appomattox: Nine April Days* (1959)
Philip Van Doren Stern, *An End to Valor: The Last Days of the Civil War* (1958)